INFORMAL
EMPIRE

INFORMAL EMPIRE

Mexico and Central America in Victorian Culture

ROBERT D. AGUIRRE

UNIVERSITY OF MINNESOTA PRESS

MINNEAPOLIS • LONDON

OCT 0 8 2005

A portion of chapter 2 was previously published in *Genre: Forms of Discourse* 35, no. 1 (2002): 25–34. A portion of chapter 4 was previously published in *Victorian Review* 29, no. 2 (2003): 42–63. Reprinted with permission.

The map of the Maya region on page vi is from *The British and the Maya,* by Elizabeth Carmichael. Reprinted with permission of the British Museum Company Limited.

Published by the University of Minnesota Press
111 Third Avenue South, Suite 290
Minneapolis, MN 55401-2520
http://www.upress.umn.edu

Printed in the United States of America on acid-free paper

Library of Congress Cataloging-in-Publication Data

Aguirre, Robert D.
Informal empire : Mexico and Central America in Victorian culture / Robert D. Aguirre.
p. cm.
Includes bibliographical references and index.
ISBN 0-8166-4499-3 (hc : alk. paper) — ISBN 0-8166-4500-0 (pb : alk. paper)
1. Mexico—Relations—Great Britain. 2. Great Britain—Relations—Mexico. 3. Mexico—Foreign public opinion, British. 4. Central America—Relations—Great Britain.
5. Great Britain—Relations—Central America. 6. Central America—Foreign public opinion, British. 7. Great Britain—Civilization—American influences. 8. Mexico—Antiquities—Collection and preservation—Great Britain. 9. Central America—Antiquities—Collection and preservation—Great Britain. I. Title.
F1228.5.G7A34 2004
327.72041′09′034—dc22
2004018507

The University of Minnesota is an equal-opportunity educator and employer.

12 11 10 09 08 07 06 05   10 9 8 7 6 5 4 3 2 1

For Danielle, *compañera y luz*

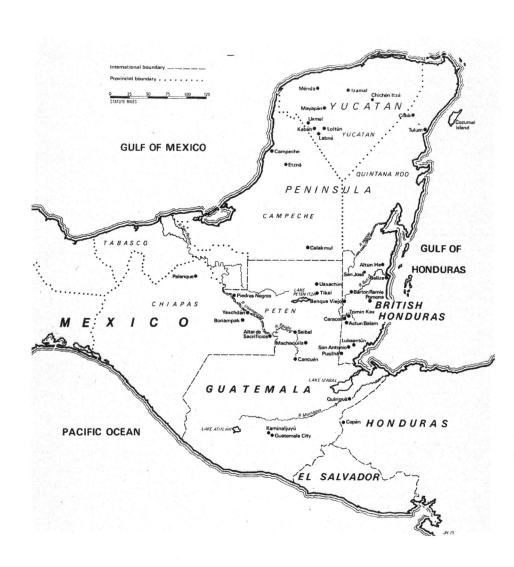

International boundary ———
Provincial boundary • • • • • • •

0   25   50   75   100   125
STATUTE MILES

GULF OF MEXICO

Mérida •   • Izamal
          • Chichén Itzá
Mayapán •   YUCATAN
     Uxmal •   Cobá •
  Kabah • Loltún •   Tulum •   Cozumel
    • Labná •   YUCATAN   Island
Campeche •

Etzná •   QUINTANA ROO

PENINSULA

CAMPECHE

TABASCO   Calakmul •

Palenque •   Altun Ha •
                    San José •   Belize •
          Piedras Negras • Uaxactún •   Barton Ramie •
                    LAKE   • Tikal   Pomona •
                  PETEN ITZA Benque Viejo •
CHIAPAS   PETEN   BRITISH
  Yaxchilán •   Tzimin Kax • HONDURAS
Bonampak •   Caracol • Actun Balam •
MEXICO   Altar de
          Sacrificios • • Seibal
              Machaquilá •   Lubaantún •
                    San Antonio •
                         Pusilhá •
              • Cancuén

                    LAKE IZABAL

GUATEMALA   Quiriguá •

              R. Motagua
LAKE ATITLAN   Copán • HONDURAS
          Kaminaljuyú •
PACIFIC OCEAN   • Guatemala City

GULF OF
HONDURAS

EL SALVADOR

JH 73

CONTENTS

ACKNOWLEDGMENTS

Many people and institutions have contributed to making this book, and I am grateful to be able to thank them here. A series of superb teachers—among them Scott Lubbock, Nello Carlini, Joseph Gallo, Robert Bloesser, Eloise Hay, Lee Bliss, Robert Erickson, Tom Steiner, Garrett Stewart, Marjorie Garber, Joel Porte, Bruce Robbins, Robert Kiely, and Deborah Nord—impressed upon me the rewards and ethical import of scholarly life. In Los Angeles, Christopher Grose listened patiently as I expressed my first ideas; his catholicity of mind and gift for friendship continue to be an inspiration. Other friends, particularly John Friedman and Alice Kimm, were equally unstinting in their support. I would have never written this book without the wise counsel and firm faith of Raphael Gunner, who insisted at a crucial moment that I stay the course.

I am indebted to my colleagues at Wayne State University for generous advice and intellectual companionship. I thank particularly Barrett Watten, Sheila Lloyd, Ted Pearson, Walter Edwards, Bill Harris, Todd Duncan, Kathryne Lindberg, Cynthia Erb, Henry Golemba, Lissy Sklar, Ken Jackson, Janet Langlois, and Ross Pudaloff. As English department chairs, Robert Burgoyne and now Richard Grusin have provided ideal conditions in which to work; they encouraged me when I wavered and stood behind me at every step. Arthur Marotti, Les Brill, and John Reed commented on several grant proposals. Michael Scrivener read an early version of chapter 2, Cannon Schmitt and John Reed versions of chapter 3, and Anca Vlasopolos a draft of chapter 4. From my first arrival in Detroit Gerald

Maclean and Donna Landry have given new meaning to the word "mentors"; a list of their acts of generosity would exceed all bounds. Suffice it to say they always found the time, *usque ad finem.*

Several other friends and colleagues have also given inordinately to this project. In London, Ross Forman and Jesus Garrido were gracious and intellectually stimulating hosts. At the British Museum, Colin McEwan lent generously of his time and his department's resources; this book would have been impossible without his help. Ian Graham took time from his own work to share ideas about Osbert Salvin and Alfred P. Maudslay; my larger debt to his years of painstaking scholarship is writ large throughout this book. Like all who work in the archive of Victorian popular culture, I owe a tremendous intellectual debt to Richard Altick, whose *Shows of London* is a towering monument in this field. Along the way Carol Ann Johnston provided ample funds of wit and fellowship and topped it off by going over the entire manuscript with a fine-toothed comb. A year generously funded by the Andrew W. Mellon Foundation allowed me to enjoy the riches of the John Carter Brown Library, where Norman Fiering, the library's staff, and the other fellows (notably David Hancock, David Kazanjian, and Karen Racine) combined to create a fertile intellectual atmosphere in which to read and write. Karen has continued to share her vast knowledge of Latin American history, and I thank her particularly for reading the entire manuscript with a critical eye. Thanks to Nancy Armstrong, Kirsten Gruesz, and the anonymous readers for the University of Minnesota Press for their insightful comments, and thanks also to Richard Morrison for believing in the project and seeing it through.

Portions of this work were delivered before helpful audiences at the Modern Language Association, the Interdisciplinary Nineteenth-century Studies Association, the Victorian Studies Association of Western Canada, the Congreso de las Américas, the Northeastern Victorian Studies Association, the Wayne State University Humanities Center Annual Conference, and the John Carter Brown Library. For invitations to address the British Museum Americanist Seminar and the University of New Mexico, I am grateful to Colin McEwan and Gail Houston.

I am also happy to acknowledge several rounds of institutional funding from Wayne State University that enabled visits to libraries and archives in London, Oxford, New York, Chicago, Berkeley, and Los Angeles. Thanks also to Arthur Marotti for finding the money to send me to the Newberry

Library. For funds to reproduce images and defray permissions costs, I am grateful to the Wayne State University Humanities Center and its director, Walter Edwards, the College of Liberal Arts, the Department of English, and the Office of the Provost.

For permission to reproduce previously published parts of chapters 2 and 4, I thank Susan Hamilton and Tim Murphy, respectively.

I owe special thanks to the staff of the many libraries, museums, and archives in which this project was carried out. In the UK: the Pitt Rivers Museum; the John Johnson Collection, Bodleian Library (especially Julie Lambert); the British Library; the City Museum of Bristol; the Linnaean Society of London; the University of London Library; the Society of Antiquaries of London; Kew Botanical Gardens and Library; the library of the Royal Anthropological Institute; the British Museum (especially Christopher Date and Janet Wallace); the Victoria and Albert Museum; the libraries of the Natural History Museum (London); and the Public Record Office. In Canada: the National Library of Canada. In the United States: the Huntington Library; the Getty Research Library; the UCLA libraries; the Bancroft Library; the Harvard University libraries (especially Gregory Finnegan, Annette Fern, and Fred Burchstead); the John Carter Brown Library; the Brown University libraries; the New York Public Library; the Cleveland Public Library; the Detroit Public Library; the University of Michigan libraries; the Library of Congress; the Newberry Library; and the American Antiquarian Society. Special thanks to the staff of the Wayne State University libraries, particularly the Inter-Library Loan Office, for expert and tireless work.

My deepest thanks go to family members scattered across the United States, Canada, Mexico, and El Salvador, all of whom have been both wonderfully generous to me and genuinely curious about this project. Special thanks to Ingeborg and Frank Aguirre for inspiration and example, to Eleanor Aguirre for leading the way, and to Robert and Gemma Price for many kind acts of hospitality. Thanks also to Mateo and Stefan for their wit, playfulness, humor, and love for stories. And for her enduring patience and unfailing love, for her countless hours of close, critical scrutiny of my ideas and words, and for her quick brilliance of mind, I thank Danielle Price. All writers should be so fortunate.

INTRODUCTION

Spanish America is free, and if we do not mismanage our affairs sadly, she is English.

—GEORGE CANNING (1824)

Nothing but Anglo-Saxon energy will ever stir this sluggish pool [of Central America] into life.

—*Household Words* (1851)

I could see the guide was troubled. He had a feeling of responsibility, and no Mexican cares for that. It's like a disused limb they have learned to do without.

—GRAHAM GREENE, *The Lawless Roads* (1939)

In 1994 the British Museum opened the Mexican Gallery. Over the entrance, a massive stone carving of the Aztec fire serpent, *Xiuhcoatl,* stands guard; against the rear wall hang richly figured lintels from the Mayan city of Yaxchilán; in between are arrayed a carved bust of *Quetzalcoatl* (the plumed serpent), turquoise mosaic masks, finely wrought jade figurines, the tools of blood sacrifice, and other pieces from the museum's vast pre-Columbian holdings. That the British Museum contains antiquities from Egypt, Mesopotamia, Greece, Rome, and the Orient is little cause for wonder; some trace of these places was always there already, rooted in ancient texts and centuries of cross-cultural contact. Considered by the Victorians as the "national institution *par excellence,*"[1] the museum has long imaged the nation's power to possess and dispossess, to order and reorder, to make and remake.[2] History is reflected in its contents. But what does the British Museum have to do with ancient Mexico? What spurred the museum to seek out pre-Columbian artifacts, to transport them across the Atlantic, and to display them in Bloomsbury? What stories are interwoven with the desire for these objects?

On such questions the Mexican Gallery is largely silent. Objects lie visible behind glass, but their passage along a circuit of exchange—comprised of travelers, collectors, middlemen, auctioneers, and museum keepers—remains opaque. Cryptic legends accompany each object: Ethno. St.373, Ethno. Q87 Am.3, and the like. But these codes resist decipherment, speaking a language for those behind closed doors—keepers, research assistants, and archivists—not the viewing public. The museum's official guidebook to the gallery devotes only a few sentences to the history of the collection, burying details about provenance under illustration and photography acknowledgments.[3] In the Mexican Gallery, the objective aspect of collecting (what the things are) reduces the subjective side (who the collector is, or what drives the collector) to insignificance.[4] Yet an anxiety over the historicity of objects is not confined to the Mexican Gallery, or even to the British Museum, but is symptomatic of museums more generally, insofar as they seek to conceal or naturalize the social and historical processes responsible for the building up of their collections. Museums, at least as traditionally defined, must resist historical investigation, if only to prevent them from being "investigated, challenged, opposed or contradicted" as a product of history itself.[5] Once the institution is opened up for scrutiny, individuals or nations may contest its right to hold certain objects, weakening the rationale for its existence as we know it. It is easy to see why museums, more embattled than ever, do not take well to investigation, much less contradiction or challenge.[6]

Beginning with and returning at several points to the history of pre-Columbian collections in Britain, this book examines select episodes in the British engagement with Mexico and Central America between 1821 and 1898, episodes in which the imperial desire for objects, rather than territory, played a defining role.[7] In political terms, these dates mark the rise of an independent Latin America, the ascendance of British political and commercial influence in the region, and the eventual waning of that power before an increasingly expansionist United States. In economic terms, they define a period of massive British investment and trade, in which Latin America received about 10 percent of Britain's exports, a portion second within the empire only to India.[8] In cultural terms, these years witnessed an extraordinary burst of representations that occurred between the first European museum exhibit of Aztec antiquities (mounted in London) and the absorption of pre-Columbian materials into the

British novel via the work of H. Rider Haggard, G. A. Henty, and others. Most broadly, my aim is to offer an alternative reading of the nineteenth-century circum-Atlantic world, one that, while not devaluing such important concerns as the slave trade or U.S./British relations, argues for the significance of the extensive traffic and exchange in cultural goods between Britain and Latin America. A second object is to draw attention to a rich body of narratives, visual representations, museum collections, and government documents that for various reasons have either escaped the attention of critics altogether or have become so deeply confined within the limits of particular disciplines as to render them invisible to outsiders. The relative marginality of Spanish in traditions of humanistic scholarship; the dominance of colonial and postcolonial studies; the near obsession with the European novel as the *sine qua non* of imperial representation; and the surge of scholarly interest in Western discourses of the East, sparked in large part by Edward Said's *Orientalism* (1978) but elaborated and refined through a still-growing series of studies—these have combined to skew our understanding of British imperialism and obscure the importance of Britain's engagement with Latin America, an engagement whose ideologies, images, and stereotypes shape our perceptions to this day.[9]

More particularly, I shall argue that, in the wake of Alexander von Humboldt's journeys (c. 1800), which made Latin America an object of intense scrutiny after 300 years of Spanish domination, the British quest for and representation of pre-Columbian antiquity became a crucial cultural arm of the larger political and economic strategy historians call informal imperialism. Born from the difficulty of militarily dominating a newly independent Latin America as well as the strain of managing extensive colonial commitments elsewhere, British informal imperialism carved out an area of competitive advantage based largely on trade and economic policy but buttressed strongly by myriad cultural activities on the ground. The most significant of these were archaeology, which produced not only knowledge but also treasures to fill the nation's museums, and ethnology, which provided a rationale for ranking white Europeans above dark and mixed race peoples found across the horizon of empire. The development of these disciplines in tandem with fresh opportunities for travel and economic adventuring in Latin America combined to create a powerfully effective way of doing the cultural work of informal imperialism, which

xvi

was heavily dependent on knowledge. Because outright colonial domination was never seriously an option, other forms of (softer) domination
developed to replace it, and these took advantage of strengthened appara-
tuses of knowledge, such as museums and freak shows, at home. And just
as the Foreign and Colonial Offices opened doors for British travelers
and archaeologists, so did imperial administrators profit in crucial ways
from the knowledge these informants created: their maps, textual and
verbal representations, collections, contacts, and experience in the field.[10]
The cultural forms engendered by this engagement—travel narratives,
museum exhibitions, panoramas, diplomatic correspondence, ethnological freak shows, and adventure novels—lent crucial ideological support to
the work of informal imperialism, shaping an audience receptive to the
influx of British power in the region.

To create visually seductive panoramic displays that portrayed foreign
land as rich, available, and conquerable; to represent the interiors of Central America and Mexico as empty and the population as destined for decline or extinction; to shape the racial attitudes of mass audiences through
theatrical displays of racially enfreaked Mexicans and Central Americans;
to encode pernicious stereotypes from those same displays into "scientific"
discourses of hybridity that upheld notions of British cultural superiority;
to build racial ideas into the justifications for dismembering, transporting, classifying, and storing away the best examples of pre-Columbian
material culture in distant museums and private collections, even while
de-legitimating the cultural achievement of indigenous peoples by insist-
ing that pre-Columbian civilization could not have arisen apart from
Egyptian, Asiatic, or Hebrew influences; to define pre-Columbian culture
in ethnographic not aesthetic terms, thus denying its status as "art" and
relegating it to a position far below the cultural productions of comparable societies; to represent indigenous Central Americans and Mexicans
as hopelessly backward and unknowable, Creole elites and *mestizos* as
untrustworthy, and both as incapable of appreciating or protecting the
cultural riches they had inherited from their ancestors; to formulate a discipline of pre-Columbian studies defined as the province of British elites
largely without recourse to, and frequently with disdain toward, Mexican and Central American intellectuals and government officials, to say
nothing of the indigenous; to desire and disparage, covet and loathe, raise
up and bring down, plunder and neglect: varying, uneven, and frequently

self-contradictory though they were, these constitute the principal characteristics of the ideology and cultural forms through which Britain
constructed its relationship to nineteenth-century Mexico and Central
America, particularly as regards the material and symbolic appropriation
of the pre-Columbian past.

I shall not argue, however, that these forms and their enabling ideologies were unfailingly hegemonic, a seamless fabric of knowledge and
power unfurling like a royal proclamation or imperial map, transforming
distant lands and alien cultures into settled possessions. Power is rarely
that simple. The site of contact was jagged, marked by mutuality, contin-
gency, and what Homi Bhabha, in an influential formulation, calls "ambivalence."[11] In fact, the cultural work under examination here reflected
both the capabilities and limitations of the policy it served, a policy that,
given its improvisational quality, in some ways hardly deserves the name.
Indeed, as will become clear in my discussion of the British government's
ultimately unsuccessful attempt to cart off a choice selection of Mayan
ruins, the empire could be bungling to the point of failure. Many more
schemes were imagined than bore fruit; the empire's reach, to adapt Robert
Browning, always exceeded its grasp. The interaction among heterogeneous and differently motivated representations was, moreover, uneven:
at times there was symmetry and crossover, and thus combinatory force;
at others, contradiction and conflict, and therefore blunted effectiveness.
Informal imperialism, in short, was ad hoc; it did not originate in a master plan and thus it developed and was frequently enacted in contradictory
ways. That it was de-centered gave it some of its unusual success, but it
also meant that different parts of it frequently operated in ignorance of
other parts; it was never a unified strategy. In contrast to the French model
of pre-Columbian research, which assumed a highly centralized form
when Napoleon III, emulating Napoleon's *Institut de l'Égypte,* set up the
Commission scientifique de Méxique at the beginning of the French occupation of Mexico (1864–67),[12] British power in the Americas was largely
dispersed and fragmentary, even within disciplined bureaucracies such as
the British Museum and the Foreign and Colonial Offices. This was due
in large measure to sheer overreach; information generated by the empire,
as Thomas Richards points out, flowed into the metropolis at a rate far
greater than it could be processed, reducing the vaunted imperial archive
to little more than a grab bag of miscellanies.[13] Conditions in the field

were never as smooth as they appeared in maps, consular dispatches, travel narratives, exhibitions—nor, for that matter, as they seem through the retrospective lenses of imperial history. As I show, moreover, Mexicans and Central Americans proved themselves capable of effective counteraction and resistance. This, too, is an important part of the history of informal imperialism.

If Britain's engagement with Mexico and Central America eschewed an outright model of military domination and settlement, one reason it could do so was the sheer effectiveness of its traditional colonial power elsewhere. With the Royal Navy controlling the Caribbean from ports in Jamaica and other islands and a small group of officials in Belize coordinating action on the mainland, Britain was well equipped to exert strong, if also "informal," control over Central America to the west and south and Mexico's eastern coast to the north. Indeed, as I show in chapter 3, the ability to use British Honduras as a stage for projecting British power inland was crucial. Here, formal and informal imperialism went hand in hand. Yet it is important to recognize key differences between British influence in Latin America and British rule elsewhere in the empire. Most significantly, post-independence Latin America was not necessarily postcolonial. The Creole elites who threw off the Spanish yoke during the wars of independence remained culturally and socially, if not politically, identified with the Spanish metropole and thus with Europe, reproducing European hegemonic structures within the newly independent nation-states they formed. After independence they continued to look to Europe, fashioning their nations "in the image of the motherland," suffusing their culture with "European ideals, practices, and material objects."[14] Creole elites also strove to weaken "Indian" identities and economic power, even as they adapted the material culture and iconography of the distant, pre-Hispanic cultures to serve a new *mestizo* or mixed ideal of national and individual identity. European knowledge about pre-Columbian antiquities was heavily dependent on existing Creole scholarship, partly because Creole intellectuals and antiquarians were eager for Europeans to appreciate the greatness of the pre-Hispanic past. That eagerness, however, could also lead to deep complicity with the acquisitive impulses of European elites, and Creoles at points bargained away their nations' cultural inheritance for the political and economic equivalent of a pot of porridge. The traffic in the material remains of the indigenous past, therefore, cannot be reduced to a single, essentialized meaning; it was, and remains, a highly contested subject. I have not pretended to know, moreover, what the pre-Columbian past meant to the "Indians" who are represented from time to time in the discourses I study here. The archives that shape my inquiry, whether British or Spanish, are not transparent or all-inclusive; they are ideological constructs in themselves. Here, at least, the subaltern does not speak, except through the voices of British and Spanish elites. Hence, I limit myself to suggesting the ways in which the indigenous presence that haunts these discourses constitutes a kind of colonial unconscious, an anxious, ambivalent reminder of violent or symbolic dispossession. The British engagement with Mexico and Central America was principally, though not exclusively, a matter between elites.

Although diplomacy, treaty-making, and cultural exchange lay at the center of Britain's response to the newly independent region, these methods, as the Victorian racial theorist Robert Knox observed in 1850, could be as coldly efficient as any violent coercion:

> Ask the Dutch Boer whence comes his contempt and inward dislike for the Hottentot, the Negro, the Caffre; ask him for his warrant to reduce these unhappy races to bondage and to slavery. . . . If he be an honest and straight-forward man, he will point to the fire-arms suspended over the mantelpiece—"There is my right!" The statesmen of modern Europe manage such matters differently; they arrive, it is true, at the same result—robbery, plunder, seizure of the lands of others—but they do it by treaties, protocols, alliances, and first principles.[15]

Indeed in the Latin American context, soft tactics frequently merged with hard. As the British Foreign Secretary Lord Palmerston put it in 1850: "These half-civilized governments such as those of China, Portugal, Spanish America, require a dressing every eight to ten years to keep them in order."[16] Buenos Aires and Montevideo were temporarily seized in 1806-7; plans for a raid on Mexico were only aborted by Napoleon's invasion of Spain. The Falklands came under British control in 1833, a fleet was sent in 1843 to protect the independence of Uruguay, and the Royal Navy anchored off Veracruz in 1859 demanding the Mexican government pay interest on debts owed to British investors.[17] Frederick Chatfield, who served as Britain's chief diplomatic representative in Central America from

1834 to 1852, deftly employed the threat of naval blockades to enforce co-operation, though his attempts at coercion, like that of other British consuls, were frequently reined in by more cautious superiors at Whitehall. On the whole, however, British punitive measures and territorial aggression were infrequent—this despite Andrew Jackson's fears that Britain would throw an "iron Hoop" around the United States by controlling Canada, Oregon, California, Texas, and Cuba.[18] Of course, the greatest threat to Mexico's territorial integrity ultimately came from the United States itself, whose victory in the war of 1846-48 sheared away the upper half of Mexico's territory, some 890,000 square miles. Further, when Britain signed the Clayton-Bulwer Treaty of 1850 with the United States, it agreed to forswear the acquisition of territory in Central America and cooperate with the United States in building an interoceanic canal. Thereafter, British influence gradually waned as the United States asserted its power in the hemisphere, culminating in the Spanish-American War of 1898.

Gunboats and blockades aside, Britain's primary interests in the region were driven by exchange, trade, and commerce. When, in the 1820s, Britain formally recognized the political independence of the Latin American republics, it did so by signing commercial treaties. Thereafter trade, along with the traditional protection afforded the lives and property of British subjects, formed "the preoccupation of British diplomacy."[19] In imperial historiography, the fundamental place of trade in the Anglo–Latin American relationship has made Latin America "the crucial regional test of theories of informal imperialism,"[20] whether described as "gentlemanly capitalism," "imperialism of free trade," or "business imperialism."[21] In an influential formulation John Gallagher and Ronald Robinson, following the late Victorian imperial theorist John Seeley, describe nineteenth-century Britain as an "expanding society," and the dissemination of language and culture from the imperial center as "radiations of the social energies of the British peoples." The character of any form of imperialism, they argue, is "largely decided by the various and changing relationships between the political and economic elements of expansion in any particular region and time." Nineteenth-century British policy toward Latin America was therefore a "spectacular example of a policy of commercial hegemony in the interests of high politics . . . informal political supremacy in the interests of commercial enterprise."[22] Subsequent historians have questioned several aspects of this theory, particularly the extent to which Britain's control of trade and investment amounted to imperialism per se, but the primacy of trade, and therefore the necessity of some kind of collaborative interaction, is not generally in dispute.[23]

A purely economic and political understanding of exchange, however, only takes us so far. As Knight points out, the British came "bearing not only guns and gifts but also intangible ideas: economic liberalism, parliamentarism, monarchism, anti-slavery, Protestantism, sport, [and] racism."[24] They also influenced fashions: the British traveler William Bullock, whom I examine at length in chapter 1, reports that during his 1823 journey from Veracruz to Mexico City he gave a volume of Rudolph Ackermann's fashions to the women of Jalapa, only to find on his return through the town six months later that "instead of their universally appearing in black, as formerly, many were now to be seen in the last fashions of England, in white muslins, printed calicos, and other manufactures of Manchester and Glasgow."[25] Since Latin America attracted relatively few British immigrants, the export of ideologies and practices was all the more necessary for the creation of "congenial collaborating élites" who could be depended upon to grease the machinery of finance and trade.[26] And so they did. Yet Knight's paradigm is itself limited by the emphasis on the *dissemination* of British attitudes from center to periphery, echoing the notion in Gallagher and Robinson (and behind them Seeley) of the "radiations" of British social energies from a fixed, knowable center to its equally stable perimeter. We need to consider, rather, the ways in which center and periphery were mutually constitutive, formed by the back and forth movement of persons, capital, ideas, and objects. Latin American elites, for instance, did not passively await British influence but actively sought it out, journeying to London, taking up residence, and forming a lively expatriate community.[27] Thus center and periphery, metropole and colony, must be examined in the same analytical frame.[28] And we also need to understand how the center/periphery model was also a part of Latin America's internal political and cultural geography, that is, the ways in which hegemony was exerted from within as well as from without.

In the specific context of the transatlantic movement of objects and ideas, Alexander von Humboldt's influential journeys in the South American interior established a key pattern. As his *Personal Narrative* makes clear, Humboldt traveled not only to take measurements and draw maps, but also to collect and ship back to Europe the specimens he had gathered, "forty-two boxes containing a[n] herbal of 6,000 equinoctial plants, seeds, shells and insects, and geological specimens from Chimborazo, New Granada and the banks of the Amazon." Antiquities also formed part of the haul. The transport of these objects, carried by twelve to twenty loaded mules and assisted by indigenous laborers, "created unbelievable difficulties," but Humboldt was so concerned with his collections that he sent "duplicates of all [he] had collected" back to Europe.[29] Charles Darwin, keenly aware of his predecessor, followed the blueprint, as did scores of British travelers throughout the nineteenth century. The desire for empirical knowledge was inseparable from the imperial desire for things. What these travelers took—rocks, minerals, fossils, plants, seeds, insects, the skins of mammals, birds, fish, and reptiles, ethnographic artifacts and human crania dug from the earth, carved pieces sawed from pre-Columbian temples, even human beings lifted from their native haunts—altered not only the places from where they were removed but also the cultures that received and displayed them, bought and sold them, stored and exhibited them. This is not to suggest that economic and political exchange were unimportant, but rather that we need a more flexible account of the circuits of exchange by which objects moved in both directions across the Atlantic, one sensitive to the role of culture and its complex affiliations with economics and politics. Such an account is especially necessary for understanding how British informal imperialism worked in Latin America; for explaining why consular officials tramped through the jungle in search of buried cities and archaeologists served as diplomatic officials; why merchants and traders turned up in Bloomsbury to sell their collections to the British Museum trustees; why the Royal Navy carried persons to Latin America and cultural artifacts back to Britain.

One way to understand these intricate circuits is through an analysis of what Arjun Appadurai calls the "social life of things," which means focusing on the things that are exchanged as well as the "functions" of exchange. The value of this approach, it seems to me, lies in its imaginative definition of commodities and dynamic model of "things-in-motion." It means paying attention not only to textiles, minerals, and manufactured goods, but also to everything from paintings (in an art market) to women (in a marriage market), the whole complex intersection of "temporal, cultural, and social factors" that shape "commoditization."[30] This model of imbricated forces informs my discussion of the ways objects largely outside the British imaginary (pre-Columbian sculpture, indigenous codices, human "curiosities" from Central America) were ascribed different kinds of value (ethnographic, economic, and political) and, in turn, functioned within the larger system of relations governing British interest in Mexico and Central America. For example, in a formulation with important implications for museum studies, Appadurai follows Jacques Maquet in describing the processes by which things intended for other uses are "diverted" into the "commodity state." In the museum context, we must also consider the violence, dismemberment, and defacement that frequently accompanied the metamorphosis of one nation's cultural patrimony into another's "artifact" or imperial trophy. Although British archaeologists, travelers, and government officials justified their plunder by invoking the rhetoric of cultural salvage (rescuing artifacts from the "abandoned" sites where they lay), such actions stripped away both the objects and their meanings in the symbolic systems in which they functioned. As Mieke Bal argues, when an object becomes a sign in another system of value "the object is turned away, abducted, from itself, its inherent value, and denuded of its defining function."[31] The museum establishment recruited ethnographic objects to formulate the scientific criteria by which to rank societies in relation to each other. Such objects helped define stages of social evolution and became convenient "markers of difference which allowed administrative authorities to identify and recognise the local affiliations of the populations under their jurisdiction."[32] The ways in which objects enter the "commodity phase" of their careers are neither simple nor ideologically innocent, but shaped by radical asymmetries of economic, political, scientific, and military power, and built on self-reinforcing cycles of desire and accumulation.

In addition to understanding how pre-Columbian objects could be diverted into other uses beyond which they were originally intended and ascribed new values in complex systems of exchange, we need to grasp the processes by which such objects entered into scientific discourses such as ethnology and anthropology (a subject I explore in chapter 4). In *Science in Action* Bruno Latour presents a powerful model for describing how it is possible to "act at a distance on unfamiliar events, places and people."[33] To have the greatest influence on others you must maximize the power of "mobilization"—coming back from your journey "with the things" in order to induce "others to go out of *their* ways," following the track you have laid down. The things you bring back must not only be mobile but also "*immutable, presentable, readable,* and *combinable* with one another."[34] This formulation helps us understand the recurrent impulse in European science to finance expeditions to gather, transport, assemble, and display immutable mobiles in the metropolis, or "centres of calculation."[35] But the gathering of objects (and even their assemblage into collections) is insignificant and ultimately unsustainable without a further transformation into "inscriptions," the flat packages of information that are the very currency of knowledge. Here, Latour provides several vivid examples: you cannot bring an entire population to the census office, only the forms; laboratory rats do not matter, only written observations about them; coastlines and mountain ranges cannot be mobilized, but only their maps and charts.[36] Inscriptions help solve the problem of scale; they reduce a world of ungainly objects into flat packages of information that can be reproduced, reshuffled, recombined, superimposed over one another, made part of a written text, and, most crucially, merged with "geometry" (i.e., three-dimensional relations) to represent and manipulate the world out there.[37]

To test this theory in the Anglo–Latin American context I analyze not only objects and their traffic, but also their reduction to and expansion in paper. I track several such transformations: a heterogeneous mass of artifacts into the neatly summarized *Synopsis of the Contents of the British Museum;* a vast circular canvas of a panorama into a twelve-page guide; the enfreaked human body into tables of measurements, combined in turn with other measurements into the ethnological treatise, and then into large-scale taxonomies of racial difference; far off pre-Columbian ruins into drawings and reports, which are then enfolded into dispatches, shipped across the Atlantic to enter an archive of related reports, drawings, and dispatches that, properly docketed and indexed, can be summoned from the files and placed on a government minister's desk, enabling him to plot the ruins' removal. By observing such techniques we may thus better understand and explain "how the few may dominate the many."[38] Yet we must also grasp how fragile and far from foolproof such techniques necessarily are: the well-kept files may break down; information may overwhelm attempts to synthesize it; mobiles may be misplaced, forgotten, or sunk to the bottom of the sea; maps and plans may be incorrectly filed, only to turn up years after being commissioned.[39] Inscriptions, especially more complex forms such as maps, dispatches, travel narratives, and works of fiction, must still be interpreted, their signs correctly understood. Moreover, those who are the distant targets of domination may learn to wield their own mobiles and inscriptions, vitiating and sometimes wrecking the imperial will to power.

Hence, I also examine stratagems of resistance, particularly among the Latin American Creole elites, though also at key moments among the indigenous. This is indeed one of my key differences with Said's *Orientalism,* whose rigid binaries (us/them; West/East) and strict Foucauldian model of discourse allow for very little resistance on the part of the Orient, flattening out the always conflictual, contingent, heterogeneous, and partial quality of imperial practices. Here, I follow Nicholas Thomas in maintaining that only "localized theories and historically specific accounts" can shed much light on "the varied articulations of colonizing and counter-colonial representations."[40] Mary Louise Pratt's *Imperial Eyes,* in this regard, has been enormously helpful, particularly its application of "transculturation" to explain the ways "subordinated or marginal groups select and invent from materials transmitted to them by a dominant or metropolitan culture," and "autoethnography" to describe "instances in which colonized subjects undertake to represent themselves in ways that *engage with* the colonizer's own terms."[41] Her scrupulous attention to Alexander von Humboldt and discussion of how subsequent British travelers employ the rhetoric of innocence to mask the expansionist agendas of their projects lie behind my own work on William Bullock, who self-consciously follows in Humboldt's footsteps. Pratt's cursory attention to New World archaeology (132–37), however, in leaving to the side the massive removal of pre-Columbian artifacts that accompanied British travel to Latin America, bespeaks a theoretical bias my work seeks to challenge. As is clear with reference to Humboldt, travelers came to take away not merely information but also material things of all sorts. Among the most spectacular and widely disseminated were indigenous objects from the pre-Hispanic past: codices (or painted books), carved glyphs from Mayan temples, sculpture, pottery, finely tooled works in mosaic and gold. In paying but little attention to the appropriation of material culture, Pratt seems to me to follow too closely on Said's description of orientalism as a "textual universe," in which the impact "was made through books and manuscripts, not, as in the impress of Greece on the Renaissance, through mimetic artifacts like sculpture and pottery."[42] Yet even a brief examination of the Egyptian collections in European and U.S. museums suggests the importance of material appropriation, and this is no less the case in Latin America, which witnessed the wholesale removal of its most precious cultural artifacts. I argue that it is imperative to consider not only finished texts, consumed in the library or study, but also related forms of visual or material culture that disseminated information about the Americas to mass audiences (exhibitions, fairs, panoramas, and freak shows) while *embodying* the imperial power to possess and remove.

The chapters that follow analyze a series of individual forms and practices that, taken together, represented Mexico and Central America to British audiences. In the first chapter I consider the Mexican productions of the colorful showman and museum entrepreneur William Bullock (c. 1773–1849). In 1824, after returning to London from a six-month journey to newly independent Mexico, Bullock published a travel narrative, arranged a panoramic display, and mounted the first European museum exhibit of Aztec antiquities at the Egyptian Hall, his elaborate display space in Piccadilly. Mingling spectacle and science, Bullock's exhibition kindled Britain's obsession with the pre-Columbian past, while promoting investments in Mexican mining and manufactures. The British Museum purchased the collection after the exhibit closed, installing it first among the "artificial curiosities" and later in the ethnographical room, opened in 1846. Today, several of Bullock's objects are prominently featured in the Mexican Gallery. Discussing the exhibit's relation to narratives of collection and imperial acquisitiveness, I explore how symbolic meanings were attached to the appropriation of objects during this period. I also demonstrate that as early as the 1820s Mexican elites resisted the looting of their cultural heritage, warning of the depredations caused by foreign travelers, introducing legislation to stanch the outflow of antiquities, and interpreting their own past in museums and historical narratives. Such actions refute the oft-repeated British view that no one in Mexico cared about pre-Hispanic artifacts (and hence that they could be removed with impunity); they also show how the British will to power was compromised and undercut.

Museum collections demonstrated the nation's reach and grasp, bringing the exotic world home, reducing it to size, placing it in new structures of knowledge, and absorbing it into the national imaginary. In chapter 2,

I study this theme through an analysis of one of the century's most distinctive visual forms, the panorama, considered here as proto-cinematic entertainment and a powerful technology that projected the viewpoint of travelers in the field onto the screen of mass culture back home. Instead of offering a grand overview of the form, I focus on a historically contained sequence of panoramic views of Mexico City, beginning with one that Robert Burford, in collaboration with Bullock, exhibited to wide acclaim in his Leicester Square rotunda in 1825–26. I trace the genealogy of the site represented on the panoramic canvas and in the accompanying printed guide, first to the Spanish colonial narratives that installed the view in the European mind, and second to eighteenth-century English translations of the conquest narratives that employed the familiar modes of the sublime and the picturesque to give it a distinctly English flavor. To form a contrast, I then move to the 1840s and across the Atlantic to examine the ideological uses of panoramic vision in William H. Prescott's *History and Conquest of Mexico* (1843) and in a triumphal panorama of the Mexican War exhibited in the United States. Drawing on recent work in visual theory, I demonstrate how the panorama served not only as domestic entertainment but also as a machine for producing imperially minded viewers. I close by exploring a variety of Mexican responses to this powerful form of imaginative possession.

After the British Museum purchased Bullock's collection in 1827, travelers, private collectors, naval officers, and diplomatic personnel beat a path to Bloomsbury to sell or donate their pre-Columbian collections, most of which came from Mexico. But during the early 1840s attention shifted farther south, to the lost Mayan cities of Central America. In chapter 3, I discuss the British government's extraordinary though ultimately unsuccessful conspiracy to remove some of the most valued of these ruins: the "sculptured remains" of Copán, Quiriguá, and Tikal, which lay in Honduras and Guatemala. The American travel writer John Lloyd Stephens and the British architect Frederick Catherwood had popularized these sites in *Incidents of Travel in Central America, Chiapas, and Yucatan* (1841), a best-selling work of travel and a recognized classic of archaeological narrative. Fearful that the Americans would cart off the ruins and thus triumph in an increasingly important arena of imperial rivalry, the British Museum recruited the Foreign Office to bring them to Bloomsbury. My archive is a remarkable and heretofore-unexamined cache of letters and dispatches I "unearthed" in the Colonial and Foreign Office archives, written between 1841 and 1855, that details the vast reach of the conspiracy. I examine these documents through Latour's notion of acting "at a distance," but also through studies of epistolarity and mimetic desire, which enable a discussion of the dispatch as a specific literary and bureaucratic form, and the closed, homosocial world of imperial administration as a specific cultural site in which it flourished. Last, I consider the conflict between Central American attempts to protect a national heritage and a British imperial acquisitiveness best summed up by Palmerston, who believed that it would be relatively simple to acquire the monuments because the local people were incapable of properly valuing them.

In 1855 John Connolly, president of the Ethnological Society of London, discussed the connection between Britain's commercial relations and the study of ethnology. From about 1830 onward those relations, along with information brought back by travelers, transformed London into a leading center for anthropological inquiry and the study of racial difference. Yet a parallel and competing culture of popular freak shows also shaped these discourses, frequently in ways that threatened the learned societies' control over their discipline. In chapter 4, I address a particularly rich instance of this overlap, the poignant career of Máximo and Bartola, the so-called Aztec Lilliputians. The children, who had abnormally small heads, were taken in 1851 from El Salvador to London to be exhibited as living descendants of the "lost city" of "Iximaya." After appearing before Queen Victoria and other members of the nobility they were examined by leading ethnologists and medical doctors, including Richard Owen and Robert Knox, whose studies were published in the leading anthropological and medical journals. As the controversy over their origin raged, scientific opinion turned to the problematic status of the *mestizo,* the mixed progeny of European and indigenous stock who formed the bulk of Latin American peoples. Dr. Karl Ritter von Scherzer, who was then exploring the ruins of Central America for the British Museum, pronounced the children nothing more than racially mixed degenerates. Articles in *Household Words,* the *Athenaeum,* and the *Illustrated London News* carried on the debate. Tracking the story to the mention of a lost city in Stephens and Catherwood, I open up for scrutiny the entangled worlds of travel, spectacle, and ethnological inquiry during this period. I argue that ethnological displays, in presenting the descendants of the ancient Central American civilizations as hopelessly degenerate, gave crucial ideological support to the dispossession of cultural property—a dispossession that was ongoing even as the children were exhibited in London.

D. H. Lawrence's *Plumed Serpent* (1926) is an important monument in the primitivist project of modern culture. Yet in the final decade of the nineteenth century, popular novelists such as H. Rider Haggard anticipated many of its pre-Columbian themes, while bringing the material developed by the British engagement with Mexico and Central America into the British novel. My final chapter examines Haggard's *Montezuma's Daughter* (1894), arguing that it reformulates the fascination with pre-Columbian antiquity into a parable of masculine desire, racial fear, and imperial nostalgia. An awareness of Britain's missed opportunities in Latin America informs the novel's structure and rhetoric, which is characterized by a lament for the heroic age of Elizabethan exploration and the lost riches of ancient Mexico. In the context of increasing U.S. dominance in the hemisphere, foreshadowed by the Monroe Doctrine of 1823 and consolidated by the Spanish-American War of 1898, Haggard's novel both imagines and laments a colonial empire that might have been but never was, offering an important retrospective on the entire period of cultural inquiry examined in this book.

The following chapters thus offer an expanded account of British informal imperialism in Mexico and Central America, one focused not merely on trade and politics but on the transatlantic networks of culture that accompanied and enabled them. Pre-Columbian objects circulated within these networks, evoking feelings of desire and envy, mastery and dispossession, pride and disgust. The history of those affective relations, I argue, has been erased not only by the modern museum gallery but also by literary history, which has ignored the transatlantic transport and traffic of objects, persons, and ideas, or limited it to the well-known lines of transit between Britain and the United States. There is a great deal more to be done in this area, of course, beginning with the untold stories residing in objects not examined here and extending to the scores of British travel writings and fictional narratives about the Americas that molder on library shelves awaiting the curious reader. This study is offered in the hope of urging on that work.

chapter 1

"OPEN FOR INSPECTION"

Mexico at the Egyptian Hall in 1824

George Canning, in the playfulness of his wit, expressed a hope that the consuls he was despatching to the New World might possess half the information Bullock's Museum could afford.

—WILLIAM JERDAN, *Men I Have Known*

Colorful, entrepreneurial, an amateur in the classic British sense, the museum showman William Bullock (c. 1773–1849) looms large in the nineteenth-century British encounter with Mexico, inaugurating a set of interlocked practices (traveling, collecting, exhibiting) whose impact resounded throughout the period examined in this book. On 11 December 1822 he sailed from Portsmouth to Mexico, arriving at Veracruz in late February 1823. The journey, the first by a British traveler since the seventeenth century, shimmered with possibility.[1] After declaring independence from Spain in 1821, Mexico sought formal recognition from Britain (granted in 1824), and, perhaps more important, investment capital.[2] British merchants and bankers clamored for a trade agreement with a nation whose wealth was the stuff of legend; scientists and antiquarians sought information beyond what had been hinted at in Alexander von Humboldt's travels, which focused principally on South America.[3] As he described it in his 1824 travel narrative, Bullock's landing was freighted with symbolism: "I had scarcely put my foot down upon [the pier] when I observed that it was partially paved with pigs of iron, each bearing the broad arrow of the king of England." Hence, "the first step an Englishman takes in New Spain" is on "English property" (*SMR*, 15).[4] Bullock took the royal imagery as a sign of the "good understanding and commercial intercourse" he hoped would develop between the two countries. Indeed, within a week of Bullock's landing, Britain's first diplomatic representative, Patrick Mackie, arrived in Veracruz bearing official letters asking him to ascertain whether Mexico's leaders were disposed to "friendly relations and commercial intercourse with Great Britain."[5] The nearly identical phrasing suggests how closely Bullock's enterprise mirrored that of the state.

On returning to London from his six-month journey, Bullock staged a stunning series of representations, each of which put Mexico on display for the British public: a 500-page illustrated narrative, *Six Months' Residence and Travels in Mexico* (1824), which was in a second edition by 1825 and quickly translated into French, German, and Dutch; a large-scale panoramic painting mounted in a specially built theater in Leicester Square (see the following chapter); and the first European museum exhibit of Aztec and contemporary Mexican artifacts, displayed at his elaborate showcase in Piccadilly, the Egyptian Hall.[6] The first edition of Bullock's narrative, some 1,500 copies, sold out within days, and his Mexican representations received wide coverage in the periodical press, with substantial reviews in the *Times, New Monthly Magazine, Literary Gazette, London Magazine,* the *Classical Journal, Gentleman's Magazine,* and the *Edinburgh Magazine*. The exhibits were regarded not merely as entertainment, but as knowledge useful to the state; the *Literary Gazette* concurred, observing that the exhibits were "calculated to be very beneficial to [the] country."[7] As the rhetoric of "calculation" and "benefit" suggests, the periodical press understood the exhibits' value primarily in the economic terms we have come to associate with informal imperialism. Bullock's productions played nicely into this logic by throwing the bright light of publicity on Mexico's cultural and economic resources, presenting them as available for inspection and control. The Mexico he described was "one vast field for the exercise of British capital, machinery, and industry" (*MM*, 4). Functioning as a vivid metaphor for the empire's extractive reach and epistemological mastery, the exhibits laid the ideological groundwork for British informal imperialism in the region.[8]

In a version of what Mary Louise Pratt terms "anti-conquest," a rhetorical strategy by which travelers seek to "secure their innocence,"[9] Bullock represented himself as a "mere searcher after Antiquities" (*AMM*, iii), driven by "motives of curiosity only" (*SMR,* 24). But these self-representations only masked a larger ambition of turning cultural inquiry to economic advantage, of unearthing and extracting precious metals as well as buried sculptures. The *Times,* in its account of Bullock's exhibition, saw this clearly, reporting that in "ransack[ing] the superb capital of Mexico," Bullock's only difficulty lay in "how to collect the best and carry off the most."[10] Like other early travelers to Spanish America (George F. Lyon, Robert W. H. Hardy, Mark Beaufoy, and Henry G. Ward), whom Jean Franco calls "missionaries of capitalism,"[11] Bullock believed in the "mutually conducive" and "reciprocal advantages" of free trade (*AMM,* iii–iv), one of the deepest of capitalist beliefs. Mexico, he wrote, adapting Adam Smith's metaphor, lacked only the "fostering hand of a free, enlightened and enterprising" nation and the "knowledge imparted by modern science" to usher it into a prosperous and technologically sophisticated modernity (*AMM,* iv). Historians of informal imperialism have pointed out that British overseas capitalism was heavily reliant on precisely the kind of insider knowledge Bullock proffered; access to and control of information was the very linchpin of the gentlemanly capitalism that underwrote imperial expansion from the City of London.[12] Bullock embraced the relationship between knowledge and laissez-faire capitalism, filling his narrative and exhibition catalogues with information he felt might be valuable for British road-builders, railway engineers, farmers, merchants, and especially miners. Goaded in part by Bullock's account of a soil "inexhaustible in the precious metals" (*AMM,* iv), British investors sunk millions of pounds into Anglo-Mexican mining companies, including the Mexican Company, directed by Bullock himself. The resulting boom and crash of these investments wreaked great havoc in Britain, but even more in Mexico, which soon discovered the political cost of economic dependence.

A notable early speculator in Mexican futures was young Benjamin Disraeli, who, backed by the financier J. D. Powles, dashed off three pamphlets in 1825 to reassure investors—against fears of another South Seas bubble—that the mines were laden with ore. Issued anonymously, these pamphlets were the future statesman's initial foray into print and provided lively material for *Vivian Grey,* his first novel, published in 1826–27, with its account of a party at which the talk was of "the latest anecdote of Bolivar . . . 'new loans,' . . . 'liberal principles,' and 'steamboats to Mexico.'"[13] Though the epigraph to Edward Said's *Orientalism* has given a new ring to Disraeli's statement that "the East is a career," Disraeli's own *bildungsroman,* along with that of many others throughout the century, suggests the advantages of *westward* careers.[14] By as early as 1825 Disraeli was claiming to have read "every book on the subject" of Mexican mining,[15] no doubt including Bullock's, which was constantly before the press. Like Bullock, Disraeli believed that Mexico's possession of "metallic depositories in a most eminent degree" made it an "object of intense interest to every Briton,"[16] and his stark imperialist formulation—that wealth could only be acquired by the "universality of our international relations, by making the whole world the theatre of our action"—represents the national extension of individualist careers such as his own and Bullock's.[17] As Disraeli put it, "IN PROPORTION AS THE ENERGIES OF AMERICA ARE DEVELOPED AND HER RESOURCES STRENGTHENED, WILL THE POWER AND PROSPERITY OF ENGLAND BE CONFIRMED AND INCREASED."[18]

But for Henry George Ward, the British *chargé d'affaires* in Mexico from 1825 to 1827, the expectations of 1824 led all too rapidly to the "despondency of 1828"—a turn of events Harriet Martineau later called the "spectacle of intoxication and collapse."[19] With Bullock in mind, and possibly London speculators such as Disraeli also, Ward deplored the advantage taken by those who were "enthusiasts, while many had no better object than to turn the enthusiasm of others to account."[20] Yet painful as were these cycles for British investors, their effect on Mexicans was devastating. Today, Mexico frequently stands as an example of the developing world's crippling bondage to globalization, but a good measure of its current economic woes can be traced to the first years after independence, when the sudden penetration of its markets by a massive British "trade offensive," the default of two massive loans, and the withdrawal of investment after the mining bubble collapsed plunged it into economic vassalage, forming a key episode in what Carlos Marichal calls "a century of debt crises."[21] The political repercussions were equally profound, as British subjects became enmeshed "in the political and economic life of the country" until about 1888. If nothing else, the "embarrassment" engendered by the nation's massive obligations put Mexican consular and diplomatic personnel at a strategic disadvantage against their British counterparts for decades.[22]

It was in this context that Bullock opened his two-part museum exhibition, which ran from April 1824 to September 1825. The exhibition explicitly linked enterprise and knowledge, one part addressing the newly independent state's potential as a field for Britain's economic ventures, the other its indigenous past. In "Modern Mexico" (Figure 1), Bullock exhibited a carefully "classed and arranged" array of objects: models of Mexican costumes illustrating "persons of all ranks and descriptions"; examples of Mexican leatherwork, embroidery, and dyed textiles; a collection of mineralogy, "in which the pure ores of gold and silver are seen in their native state"; exotic vegetables and fruits, including avocados, melons, and mangos (rich as the "clotted cream of Devonshire"); animals, birds, fishes, all carefully preserved by Bullock himself, who was a master taxidermist—indeed everything that could "throw a light" over Mexico's "productive industry" (*AMM*, 8–13). A Mexican native, José Cayetano Ponce de Leon, whom Dorothy Wordsworth found "not the least interesting object" in a "very amusing" exhibit,[23] emerged from a thatched hut to speak with visitors, suggesting the existence of a "docile," "simple," and "contented" population who could be counted on to work the mines, British steam technology notwithstanding (*AMM*, 6; 8). The entire exhibit was suffused with economic imagery: Bullock displayed his collection of 170 stuffed hummingbirds in a case painted with a view of a "silver mine of

Figure 1. Agostino Aglio, interior of the exhibition of "Modern Mexico." Courtesy of the Bancroft Library, University of California, Berkeley.

del Bada . . . presented to Mr. Bullock by the Mexican Government"; the birds themselves he compared to the "brightest gems" (*AMM*, 12; 9), a trope echoed later in the century in Martin Johnson Heade's series of hummingbird paintings, "The Gems of Brazil." Even Bullock's miniature wax models of indigenous and Creole Mexicans were inflected with economic assumptions. Their hierarchical arrangement mirrored that of the British spectators (*AMM*, 10; 17), thus supporting Roland Barthes's thesis that classificatory schemes underwrite social containment by grouping objects and spectators alike into fixed categories; "the word 'class,'" he writes, "applies to both notions."[24] The lithographs produced for Bullock's travel narrative show a populace recently emerged from a protracted struggle for political independence as ordered, settled, and safely postrevolutionary, ready for employment in the service of British industry (Figures 2 and 3).

"Ancient Mexico" (Figure 4), by contrast, was dominated by archaeological and ethnographic imagery, and featured objects that underlined the brutality—"more monstrous and bloody than the Egyptian" (*AMM*, 20)—as well as the cultural advancement of Aztec civilization, and thus the sophistication of an imperial science that could hold both in tension. The hall was filled with sculptures, painted books (codices), and early postconquest maps, described alternately in the catalogues as grotesque and culturally advanced. Towering above them all were three massive plaster casts of Aztec monuments that had been discovered in the 1790s during street repairs in Mexico City: the fearsome nine-foot high *Coatlicue*, her necklace adorned with severed hands (Figure 5); the *Piedra de Tizoc*, a giant cylindrical slab bedecked with symbolic carvings (Figure 6); and the *Piedra de Sol*, or calendar stone, nine feet in diameter, illustrating the Aztec's complex grasp of time (Figure 7).[25]

The exhibits suggested the extractive powers of British imperialism, not only by bringing things back once, but doing so in ways that could be infinitely reproduced. In Bullock's exhibits we see the emergence of a powerful formula, in which an instance of travel, collecting, and exhibiting begets a "cycle of accumulation" that brings ever more objects across the Atlantic to museums and private collections in Britain.[26] The process is well illustrated by the history of Bullock's collection, which in 1827 was absorbed into the British Museum. At that time the museum had only a handful of pre-Columbian artifacts, but by century's end it had amassed

Figure 2. "Mexican Indians Going to Market," from William Bullock, *Six Months' Residence and Travels in Mexico* (1824). Courtesy of the John Carter Brown Library at Brown University.

Figure 3. "Mexican Gentlemen," from William Bullock, *Six Months' Residence and Travels in Mexico* (1824). Courtesy of the John Carter Brown Library at Brown University.

one of the world's greatest collections—a status it retains today.[27] Between 1828 and 1857, the museum acquired thirteen separate pre-Columbian collections, totaling well over 2,000 artifacts, most collected by travelers, military officers, consular officials, and the like. Present estimates put the Mexican collections alone at over 7,000 objects. And in a fitting homage to the importance of Bullock's collections, the museum's Mexican Gallery prominently features several of the artifacts Bullock first brought to London.[28]

The visual presentation of archaeological and ethnographic materials, along with their transformation into "inscriptions" via the detailed exhibition pamphlets, constituted a significant advance in museum ethnography and a marked globalization of London's exhibitionary culture. The exhibits meshed closely with Bullock's travel narrative, which narrated key aspects of Mexican history and supplied detailed ethnographic information about its populations, customs, and practices. The show's anthropological dimension—itself economically inflected—was embodied not only in the person of Bullock's Mexican informant, José, but also in the structure of the exhibit itself. Partitioned between "Ancient" and "Modern" Mexico, the design suggests the anthropological trope called the "denial of coevalness," whereby the other is shut out from the present, progressive

Figure 4. Agostino Aglio, interior of the exhibition of "Ancient Mexico." Courtesy of the John Carter Brown Library at Brown University.

Figure 5. *Coatlicue,* as photographed by William Henry Jackson. Library of Congress, Prints and Photographs Division, Detroit Publishing Company Collection, LC-D43-T01-1132.

historical moment in which the anthropologist or cultural observer exists.[29] In the Mexican context, this trope doomed the indigenous and the poor to a temporal no-man's land outside modernity, separated both from the noble past embodied in the ruins and any present stake in their ownership. Pratt discusses how European travel discourses "deterritorialize indigenous peoples,"[30] but Bullock's productions also disempowered Creole elites, clearing the way for the accelerated removal of Mexico's cultural treasures to distant museums. The exhibits may thus be understood to have formed the cultural parallel to the economic hopes of Disraeli and others who predicted that Mexico's mineral wealth would line the pockets of British investors.

In what follows, I begin by tracing Bullock's role in important late-eighteenth- and early-nineteenth-century museums, paying particular attention to the techniques of ethnographic spectacle that he later employed so effectively in the Mexican exhibitions. I then examine the exhibits

Figure 6. The *Piedra de Tízoc*, as formerly exhibited in the Museo Nacional, Mexico City. Courtesy of Research Library, Getty Research Institute, Los Angeles.

themselves, arguing that their implicit ideologies meshed perfectly with the developing strategy of informal imperialism, symbolizing the ability of cultural elites to dominate from a distance both economically and culturally. In a further step of the argument I consider the afterlife of the exhibits in a series of textual inscriptions that restructured the unwieldy world of three-dimensional objects into flat packages of information available for subsequent combination, reproduction, and citation. Last, I analyze how Mexican cultural elites, who claimed the material culture of the Aztecs for their own nationalist cause, employed legal and cultural arguments to contest the plunder carried out by foreign visitors. Antiquities figured

Figure 7. The Piedra de Sol, from Claude Désiré Charnay, *Album fotográfico mexicano* (c. 1860). Photography Collection, Miriam and Ira D. Wallach Division of Art, Prints, and Photographs, New York Public Library, Astor, Lenox, and Tilden Foundations.

prominently in these discourses, just as they did in British ideologies of cultural dominance. While British travelers were busily carting off Aztec (and later Maya) relics, Mexicans built museums of their own and wrote legislation prohibiting the export of the nation's cultural property—a struggle over the possession and meaning of the past that reverberates to this day.

FROM ARTIFICIAL CURIOSITIES TO MUSEUM ETHNOGRAPHY

Despite making lasting contributions to natural history, collecting, travel, and museum display, Bullock has escaped the attention of biographers.[31] Although I sketch some outlines of his life here, I am principally concerned with the way Bullock's collecting and exhibitionary practices figured in national identity and imperial self-fashioning. The most immediate context for this discussion is the eighteenth- and early-nineteenth-century history of commercial and scientific expeditions that, in exploring geographical frontiers, expanded European knowledge of distant cultures and helped created the science of ethnography: Alexander MacKenzie's journey to Northwest Canada; Mungo Park's expeditions to Western Africa; Alexander von Humboldt's trek through South America; and above all Captain Cook's voyages to the South Seas. But although Bullock was influenced by these heroic exploits, I shall argue that he put his own, unique stamp on them by combining travel, collecting, and museum exhibition into a unified process, one whose most impressive result was the Mexican ensemble of 1824–25.

Bullock's career as a collector, which began in the mid-1790s in Sheffield, gained steam after 1801 when he moved to Liverpool. His first venture was a museum operated from his house at 24 Lord Street, but soon he was advertising his wares as the proprietor of the Liverpool Museum in Church Street.[32] The inventories of his museums show that he took good advantage of the port's brisk dockside traffic in exotic material brought home by sailors and ship captains. His eye was particularly drawn to "curiosities," a term, as Nicholas Thomas observes, that implies qualities both in certain objects and those who desire them. Gaining currency as an ethnographic category after Cook's South Seas voyages, curiosity was at once noun (a curiosity), adjective (it is curious), and measure of the "knower's intellectual and experiential desire" (one's interest is curious).[33] In her recent book on the subject, Barbara Benedict argues convincingly that the changing fortunes of curiosity as ideal and practice were particularly well illustrated in the career of Sir Hans Sloane, whose gift of his private collection of curiosities to the nation established the British Museum. After being widely ridiculed in the late seventeenth century for being "so Curious that nothing almost has pass'd him," Sloane was recuperated as a national hero by the mid-eighteenth century, as museums "came to represent a new system of value: the British freedom of inquiry."[34] As Sloane's stock soared, so did that of curiosity, and by the early nineteenth century Bullock was able to capitalize on the renovation of curiosity that had transformed it from the scandalous pursuit of dilettantes into a positive attribute of the scientific gentleman. Still, curiosity continued to retain disreputable associations. In 1813, for example, Bullock wrote the Earl of Liverpool asking permission to display the embalmed head of Oliver Cromwell, "still entire with the flesh on," an object he called a "mere matter of curiosity."[35] The earl, however, took a dim view of the proposal, invoking the need to protect women and children who might be shocked at the sight of such a gory object. Antiquarian and moral definitions of curiosity remained in conflict.

Bullock nevertheless made a tidy business from the display of curiosities, particularly those distant in time and place from the museums where they could be seen. Bullock wrote with pride of the abundance, cost, and arrangement of his collections; on the title page to his 1810 catalogue he boasted of "seven thousand natural and foreign curiosities, antiquities, and productions of the fine arts," collected at an "expence of upwards of twenty-two thousand pounds."[36] Along with ethnographic artifacts from Africa and the Americas, Bullock acquired a large collection of objects from the South Seas, some originally obtained by Cook and Banks, others from various late-eighteenth-century travelers, collectors, and museums. In his *Treatise on the Art of Preserving Objects of Natural History* (1818), Bullock made clear the links between museum display, ethnographic narrative, and Britain's commercial enterprise: the collections embraced the "most interesting articles brought from the South Seas during the Voyages of Discovery of Captain Cook. They include the identical Idols, Weapons, and other domestic and military implements engraved in the History of those Voyages."[37] Narratives contextualized exotic objects within specific cultures and, as in Cook's case, associated them with the great deeds of travelers and explorers. The objects that accompanied or illustrated narratives, in turn, anchored them in a world of things and embodied the appropriative reach and cultural sophistication of British subjects. The removal and display of exotic curiosities helped to map the contours of a world split between the primitive producers and metropolitan consumers of curious objects. Once gathered into the centers of calculation, curiosities were indexed, labeled, catalogued, and absorbed into European taxonomic systems. Prominent among these was the Linnaean order, which Bullock followed with the conviction of a new convert (in 1810 he was elected as a fellow to the Linnaean Society of London). John Rippingham testified to the master's skill in his *Natural History, according to the Linnaean System, explained by familiar dialogues in visits to the London Museum,* a primer that used Bullock's exhibits to instruct the reader in the principles of rational classification.[38] In Bullock's museums we find the ideal of a coherently ordered world imaged through devices such as the habitat group, vivid tableaux that re-created the postures and physical surroundings of creatures in their natural surroundings (Figure 8).[39] A famous and recently recovered example, preserved at the Rossendale Museum in Lancashire, depicts a Bengal tiger struggling to escape the asphyxiating grip of a giant python; although each animal is individually realized, the display creates a sense of drama by bringing them into mortal combat.[40]

The showman's knack for theatrical flair reached its apogee when Bullock moved his museum from Liverpool to London in 1809 and commissioned a lavish new building to house his collections. The city he entered had been fundamentally transformed; a vital exhibitionary culture flourished in show halls, theaters, private museums, and meeting rooms. Just before and just after Bullock's arrival the British Museum obtained spectacular treasures, including the Rosetta Stone (1802) and the Elgin Marbles (1816), each a potent sign of Britain's control over the material remains of great civilizations.[41] Seeking his place in the new exhibitionary order, Bullock hired the architect Peter F. Robinson (1776–1858)—famous for the onion-shaped cupolas he added to the Royal Pavilion in Brighton—to design an ornate building for his collections in Piccadilly, which was completed in 1812 at a cost of £16,000.[42] Like the Royal Pavilion, the Egyptian Hall, as it came to be known, played off the nation's orientalist fantasies (Figure 9), symbolically echoing Napoleon's invasion of Egypt (what Edward Said calls the "very model of a truly scientific appropriation of one culture by another"),[43] Jomard's *Description de l'Égypte* (published 1809–28), and the British appropriation of Egyptian antiquities captured from the French.[44] The gaudy edifice, equipped with a façade inspired by the Temple of Hathor at Dendera, struck Jane Austen at least as among the most fashionable places in London.[45] More importantly, both the frame and its changing contents reinforced the ideological calculus of imperial possession I have sketched above. If the individual surrounded by his accumulated property suggests the Enlightenment concept of possessive individualism,[46] Bullock's orientalist showcase signaled the extension of that dynamic to the nation, and thus a symbolic enlargement of curious desire.

In 1819, Bullock embarked on a remarkable series of exhibitions that further deepened the connection between collecting, display, and national identity. Auctioning the heterogeneous contents of his London museum—

Figure 8. Interior of Bullock's Museum, c. 1810. Courtesy of Guildhall Library, Corporation of London.

including his 32,000 "remarkable subjects of animated nature"[47]—he turned to a series of single-subject exhibits with strong national themes. First, in 1816, came the exhibition of Napoleon's ornate military carriage, which had been captured in the war with France.[48] As Thomas Rowlandson's caricature shows (Figure 10), the exhibit set off a frenzy; visitors swarmed the carriage, clambering over and inside it, erasing the boundary between spectator and object as they engorged themselves in riotous consumption. So successful was the exhibit that after a year in London it toured the major cities and towns of England, Scotland, and Ireland, reaping Bullock a profit of over £25,000.[49] Bullock's exhibition catalogue, reprinted by Marie Tussaud when she purchased the carriage in the 1840s, rhetorically cements the association between trophy and nation, noting that it is impossible to refer to the object "without feeling a patriotic exultation" over the "wisdom of British councils" and the "valour of English arms." Bullock went on to add: "In approaching this carriage, therefore, an immediate connection is formed, with the greatest events and persons, that the world has ever beheld."[50] Yet Rowlandson's image hints at a further commingling of subjects and objects, for in the background we see posters for the Polish Dwarf (Joseph Boruwlaski) and the Hottentot Venus

Figure 9. Façade of Bullock's Egyptian Hall.

(Saartjie Baartman), figures who appeared on the British stage as human curiosities.[51] As I argue in chapter 4, the move from things to persons-*as*-things was central to the nascent disciplines of ethnology and anthropology, structures of knowledge that relied on the same mechanisms of travel and removal that fed the museum market in nonhuman curiosities. The juxtaposition of human curiosities with military spoils suggests the always-already imperial context of the emerging museum order.

It was a short step from the carriage, functioning as a synecdoche for Britain's dominance over France, to more complex exhibits gesturing toward the control of territories at the colonial periphery. In the 1820s, the Egyptian Hall was the scene of three additional exhibitions that exemplified both a more systematic analysis of "culture"—focused on the material productions of specific groups of peoples—and a closer coordination with the territorial ambitions of the nation. In 1821, Bullock displayed a cache of Egyptian antiquities looted by the orientalist adventurer, grave robber, and fellow showman Giovanni Battista Belzoni. The exhibit coincided with the British mobilization of antiquarian research in the Nile River Valley.[52] In 1822, he brought a family of Laplanders to London, evoking

Figure 10. Thomas Rowlandson, *Exhibition at Bullock's Museum of Boneparte's Carriage taken at Waterloo*. Courtesy of Guildhall Library, Corporation of London.

the polar journeys of James Clark Ross and Edward Parry.[53] And in 1824, he put on "Ancient and Modern Mexico," the fruit of his own transatlantic journey. Each exhibit was ethnographically rich, cunningly arranged, and highly successful. Each staged an exotic region that had recently come under, or was in the process of coming under, British domination, thus reinforcing the visitor's centrality in a London grown increasingly convinced of its own centrality as the hub of empire. Each demonstrated what has been called the "particularly European concern with rendering things up to be viewed," and each illustrated the art of dominating from a distance, a principal feature of which was the removal of objects to the centers of calculation in an ever-growing chain of accumulation.[54]

OPEN FOR INSPECTION

In a rhetorical figure that became a durable fixture in British representations of Mexico and Central America, Bullock portrayed his Mexican venture as an act of heroic preservation, of saving for future generations objects endangered by decay or neglect; the *Classical Journal,* which ran a lengthy review of the exhibit, agreed, noting that Bullock had "rescued" many of the "most valuable antiquities," which are now "safely brought over" to England.[55] Yet to be "rescued," these objects had first to be ripped from their proper contexts, a process that distorted their meaning by placing them into a new order, thus making them "relative to a new subject."[56] Arjun Appadurai describes this as a two-stage process, from an aesthetics of "decontextualization," in which objects are denuded, to an aesthetics of "recontextualization," in which they become laden with new significance.[57] Another way to put this is that narratives of the collection and the collector displace narratives of cultural production.[58] The first clue to that displacement is the design of the galleries that housed Bullock's collection. Ancient Mexico was placed upstairs in the "Great Room" of the Egyptian Hall, which Bullock commissioned John B. Papworth (1775–1847) to design in ornate Egyptian style.[59] The setting visually alluded to Robinson's façade and heightened the diffusionist reading of Mexican culture the exhibit sought in part to promote (Figure 11). Just as the exterior, in evoking Britain's preeminence in the East, provided an orientalist gloss to the exhibits of Napoleon's carriage and Belzoni's Egyptian artifacts, so did Papworth's "Great Room" connect ancient Mexico with ancient Egypt—

Plate 19. Vol. VIII

Figure 11. John B. Papworth's design for the interior of the Great Room at the Egyptian Hall. Courtesy of Guildhall Library, Corporation of London.

an association further emphasized by the showing of Belzoni's artifacts at the Egyptian Hall in 1821. In language that would be repeated throughout the century, Bullock's catalogue locates the Mexican past within the genealogical narrative of the West, arguing for "the close and striking resemblance" between the "Antiquities of Mexico and Egypt. The mighty Pyramid, the hieroglyphic writing, the sculptured stone, are almost alike; and their kindred origin can hardly be doubted" (*AM*, 3). Subsequent diffusionists would go further in recontextualizing pre-Columbian monuments within other cultural traditions, most famously Edward King in his attempt in the 1830s to prove that the Hebrews had settled ancient Mexico.[60] Like the British Museum's display of Egyptian antiquities, Bullock's Mexico sunders the artifacts from their native contexts, enlisting them in a cultural narrative pointing to Britain as the rightful keeper and conservator of antiquity and its material remains.

In "Modern Mexico," Bullock used a panoramic backdrop to frame the exhibit (see Figure 1), anticipating the large-scale panorama he exhibited in Robert Burford's Leicester Square rotunda the following year. The background panorama, billed here as the first "exhibited in Europe," "arrests the attention of the visitor" (*AMM*, 5), imaging imperial spectatorship by creating the illusion of standing in a privileged position over the view. The elevated position is not only associated with feelings of sublimity but also, as I argue in the next chapter, with strategies of military surveillance, technologies of mapping, and European ideologies of possession. The exhibit's panoramic backdrop reflects the travel narrative's repeated staging of elevated viewing, such as the moment the narrator ascends a hill to appreciate "a view of the valley of Mexico, with its lakes and bold outline of volcanic mountains, spread like a map before us," or when he remarks of Mexico City that "no place I ever saw affords so many interesting points for a panoramic view" (*SMR*, 119, 128). Atop the pyramids of Teotihuacán, just outside Mexico City, "we sat down to contemplate the scene of ancient wonders:—where *the eye takes in* the greater part of the vale of Mexico, its lake and city, and *commands* an extensive view of the plains beneath and the mountains that bound the west of the valley" (*SMR*, 412–13; my emphasis). Just as placing ancient Mexico within an orientalist frame suggested the eventual removal of antiquities to British museums, the "mapping" of contemporary Mexico stood as the cognitive precondition for the removal of its mineral riches to the vaults of British banks. The panoramic

tropes in the travel narrative and the exhibit serve as vehicles of mass visuality, presenting Mexico as a field to be dominated in certain imperially
minded ways.

The panoramic imagery invites the reader to share in a fantasy of possession by assuming the subject-position of the narrative "I" that "takes
in," ascends above, and maps the vista; the reader participates in and
becomes complicit with the narrator's experience, climbing up and looking down through his very eyes at the panoramic scene laid out below.
The exhibit's panoramic backdrop, in turn, installs the London visitor
within the subject position of the traveler, re-creating Bullock's experience
of "seeing" Mexico "on the spot." The *New Monthly Magazine* praised this
effect, noting that the exhibit "renders credible the veriest stories of travelers."[61] But beyond heightening the sense of the "real," the exhibit presents the land as available for a first-time view, creating the illusion that
Mexico's resources lie unclaimed, its land unsurveyed and awaiting discovery. The panorama thus provides a startling visual example of the
way in which imperial science, intersecting here with techniques of mass
spectatorship, brings "things back to a place for someone else to see it for
the first time."[62] What Bullock carries to London is not merely a view
or a collection of things, but rather ways of looking and perceiving that
reinforce imperial subject positions.

The accompanying catalogues reinforce these subject positions through
a carefully constructed discursive frame that contrasts the Spanish model
of violent military domination with the British model of gentlemanly,
informal, and "reciprocal" engagements (*AMM,* iii), a juxtaposition that
has literary analogues in the contrast between military and mercantile models of heroism, the *Amadís de Gaula* versus *Robinson Crusoe*.[63] But Bullock's
exhibition catalogues also trouble this distinction by alternately admiring
and lamenting the success of Cortés's "enterprise" (*AM,* 2)—a term that
ambivalently places the military campaign under the sign of economic
progress and the opening of distant markets. Although Bullock admires
Cortés for his strategic brilliance and stout courage, he also paints him as
a ruthless zealot responsible for "ravages and desolation" that "reduced to
ruins" a once-great culture (*AM,* 2). The Spanish conquest, according to
this latter view, "made but a slight change from the preceding era, when
the murderous idolatry of Mexico floated its temples with the blood of
human sacrifices" (*AM,* 4). Still, the catalogues narrate the conquest from

the Spanish perspective, with lengthy excerpts from Cortés's letters to Charles V and the *Historia verdadera de la conquista de Nueva España* of Bernal Díaz del Castillo, Cortés's loyal foot soldier. These sources keep the destruction of Mexico-Tenochtitlán before the reader's eyes, even as they privilege the role of the eyewitness, and thus Bullock himself, who had spent six months in direct experience with "what fell under [his] observation" (*SMR*, vi). The "abridged travel" of Bullock's exhibit, according to the *Literary Gazette*, "set that superb country before your eyes."[64]

Bullock's catalogues also look backward, reinforcing the distinction between competing imperial models by evoking the "*El Dorado* of Elizabethan times" (*MM*, 3), and thus British memories of an older conflict with Spain over the Western Hemisphere—memories that would be repeatedly stirred up by the decolonization of Latin America in the 1820s and the resurgence of British imperial might in its wake. As Disraeli put it, "The capture of a Manilla galleon will no longer afford either a peerage or a pension, and future Gondomars will not again scare the royal presence with brief but bitter denunciations of 'Piratas Ingleses.'"[65] The fascination with Walter Raleigh and the golden age of Elizabethan discovery in the Americas was manifested throughout the century. In 1826, the Raleigh Travelers' Club was formed in London, becoming the Royal Geographical Society four years later. Among its first acts was sponsoring Robert Schomburgk's expedition to British Guiana, the legendary source of Raleigh's El Dorado.[66] At midcentury, the Hakluyt Society—named after another Early Modern champion of Empire—commissioned Schomburgk to edit Raleigh's *Discoverie of the Large, Rich and Bewtiful Empyre of Guiana.* In John Everett Millais's 1870 painting, *The Boyhood of Raleigh,* the young adventurer listens to a swarthy sailor looking out over an open sea—a scene that for one contemporary reviewer suggested "El Dorado, and the palaces of Aztecs and Incas."[67] When, at century's end, the Royal Geographical Society marked the tercentenary of Queen Elizabeth's death, it did so by publishing a hagiographical essay on Raleigh by Edmund Gosse.[68] The nineteenth-century rehabilitation of Raleigh not only summoned forth the Elizabethan heyday of overseas exploration, and therefore a recuperated imperial past, but also a new horizon of possibility represented by the sudden reopening of Spanish America.

Raleigh's South American venture was a vivid reminder to British readers of the long, bitter conflict with Spain. As Gosse put it, "Contempt of

the cruel and ignorant Spaniard was always burning in Raleigh's bosom."[69]
That contempt, so vigorous in the 1590s, had a long afterlife, surfacing
repeatedly in the Black Legend, which portrayed the Spanish conquest as
barbarous and inhumanely cruel. The principal source for the discourse
was Bartolomé de Las Casas's *Brevíssima relación de la destrucción de las
Indias* (1552; English trans. 1583), which, in the editions illustrated by
the Dutch engraver Theodore de Bry, painted an unforgettable picture of
Spanish brutality in the New World. English translations of Las Casas
had a way of appearing at crucial historical moments, laying the ideological ground for other kinds of anti-Spanish interventions: a 1656 edition
translated by John Phillips, Milton's nephew, was published just as Oliver
Cromwell was mobilizing his troops for the "Western Design" in Jamaica,
and an edition published in New York was used as American propaganda
in the 1898 war against Spain.[70]

Bullock's Mexican productions ingeniously adapt the Black Legend to
the needs of informal empire by shifting attention away from the Spanish
destruction of indigenous peoples to the widespread devastation of cultural memory that thwarted curious observers like Bullock. The Spanish,
according to the *Classical Journal,* looked with "suspicious eyes" on "those
who seemed too curious in their investigations into her possessions in
the New World."[71] Indeed, Bullock decries the religious zeal that led the
Spanish clergy to burn "all the Aztec paintings, manuscripts, and hiero-
glyphical writings" (*SMR,* 400), and he finds that neglect repeated everywhere in contemporary Mexico, as if memory and historical awareness
were the primary victims of the conquest. Searching for the temples at
Teotihuacán, he finds that no one "knew or cared any thing about them";
on asking "an old Indian woman we met near the pyramids if she could
tell who made them, she replied, 'Si Signior [*sic*], St Francisco'" (*SMR,*
418–19). Bullock sums up the charge thus: "The Conquerors employed
all their means to efface every vestige and recollection of what *had been,*
from the minds of the subjugated people; . . . all their valuable books,
hieroglyphics, paintings, and historical manuscripts which could be discovered, either by art or force, were indiscriminately committed to the
flames" (*AMM,* 20). The rhetoric of darkness and Spanish ignorance but-
tresses Bullock's argument that the British are bearers of enlightenment, as
evidenced in their concern for antiquarian research, their illustrious history of scientific expeditions to far-flung lands, and their great museum

collections at home. Bullock's descriptions of the lengths to which he went scouring the land for antiquities, searching through musty archives, and molding plaster casts in the heat of the Mexican sun—all in the cause of "rescu[ing] from oblivion" what was in danger of being lost or unappreciated (*AM,* 2)—are best understood as figures for the salvific power of British civilization itself. If under Spanish colonialism, "Temples were cast down, Idols broken to pieces or buried, and all the memorials of former ages diligently obliterated," the "Catalogue will show that much has been saved" (*AM,* 2). Bullock even reports the astonishment of the Mexicans themselves, who "express[ed] surprise at the motives that could induce me to take so much pains in copying those stones" (*SMR,* 336). For Bullock, Britain's effort to collect, preserve, display, and study the material remains of the past is convincing evidence of its cultural superiority and ethical advance over Spain. Whereas Spain came to plunder and sack, Britain comes not only to trade and exchange but also to shed light on the mysteries of the Mexican past, to increase wealth *and* knowledge.

But just as Bullock characterizes British travelers as savers of the past, he also presents them as forward-looking agents of the new industrial future: innovative, progressive, and technologically advanced. Here Bullock anticipates the logic of the world's fairs, whose invariable message of European progress was advanced through the contrast between technological prowess (evidenced by photography, the steam engine, the cotton gin) and primitive backwardness (embodied in "rude" or "simple" handicrafts or curiosities). These contrasts, part of the larger logic of temporal displacement that underpinned Western assumptions of cultural superiority, are registered across Bullock's Mexican productions. Although Mexico, "owing to Spanish policy, is three hundred years behind Europe in every species of refinement" (*SMR,* 202–3), the transformative power of Bullock's entrepreneurial gaze is able to imagine an ill-repaired road becoming a path to riches: "Should the English establish a communication with the mines of Mexico . . . this road will be of the greatest importance; little is wanting towards its completion but the M'Adamizing system, and the spirit of enterprise now existing in England" (*SMR,* 39). The trade-off is explained in a familiar imperial logic: "intelligent strangers may be induced to visit her, and bring with them the arts and manufactures, the improved machinery and great chymical [*sic*] knowledge of Europe; and in return she can amply repay them by again diffusing through the world her immense mineral wealth" (*SMR*, 130). Britain will bring enlightenment and the colonies will return wealth. These representations—Mexico, backward and ignorant; Britain, technologically advanced and enlightened; Spain, cruel, superstitious, and unscientific—reinforce a progressive, industrial narrative of history that assumes Mexico's economic and cultural inferiority, and ultimately its availability for exploitation.

MAKING FLAT

For Bruno Latour, writing constitutes the "*the fine edge* and the *final stage* of a whole process of mobilization." Writing reduces ungainly, three-dimensional objects to flat, combinable "inscriptions."[72] It assembles things into tabular form, makes them available to structures of citation and reference, and creates new orders of knowledge based on the ability to "see" things all in one place. These processes were repeatedly born out in the British engagement with Mexico. Consider a small but representative example: a "synopsis" of birds collected by Bullock in Mexico. Lamenting that rare specimens were about to be "dispersed by the hammer of the auctioneer" and "for ever lost" (recall Bullock's language about Aztec antiquities), the naturalist William Swainson seized on his friendship with Bullock to arrange a synopsis, which he published in 1827.[73] The synopsis reduced 101 species of birds—101 very *mutable* mobiles—to a single, flat, combinable, reproducible text of a mere eighteen pages that allowed the reader to see the birds, and to see them whole (the root meaning of "synopsis"). The birds, or rather their textual inscriptions, could now enter the discourse of ornithology. Latour writes that collections have impact only while "the archives are well-kept, the labels are in place,"[74] a point we can extend by considering in greater depth the "catalogue" as a scientific and economic genre in its own right and a crucial device in the codification of the imperial archive. In the fifteenth century the term "catalogue" referred simply to a list or enumeration, such as a "Cateloge of Popes," and it was only toward the end of the seventeenth century that it acquired the suggestion of a "systematic or methodical arrangement" in alphabetical or other order, such as a "catalogue raisonné," which appeared circa 1784 *(OED)*. The later uses suggest the emerging dominance of the taxonomic drive, associated with the Linnaean system as well as the gathering and collation of objects in public and private museums. The first enumerative guidebooks to the British Museum, for example, appeared in the 1760s. A characteristic example is *The General Contents of the British Museum: With Remarks, Serving as a Directory in Viewing That Noble Cabinet* (2nd ed., 1762). The annually published volumes of the *Synopsis of the Contents of the British Museum* began in the first decade of the nineteenth century, and were followed by descriptive catalogues to separate collections such as the Greek and Roman antiquities. The catalogues guided visitors through the increasingly large and heterogeneous collections, indexing them in a reproducible, pocket-sized brief. The catalogues Bullock published regularly for his Liverpool and London museums performed the same functions.

Catalogues were also important tools in the economic transformation of objects into commodities. In 1819, Bullock issued catalogues to enumerate for buyers, who included Walter Scott and the British Museum, collections that were to be sold at auction, including one of books, one of Roman antiquities, and another of antiquities and works of art. After the Mexican shows ended, the exhibition catalogues were also transformed into lists of goods for sale. The British Museum Department of Ethnography holds a copy of the sale catalogue, bound in with Bullock's *Six Months' Residence,* with hand-written notes showing the prices paid for each item, including the Mexican antiquities purchased by William Buckland (dean of Westminster's and president of the Geological Society of London) for resale to the British Museum. The sale catalogue also helps us follow the trajectory of private collections as they pass into the larger museum order of the nation: its methods of arrangement, display, and cataloguing as well as its schemes of value. In Bullock's case, most of the Mexican artifacts were placed in a gallery known as the Artificial Curiosities of Different Countries, adjacent to the Gallery of Antiquities containing Greek and Roman statuary, while others were exhibited in the Ante Room, next to the Elgin Marbles. The gallery's miscellaneous grouping—which included "Eskimo," "Ashantee," and South Seas objects—eroded the cultural specificity Bullock had attempted to reinforce, returning the object to the disreputable status of the curiosity. The objects did not change, only the frames, but those frames changed the meaning of the objects. Likewise, the British Museum *Synopses* strip out most of the historical contexts Bullock provided and instead fall back on mere parataxis. Bullock's artifacts remained in the gallery of Artificial Curiosities until the mid-1840s, when they were moved to the Ethnographical Room, marking the emergence of a new taxonomy and system of value that, as I examine at greater length in chapter 4, would eventually be conjoined with the imperial science of anthropology. It should go without saying that in the scale of museum meaning, ethnography fell far below aesthetics; never were the Mexican artifacts considered art. Even today, they fall under the administrative control of the Department of Ethnography.

Yet if imperial science depends on the "immutable mobile," the imperial museum depends on the commoditization of those mobiles, which links scientific inquiry to the ebbs and flows of global capital. Appadurai, as we recall, urges attention to the forces that divert objects intended for other uses into the "commodity phase" of their career. Only by focusing on the trajectories of "things-in-motion" can we "illuminate their human and social context" and the way their meaning shifts from one context to another.[75] This model, where things constantly mutate under pressure from cultural or economic forces, helps us grasp a crucial step in the mobilization of the Mexican artifacts. Although never meant to be commodities, they were bought and sold in a developing market for antiquities. Value was added to them by displays such as Bullock's, and that value increased when they entered the national collection. Their trajectory as commodities, moreover, closely followed the path of Mexico's ores and precious metals; like the ores, antiquities were dug from the earth and carried across the Atlantic—frequently by men who were both miners and amateur antiquarians. Economic and cultural plunder rode on parallel tracks.[76]

As published writing, Bullock's catalogues soon entered the citationary structure of British discourse about Mexico, becoming a key source not only in travel narratives and history, but also in the popular press. One of the more complex and frequently reiterated claims of this discourse was that Mexico encouraged foreign interest in its antiquities; as Bullock put it, the collection was "formed with the sanction and through the aid of the present Mexican Government" (*AMM*, iii). In his travel narrative Bullock makes a point of showing that Lucas Alamán, Mexico's foreign minister, not only gave him permission to make the plaster casts but also sanctioned the removal of the priceless indigenous codices, the nation's oldest written records (*SMR*, 422, 334). Bullock notes as well that General Antonio López de Santa Anna "no sooner understood that my journey was solely to acquire scientific information, than he liberally refused even to examine my letters or papers, and immediately gave me an assurance of his protection"

(*SMR*, 28). We cannot, from this distance, determine whether these claims are true, but we do know that Mexican elites saw cultural exchange as a way to promulgate new transatlantic relationships after breaking politically with Spain. This notion informs Mauricio Tenorio-Trillo's argument about Mexico's participation in the world's fairs later in the nineteenth century.[77] These spectacles, which Bullock's emphasis on culture and economics anticipates, became machines for the production of a technologically and industrially oriented modernity that Mexican elites were as invested in promoting as their European and U.S. counterparts. But Bullock's claims about the aid he received from Mexicans also paint a portrait of Mexican cultural submission while affirming the distinction, elaborated in his travel narrative, between cultures that collect antiquities (and thus preserve the past) and those that do not. The distinction also plays into the notion that Western superiority lies in its possession of writing—a claim repeatedly invoked in Bullock's Mexican productions and in the larger discourse of pre-Columbian culture they engendered.

James Clifford argues that the West's ethnographic imperative has historically been grounded in the assumption of "'bringing a culture into writing,' moving from oral-discursive experience (the 'native's,' the fieldworker's) to a written version of that experience (the ethnographic text)." The process of "writing up" functions as an act of "salvage," preserving in books the traces of cultures and epochs otherwise doomed to melt away, "vanishing in time and space." Yet Clifford, drawing on Jacques Derrida's grammatology as well as evidence from traditional societies, reminds us that "*all* human groups write—if they articulate, classify . . . or inscribe their world in ritual acts."[78] The privileging of writing thus appears as a fiction of power. Bullock's attention to Aztec picture writing is symptomatic of this fiction. While on the one hand claiming that the codices have been "rescued from oblivion, and safely transferred to England" (*MM*, 2), Bullock also treats them less as coherent writing systems (which he could not understand) than as rude or barbarous curiosities. Despite possessing a writing system, the Aztecs remain mute and unknowable, their history brought to a violent close by the arrival of Europeans, who duly record the glories of conquest in their own written texts.

An examination of the counterimperial consciousness emerging in Mexico after 1821, however, complicates the terms by which Bullock (and subsequent travelers and museum officials) justified Britain's claim to ownership of monuments and thus control over the past. This counter-discourse, though laced with its own internal contradictions, suggests the complexity of Mexico's response to the sudden arrival of the British "capitalist vanguard."[79] For if the control of antiquities—and by extension historical representation itself—was crucial to British self-fashioning, it was also central to Latin American nations in the early post-independence era, as they sought to preserve their own past and incorporate sacred objects into the national imaginary. The very government officials Bullock claims to have assisted him, Lucas Alamán and Carlos María de Bustamante, protested in their writings and legislative acts against the cultural robbery visited upon them by British travelers and antiquarians. In 1823 Alamán delivered a speech to the Mexican Congress summarizing the general condition of the newly founded nation. After discussing topics such as public works and services for the poor, Alamán made pointed reference to Mexico's libraries, archives, and museums, reminding the congress that they were filled with "highly valuable monuments of Mexican antiquity" (23). Sadly, he observed, many had disappeared, undermining Mexico's efforts to establish a museum where the ancient codices and painted books—the culture's written memory—could be read by learned and studious persons (23). Alamán's speech reflects the importance of museums and archives in the construction of New World national identities. And even with its carefully phrased passive constructions that avoid naming names—the monuments have disappeared ("han desaparecido")—it suggests a critique of imperial plunder that would grow louder over the next several years as the scale of looting came to light.[80]

Alamán's speech was immediately translated into English. Joel Poinsett, the first American ambassador to Mexico and a passionate collector of Mexican antiquities in his own right, printed a translation of the speech as an appendix to his *Notes on Mexico,* published in Philadelphia (1824) and London (1825). Benjamin Disraeli, his head swimming with speculative schemes, also published the speech in its entirety in *The Present State of Mexico* (1825). Bullock himself, in a letter to the British Museum trustees in July 1825, advised prompt action on his offer to sell the collection: "as the government of Mexico has since issued an edict prohibiting any more [antiquities] from leaving the country; in consequence of it being their immediate intention to establish a national museum in the city of Mexico, it may be fairly inferred that these are the only specimens that will find their way to Europe."[81] Finally, the next month the *Gentleman's Magazine,* perhaps on Bullock's urging, again pressed the British Museum to purchase the collection, reiterating the warning that the law forbidding export was a preliminary step to "forming a National Museum of their own upon a very extended scale."[82] Thus while Mexican elites were seeking to conserve the nation's antiquities in the service of patriotism, the announced intention of forming a museum—which was formally established in 1825—was being used abroad to hasten plunder, hinder already acquired treasures from being returned, and fuel imperial rivalries between European nations.

A few years later, after more collections of antiquities were spirited out of Mexico to foreign museums, Bustamante wrote even more directly of the threat posed by foreign travelers. In his *Mañanas de la alameda de México* (1835), a set of dialogues on native history, Bustamante cast aside Alamán's polite phrasing and laid the blame for the outflow of the nation's cultural heritage squarely on foreign capitalists and travelers. From the moment we "opened our doors to free European commerce," he wrote, many travelers have arrived seeking to study "our history," to inquire after "our origins," to copy the few remaining antiquities "left to us." Driven by their "curiosidad," these travelers bought the scarcest productions ("las más raras producciones") and took them to European museums and cabinets. Most grievous, Bustamante wrote, was the removal of the ancient maps "trabajados en papel de maguey" (executed on maguey paper) that preserved "la verdadera Historia Antigua," i.e., the true ancient history of the Mexican people.[83] Here he may have been referring explicitly to Bullock, who carried away and exhibited the so-called *Plan de Maguey* and many other rare codices, some later returned to Mexico, others sold at auction, vanishing forever from the historical record. Of these, Bustamante could not speak without feeling "profound grief." Although in 1829 Bustamante introduced legislation forbidding the export of antiquities, he noted ruefully in the *Mañanas* that "the gold that purchases artifacts is stronger than any law."[84] In 1846 Isidro Gondra, the first director of the Museo Nacional, referred to his "disgust" at Bullock's acquisition of the precious codices, and explained how, through the efforts of Mexican officials, they were eventually returned to Mexico.[85]

This is not to say, however, that the Creole reverence for the indigenous past translated into sympathy for, or action to improve, the miserable conditions under which most indigenes lived. Then as now, Mexico was sharply divided along racial and cultural lines, with the indigenous trapped at the bottom of the economic and social hierarchy. When rebellions periodically occurred, the authorities put them down in the name of social order. Even the most liberal of Creole antiquarians and historians combined "valorization of pre-Hispanic Indians, compassion for colonial Indians, and embarrassment for contemporary Indians."[86] Here again the indigenous are positioned outside modernity, a temporal move repeatedly affirmed in the writing of Mexican history. Even Octavio Paz, in his classic study of Claude Levi-Strauss, writes that for 2,000 years none of the Mesoamerican cultures "had historical consciousness."[87] As we have seen, when British travelers commented on the ignorance of the indigenous toward their monuments, they rhetorically divided them from history, and thus from progress. Nineteenth-century Creoles shared this rhetoric, imposing an internal version of center/periphery power relations to control and manipulate the indigenous past for their own political ends—ends that denied the indigenous as rightful inheritors of that past. Creole historiography, whether in its museum or academic form, perpetuated the "exclusion [of the indigenous] from the national project."[88]

Yet despite its own distortions, the Creole emphasis on the nation's written memory stands as an important rebuttal to the presumed ethnographic authority of British travelers and collectors, and an equally crucial assertion of the need for cultures to be able to interpret themselves. As the Creoles insist, not only did the ancient Mexicans have writing (and history, of course), but modern Mexicans in the post-independence period were actively engaged in preserving that past and were well aware of the steep price they had paid for economic assistance from abroad. The arrival of foreign travelers imperiled the nation's cultural memory, for they sought to appropriate, remove, and control the founding documents of Mexican antiquity, undermining the culture from within. Indeed for Bustamante, the theft of the maps and codices had left Mexicans "in the dark as to how to interpret" the few remaining texts left in Mexican archives. As European interest in pre-Columbian antiquity increased over the next several decades, curious foreigners stole away more precious objects of antiquity, depositing them in distant museums and private collections where they served other purposes, other narratives. In 1859 the Mexican Society of Geography and Statistics, a leading scientific body, published the report of a special commission calling again for stronger laws protecting cultural heritage, urging that the government claim Mexico's archaeological monuments as property of the state. Darkly, it noted the precise calculus of desire and appropriation we have examined here: "In proportion to the increased European cult for the study and possession of antiquity, so will the danger increase to those few monuments that now remain."[89] As I have argued here, the roots of this massive redistribution of property lay in Bullock's venture, whose combination of travel, collecting, and exhibiting remained a crucial feature of Britain's relationship with Mexico and Central America for decades.

chapter 2

BUENA VISTA

*Panoramas and the
Visualization of Conquest*

The traveler's testimony is also the preparation for warlike spirits.
— CARLOS MONSIVÁIS, "Los viajeros y la invención de México"

In early-nineteenth-century Britain, the collecting, removal, and display of far-flung artifacts served as a compelling metaphor for the empire's reach and grasp, an analogy intensified by shows that made explicit the association between museum collections and the extractive operations of imperialism. If exhibitions brought the public into intimate contact with artifacts, or, in Bruno Latour's formulation, "mobilized" distant objects for display in the "centers of calculation,"[1] intimacy was in some sense an effect of that power to mobilize. To inspect was also to touch or seize; exhibition rooms were drawn to human scale; houses, as Sir John Soane showed, could be museums, and museums houses. Entire cultures were miniaturized, domesticated, displayed, and made flat in descriptive lists and catalogues. These operations, which have figural analogues, tore away the frames that had originally given objects their meaning within the cultures that made them. Through metaphor, museum exhibitions configured artifacts into relationships of substitution; through metonymy, into relationships of contiguity. Each process destroyed one formation only to forge another.

The panorama, by contrast, separated the observer from the artifact through complex spatial dynamics inscribed in the built form of its architecture and the tradition of landscape viewing that informed it. Patented

in 1796 by Robert Barker (1739–1806) and featuring vast 360-degree paintings displayed in specially designed, circular theaters, the panorama was
at once a technology, an art form, and a complex instrument of power. By
the 1820s, it had become a staple of metropolitan entertainment in London, Paris, Berlin, and various cities on the eastern seaboard of the United
States; over 100 million people, according to one estimate, saw these productions.[2] In Britain, the panorama attracted the attention of figures
such as Wordsworth, who accused it of "taking in / A whole horizon's circuit . . . with power," and Ruskin, who praised it as an "educational institution of the highest and purest value."[3] Its visual poetics look back to
eighteenth-century developments in landscape theory and the sublime,
while its status as mass entertainment points forward, as Walter Benjamin
notes, "beyond photography, to films and sound films," suggesting the
desire for cinema long before its realization.[4]

In this chapter I investigate the function of panoramic representations
in the British encounter with Mexico, focusing in detail on how Bullock's
panorama, staged in tandem with his museum exhibition, encoded spatial
and imaginative relations that were crucial to Britain's informal empire in
Mexico. In arguing this point, I first trace the discourse of imperial vision
back to the Spanish colonial narratives that informed Bullock's Mexican
representations. Then, for contrast, I analyze how panoramic tropes were
appropriated by two U.S. cultural productions that were indebted to
Bullock but which diverged from him in significant ways: William H.
Prescott's *History of the Conquest of Mexico* (1843) and a scrolled, or moving, panorama exhibited by Mexican War veteran Corydon Donnavan in
the late 1840s. I use these examples not to offer a comprehensive account
of the panorama, but rather to examine the panorama's function as a potent
ideological weapon in the cultural armature of informal imperialism.

MANAGING ATTENTION

In a peculiar example of imitative form, discussions of the panorama have
generated masterly overviews and grand syntheses, while ignoring the particular historical contexts of individual panoramas. Over 300 panoramas
were exhibited in the United States and Europe, yet critics have examined
only a handful in any detail. The standard history of the British panorama, Richard Altick's *Shows of London*, situates the form within a broad

cavalcade of domestic spectacle between 1660 and 1850; Stephan Oettermann's *Panorama: History of a Mass Medium,* taking a similarly wide view,
traces the panorama's origin to a new awareness of the horizon aided by
balloon and mountain ascents, advances in the theorization of landscape,
interest in the sublime, and the growth of urban populations eager for
new amusements.[5] More recently, students of what Nancy Armstrong calls
"mass visuality," such as Susan Buck-Morss and Anne Friedberg, have
turned to Walter Benjamin's *Arcades Project* to probe the formation of
subjectivity in relation to mass spectacle, the emergence of the modern
city, and the culture of consumption.[6] In "Paris, Capital of the Nineteenth
Century," Benjamin accorded the panorama a key place among the representations and practices that defined modernity for a newly mobile urban
bourgeoisie: shopping arcades; the world's fairs; glass and iron buildings such as the Crystal Palace; the *flâneur;* and urban design, specifically
Haussmann's redesign of Paris, the true purpose of which, he argued, "was
to secure the city against civil war."[7]

Benjamin's grasp of the place of architecture in social regulation anticipates Michel Foucault's work on discipline, which takes as its principal
site Jeremy Bentham's panopticon, designed nine years before Barker's
panorama. In a series of letters written in 1787 and published in 1791,
Bentham boasted that his "inspection house" was merely a "simple idea in
Architecture."[8] Yet the panopticon, as Foucault argued, represented nothing less than a fantasy of total knowledge, embodied within an influential
instrument of regulatory control.[9] A comparison of Bentham's panopticon
(Figure 12) with Robert Mitchell's panorama (Figure 13) suggests that
Bentham's insistence that his design should be understood as fundamentally architectural was not wholly disingenuous. Each was a circular building arrayed around a central viewing tower, a design that organized the
relations between subject and object, knower and known, into a highly
charged "field of inspection" that could be "dilated" to any extent.[10] The
panopticon enabled the inspection of criminalized bodies; the panorama,
visual images painted in the round. The field of inspection also mapped a
relational dynamics in which power depended entirely on one's physical
and thus subjective position. The prisoners' views were blocked by walls
jutting out from each cell and by a lighting system that illuminated the
prisoner but concealed the supervisor, while the elevated tower granted
the most privileged view, a full 360-degree sweep.[11]

The design of European schools, factories, workhouses, and asylums gradually incorporated the relation between vision and power as well as the dynamics of subjectification that was its corollary.[12] Neither Benjamin nor Foucault, however, with their attention fixed on Europe, examines how such technologies were mobilized for the imperial project. Like most students of panoramic or panoptic representation, they emphasize either the fashioning of domestic subjects for rituals of consumption or the disciplining of docile bodies for service to the state. Yet, while Bentham failed to persuade Parliament to build his prison,[13] the model was successfully exported, providing a noteworthy example of how metropolitan technologies of representation and social control found new applications abroad. In his comprehensive code for Venezuela (1810), Bentham proposed the construction of a "panopticon polychreston," a circular school whose central hall could serve as church, court, concert space, or assembly room.[14]

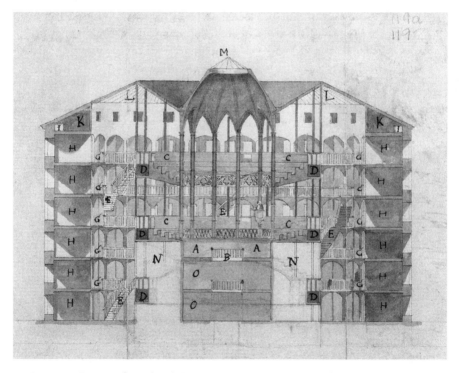

Figure 12. Section of Bentham's Inspection House. Jeremy Bentham Papers (119a/119), University College London Library Services.

Ten years later, he corresponded with Spanish American leaders to encourage the construction of the panopticon—a project eventually realized in the design of various Latin American penitentiaries.[15] The panorama, as well, was nearly exported to Latin America. In 1827, the Chilean lawyer and statesman Mariano Egaña (1793–1846), who had been living in London, wrote two lengthy letters to his father describing his hopes for bringing the panorama to Chile; only the great expense prevented it from gaining a foothold there.[16]

To understand further how the panorama's dynamic of power operated in the imperial context, we must consider not only Foucault's emphasis on the "surface of application,"[17] but also the subjectification of the *observer*, standing in the high tower. Jonathan Crary, in an important book on nineteenth-century technologies of vision, defines the "spectator" as one who passively looks, the "observer" as one who is "embedded in a system of conventions and limitations." For Crary, the 1820s and 1830s marked a new set of articulations between the body and institutional modalities of

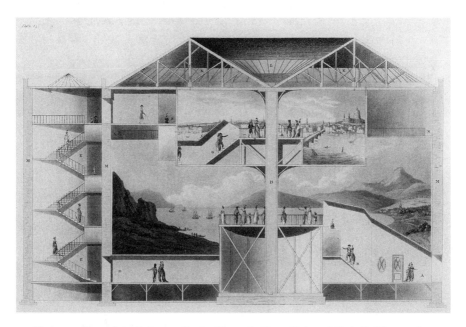

Figure 13. Plan of the Leicester Square Rotunda, from Robert Mitchell, *Plans and Views in Perspective of Buildings Erected in England and Scotland* (1801). Courtesy of Yale Center for British Art, Paul Mellon Collection.

power that redefined the "observing subject." Though he focuses principally on forms such as the camera obscura and the stereoscope, and pays
little attention to the imperial dynamics of visual technologies, Crary's
emphasis on the "management of attention" merits consideration here.[18]

How did the panorama's architectural design structure the relations
between an embodied observer and the images it purveyed? First, because
concealed skylights illuminated the image while shrouding the observer
in darkness, the entire apparatus obscured the panorama's function as a
machine for the production of vision. The panorama created "not only a
spectacle but a spectator with a particular relation to 'reality',"[19] a reality
controlled, as in the darkened cinema, by the manipulation of light and
images. Visitors ascended the observation tower by interior staircases that
hid the panoramic image from their gaze until they emerged onto the
viewing platform. "The top and bottom of the picture," as F. W. Fairholt's
Dictionary of Terms in Art (1854) described it, were "concealed by the
framework of the gallery; . . . an almost infinite space and distance can
be represented with a degree of illusion quite wonderful."[20] The effect
was overwhelming, not merely from the vast scale of the spectacle—some
exceeded 20,000 feet in area—but from the abruptness with which the
observer was subsumed within the image. The panorama's circularity and
its lack of a frame denied the stabilizing comfort of single point perspective
on which realist painting had relied since the Renaissance. A reviewer for
Blackwood's captured the panorama's dizzying collapse of space and time:

> Vesuvius in full roar and torrent, within a hundred yards of a hackney-coach
> stand; . . . Switzerland, with its lakes covered with sunset, and mountains
> capped and robed in storms . . . stuck in a corner of a corner of London . . . ;
> and now Pompeii, reposing in its slumber of two thousand years, in the very
> buzz of the Strand.[21]

Unlike the ascent up a peak, a mainstay of the Romantic quest for the
sublime, there was no gradual dawning, no physical effort invested in the
arrival at the summit, nor the prospect of a slow descent. The observer was
plunged violently *into* the illusion.

Yet if one effect of the panoramic illusion was to surround the observer
with a totalizing image, another was to place the observer—as in the topo-
graphical tradition of British prospect poetry—in a superior position *over*

the represented landscape, to play on the psychological associations of height, and thus to promote a vision of the land as available for domination or control. As Mitchell's design shows, the vantage point enjoyed by and enjoined on the observer was elevated above the painting, at eye level with the horizon. The observer's commanding view suggests both Bentham's "supervisor" in his high tower and Edmund Burke's claim that he knew of "nothing sublime which is not some modification of power." Indeed, Burke held that vastness was most sublime when experienced from a dizzying height: "an hundred yards of even ground will never work such an effect as a tower an hundred yards high."[22] There are several ways to understand this power. In Victorian fiction towers frequently suggest narrative omniscience or epistemological mastery of other kinds: in *Bleak House* (1853) the all-knowing Inspector Bucket "mounts a high tower in his mind, and looks out far and wide"; in *The Mill on the Floss* (1860) Maggie Tulliver meditates on the astronomers who "live up in high towers," guarding masculine realms of knowledge.[23] For an increasingly class-conscious populace, the ascent to the high platform may also have functioned as a "metaphor for social aspiration and social dominance."[24] Indeed, some accounts of the panorama suggest a two-tiered structure based on social standing, with a lower painting giving a "compromised view" set below another, which offered the "correct perspective"—for a higher price, of course.[25]

In geographical terms, the panorama symbolized the center/periphery relation at the heart of imperial ideology; within its double center—the observation deck and London itself—one took in the pictured terrains projected on its screens.[26] In seemingly collapsing vast distances, the panorama suggested the idea of an expanding, limitless empire that was capable, through a variety of means, of mobilizing the periphery for consumption at home, often in celebratory ways. Henry Aston Barker, whose father invented the panorama, played a notable role in linking the panorama to expansionist national agendas. His sketches of the battle of Waterloo, quickly transformed into circular images, caused an immediate sensation, securing the panorama's importance as a tool for the making of imperial subjects.[27] When the Royal Highland Regiment returned to Edinburgh from the war, they were admitted free to the panoramic view of the battle; so effective was the realism, and so limited their own perception of the battles in which they had fought, that to grasp what they had experienced as soldiers they had to become "spectators" of the panoramic representation of it.[28] In 1860, on the eve of a great period of imperial growth, the popular magazine *Chambers's Journal* looked back at fifty years of panoramic entertainment to remark that the panorama of Waterloo "was the most popular and lucrative" of any exhibited.[29] Victorian imperialists of a later generation drew on the panoramic trope of a limitless horizon to represent an empire on which the sun never set. Edward Hertslet, a noteworthy Foreign Office archivist, described Downing Street as "the greatest street in the world, because it lies at the hub of a gigantic wheel which encircles the globe under the name of the British Empire."[30]

By the early nineteenth century, the panorama spurred public interest in imperial exploration, forming the popular analogue to bodies such as the Royal Geographical Society, whose charter (1830) made clear the relationship between the expansion of geographical knowledge and "the welfare of a maritime nation like Great Britain, with its numerous and extensive foreign possessions."[31] Crucial here is the panorama's status as popular culture, which Annie E. Coombes, following Tony Bennett, defines as the "area of exchange" between classes.[32] While the form appealed to such figures as Wordsworth and Ruskin, it also captivated, according to nineteenth-century panoramist John Vanderlyn, "all classes of Spectators, . . . for no study nor a cultivated taste is required fully to appreciate the merits of such representations."[33] At the level of mass visuality, the panorama furnished an ever-changing series of new geographical terrains, figuring them as already or soon to be contained. In 1834, Robert Burford mounted a panorama celebrating James Clark Ross's discovery of the North Magnetic Pole in 1831. In 1834–35, the British architect and traveler Frederick Catherwood exhibited panoramas of Karnak and Jerusalem reflecting the mobilization of British antiquarian research in the region after Napoleon's defeat. And in 1836, Burford displayed a panorama timed to publicize Lt. William Smyth's journey from Lima across the Andes in search of a passage to the Atlantic.[34] Like travel literature, panoramas provided an experience of the "real" geared to the logics of imperial geography, immersing the observer in images that acted powerfully on the body itself. In Latourian terms, the form imaged the possibility of acting at a distance, mobilizing distant places for visual cognition in the metropolis. As the charter of the Royal Geographical Society suggested, the production of that knowledge enabled the manipulation and control of the periphery from distant metropolitan centers.

MEXICO IN LEICESTER SQUARE

As we saw in the previous chapter, Bullock experimented in the early 1820s with panoramic visuality both in his travel narrative and in the museum exhibitions, complementing the representation of fine-grained particulars with suggestions of totality. If the use of the panorama in these forms gestured toward an all-encompassing view, the full-scale panorama that Bullock mounted in Leicester Square in 1826 took that possibility to its conceptual and affective limit. Here, visitors were invited to take in Mexico through a mass-cultural technology that, like the museum exhibitions, reinforced collective identities and a sense of national belonging. Since Mexico, unlike Paris, London, or other familiar scenes represented in panoramas, was almost entirely unknown to the wider British public, and was already being cast as "one vast field for the exercise of British capital, machinery, and industry,"[35] Bullock's panorama must be understood as part of a larger system of representations that served the goals of British informal imperialism in the Americas.

This visually imagined subjugation was effected not only through the specialized architectural and scenic techniques common to all panoramas, but through the language of the textual guide that accompanied the display, a guide which, in explaining the view and reducing it to writing, translated the necessarily ephemeral experience of being in the panoramic theater into a portable text that could be cited, indexed, and combined with other discourses. In twelve lively pages, Bullock's printed guide reinforced the aesthetics of visual domination by situating the painted image with reference to carefully chosen historical antecedents, narratively framing the circular image to ensure a particular reading of it. The pamphlet also ordered the viewing experience by providing commentary on thirty-eight locations within the painting, ranging from key buildings to geographical features such as lakes, volcanoes, and mineral springs. Two fold-out plates indexed these sites both to the commentary and to the panoramic image before the viewer (Figure 14). Not simply descriptive or enumerative, the pamphlet was suffused with the commercial ideologies central to Britain's relationship with Mexico in 1825–26, when investors and financiers, after the initial enthusiasm for Mexican mines, began to fear a crash. Bullock's display of a rational and orderly Mexico countered those fears by representing Mexico through the same technology used to depict the rational and orderly cities of Europe; Mexico was depicted as a safe place for British money. But by subtly alluding in the guide and in the image to a history of colonial conquest and vassalage, Bullock's panorama also underlined Mexico's long submission to Europe. For although a military occupation was out of the question, new forms of domination, troped as mutually beneficial exchange, could be easily imagined from within the pleasure dome of the panorama.

The opening description of Mexico City is "taken" from a godlike, panoramic perspective; the narrator describes it as resting in the "centre of a vast plain" surrounded by mountains to the height of 14,000 to 17,000 feet.[36] The Mexico he depicts thus appears already panoramic, as if nature,

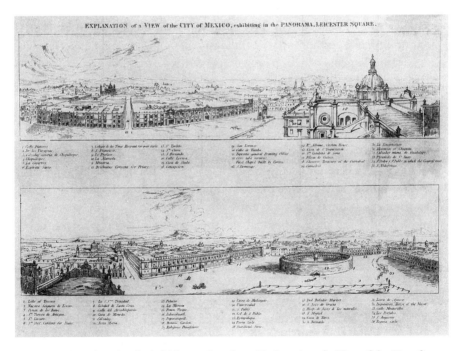

Figure 14. Robert Burford, fold-out plan, from *Explanation of a View of the City of Mexico, Exhibiting in the Panorama, Leicester Square.* Courtesy of Research Library, Getty Research Institute, Los Angeles.

and not a European aesthetic tradition, had composed it as landscape. This strategy, like the panorama's lighting scheme, naturalizes vision itself by concealing the apparatus that makes it possible. In the description quoted below, a "vast amphitheatre" encloses the scene, suggesting that the land, in a sublime mode, stages itself for visual consumption by the imagined traveler. What nature has wrought, moreover, exceeds the power of language, thus the necessity of the visual experience:

> viewed from an elevation in the interior [of the city], the regularity of the streets, the beauty and extent of the public buildings, the number and variegated colours of the houses, the luxuriant appearance of the surrounding valley, studded with numerous towns and villages, and the extensive lakes . . . the whole enclosed by a vast amphitheatre of lofty mountains; form a scene magnificent and beautiful beyond description.[37]

Although the scene is described in language, it is also ineffably sublime; although words are inadequate to the picture, the view can be represented on the circular canvas.[38] It is almost as if Bullock motions the observer to look up from the page to take in and assume power over the image.

In ways now familiar to us from observation decks in skyscrapers, word and image work together, with the guide referring to the image and the image returning the spectator to the guide. Using these paired modes of cognition the panorama explains the relationship between the sight of Mexico presented in London and a historically antecedent sight first experienced by the Spanish conquistadors. The relationship may be understood both as superimposition and repetition with a difference. The prior sight toward which Bullock's London panorama gestures is the first prospect of the valley of Mexico glimpsed by Cortés and his soldiers in 1520 during their long march inland from the town of Veracruz. Because Bullock's Mexican itinerary inland from the coast closely paralleled Cortés's, the panorama suggests a visual experience readable on several levels: the first view seen by Cortés (and its representations in narrative); Bullock's reprise of that vista during his own journey inland (and its representations); and last, the British spectator's view, enabled by the printed guide, inside the panorama. What this overlapped structure makes possible is a comparison of imperialisms and a renovation of panoramic vision.

In narrating the Spanish conquest Bullock repeatedly cites the vivid eyewitness account of Bernal Díaz del Castillo (1496–1584), the *Historia verdadera de la conquista de la Nueva España*. Since its first appearance in English in 1800 as *The True History of the Conquest of Mexico*, Díaz's text has been praised for its narrative vigor and earthy appeal.[39] Yet in the guide to the panorama Bullock eschews Díaz, taking his description of the valley of Mexico from the *History of America* (1777) by William Robertson, who, ironically, never set foot in Mexico. Here is Robertson's description of the conquistador's first glimpse of the valley of Mexico, as given by Bullock:

> When, in descending the mountains of Chalco, the Spaniards first beheld the plain of Mexico, one of the most striking and beautiful on the face of the earth; when they observed fertile and cultivated fields, *stretching farther than the eye could reach;* when they saw a lake, resembling the sea in extent, encompassed with large towns, and discovered the capital city rising upon an island in the middle, adorned with its temples and turrets, the scene so far exceeded their imagination, that some believed the fanciful descriptions of romance were realized, and that its enchanted palaces and gilded domes were *presented to their views*: others could hardly persuade themselves that this wonderful spectacle was any thing more than a dream.[40]

Why would Bullock choose this account over Díaz's? The principal difference is aesthetic; Robertson supplements his Spanish source by emphasizing the sublime, which he had derived from Burke, and the picturesque, which was already in the air and soon to be theorized by William Gilpin and Uvedale Price.[41] Nowhere in Díaz do we find tropes such as "stretching farther than the eye could reach," or the "gilded domes were presented to their views." Instead, we find the marvelous ("maravillar") and the legendary: "decíamos que parecía a las cosas de encantamiento que cuentan en el libro de Amadís."[42] The dazzling city, that is, seemed like the enchanted things described in *Amadís de Gaula,* the fabled work that, according to Cervantes, maddened Quixote's brain. By means of the sublime and picturesque, Robertson translates romance into the tropes of British landscape representation, with its overtones of aspiration, mastery, oversight, imaginative possession, and classification according to forms of aesthetic experience and kinds or qualities of landscape. As we have seen, that tradition deeply influenced the development of the panorama as an art form, even if the physical experience of ascending peaks to discover picturesque views was transformed into climbing a winding staircase of an urban building to emerge on a view painted in the round. It is in fact quite fitting that Bullock should prefer his Díaz filtered through Robertson, first because the *History* is historically and culturally coincident with the eighteenth-century theorization of landscape aesthetics, second because an emphasis on the aesthetic appreciation of land as an index of civilization underwrites the British project of informal imperialism at this time, helping to distinguish it, as we saw in the last chapter, from the Spanish seizure of land and resources.

If imperialism is a process "conducted simultaneously at concrete levels of violence, expropriation, collaboration, and coercion, and at a variety of symbolic or representational levels,"[43] Bullock's references to the Spanish conquest seek to contain the first form of imperialism within the second. Bullock desires his patrons, in other words, to distinguish *between* imperialisms. The Spanish conquest of Mexico exemplifies violent imperialism, while Britain's informal engagement promises to be, if not merely symbolic, certainly kinder and gentler, mutually advantageous in economic terms, appreciative of a good view, and therefore a desirable improvement over the Spanish system of colonial control.[44] The Spanish conquest is a foil, standing for violence, brutality, and ignorance—all the things Britain's cordial and aesthetically inflected relationship with Mexico will eschew, even as it seeks to profit from that "most extensive exchange."[45]

In important ways, then, Bullock attempts to circumscribe the panorama's effects, even as he draws on its power. He valorizes Cortés's bravery but rejects the territorial aggression and cultural destruction that were its most immediate result. According to his theory of post-conquest Mexican history—a view shared by British contemporaries—Mexico's current ills could be traced to three centuries of Spanish misrule, which had reduced the once-great land, "splendid but little known," to a colonial vassal, stripped of its resources and plunged into ignorance.[46] If the panorama gestures toward the conquistador's first sight of Mexico, it is only to suggest its failed promise, redeemable by a new kind of vision, embodied within the luminous and perfectly centered space of a London panorama. In turn, the enlightening power of British culture—its respect for beauty, its care for the past, its belief in progress—will liberate Mexico from the "lethargy and shackles" in which it has been so long "bound by the narrow and barbarous policy of Spain."[47] The visual scene offered to the British public, accompanied by anti-Spanish rhetoric, supports an ideology that ultimately disclaims imperial intent because it is not enacted through violence. Trade is not imperialism; exchange is mutually beneficial; cultural and economic reciprocity is in everyone's interest. In this way the panorama contributes centrally to the mystifications of informal imperialism, an imperialism that defined itself in opposition to other, less "civilized" forms of coercion, even as it employed related representational strategies.

ANNIHILATING THE DISTANCE

To examine this point from another angle, I will move across the Atlantic and forward two decades, to the years just before and after the Mexican War (1846–48), a period of American cultural history in which the archival recovery of the Spanish literary tradition by Washington Irving, W. H. Prescott, and others was closely geared to new logics of territorial expansion. Here, many of the same cultural and historical materials that figured in the initial British enthusiasm for trade with Mexico reappear, incorporated now into the narratives and ideology of Manifest Destiny. Not surprisingly, panoramic viewing emerges as a key trope, a foreshadowing of possession; the panorama as mass entertainment, as sheer technology also reemerges, managing the attention of viewers with new techniques, telling a familiar story with a new slant. I focus here on two works, one a traditional narrative history of the Spanish conquest, the other a panoramic celebration of the U.S. defeat of Mexico in the Mexican War. In each case, the panorama raises complex issues about landscape, Manifest Destiny, and the construction of Mexico as a "field" of inquiry.[48]

William H. Prescott's *History of the Conquest of Mexico* (1843), written by a functionally blind author who never visited Mexico, played an important symbolic role in the Mexican War;[49] many U.S. soldiers carried copies of the book as they marched from Veracruz to Mexico City, self-consciously following the footsteps, and the narrative, of the first conqueror Cortés in what they called the "Second Conquest."[50] Hoping to goad its troops to emulate Cortés's courage and resolve, the U.S. Navy ordered copies of the *History* to "form part of the library of every man-of-war."[51] The *History,* like the panoramas consumed in London, served as a map, neatly summarizing the geographical and cultural terrain confronting the soldiers during their march inland along the first conqueror's path. Though Prescott himself opposed the war, in writing his history he explicitly identified with the conquistadors. Describing his progress on the work to Charles Dickens, he wrote: "I am hammering away on my old Aztecs and have nearly knocked their capital about their ears."[52] The text's landscape tropes and narrative devices, moreover, easily lent themselves to the U.S. imperialist project by describing Mexico as ripe for the taking.[53] The narrative deftly manipulates what Mieke Bal terms the "focalizer," the visual and subjective point from which elements in the narrative are viewed or seen. In discussing character, Bal points out that the "reader watches with the character's eyes and will, in principle, be inclined to accept the vision presented by that character,"[54] an assumption Prescott adapts in the *History* by constructing the reader as a traveler, as in the following passage that describes the view from the top of a pyramid: "But the traveller, who will take the trouble to ascend its bald summit, will be amply compensated by the glorious view it will open to him" (2:390). In suggesting the view from a height, Prescott alludes to the panoramic trope encountered so frequently in travelers' accounts such as Bullock's; indeed, in language that recalls both Prescott's blindness and his reliance on correspondents to function as proxy travelers, he praised his predecessor as a keen-eyed observer, noting that Bullock saw "what has eluded the *optics* of other travelers" (2:390; my emphasis). Thus the on-the-spot traveler, synthesizing historian, and reader all share in the focalizing process, participating in modes of visual cognition that are also vehicles of power.

Given, then, the tradition of viewing the sight of Mexico City as *already* panoramic, let us examine Prescott's narration of that first prospect as seen through the eyes of Cortés's soldiers:

> They had not advanced far, when, turning an angle of the sierra, they suddenly came on a view which more than compensated the toils of the preceding day. It was that of the Valley of Mexico, or Tenochtitlan, as more commonly called by the natives; which, with its *picturesque assemblage* of water, woodland, and cultivated plains, its shining cities and shadowy hills, was spread out like some *gay and gorgeous panorama* before them. In the highly rarefied atmosphere of these upper regions, even remote objects have a brilliancy of coloring and a distinctness of outline which seem to *annihilate distance*. (2:51; my emphasis)[55]

As focalized through the conquerors and internalized by the reader, this visual and verbal site prepares the ground for a second conquest. Whereas Robertson drew his tropes from eighteenth-century landscape representations, Prescott's historical narrative explicitly assembles the scene as a panorama, employing not only the discourse of picturesque aesthetics, but also the panoramic figure of the "annihilation" of distance. This reflects the panorama's absorption within the literary unconscious of Prescott's age, a literary epoch whose figures of speech manifested the ideal of unlimited intellectual and political expansion; as Emerson wrote in 1836, "there is a property in the horizon which no man has but he whose eye can integrate all the parts."[56] It also suggests the course of Prescott's own intellectual development, which coincided with the panorama's rise as mass entertainment and imperial technology. Burford and Bullock's panorama of Mexico was exhibited at John Vanderlyn's New York rotunda in 1827–28 and subsequently in cities from Philadelphia to New Orleans.[57] In preparation for writing his *History* Prescott purchased a copy of Bullock's *Six Months' Residence in Mexico* from a bookseller,[58] and while working on the text became friends with Frederick Catherwood, who opened his panorama in New York in 1838, just before embarking with John Lloyd Stephens on their epic journey to the ruined cities of Central America—enterprises Prescott followed with great interest. The first scene represented in Catherwood's rotunda was, quite fittingly, as we shall see below, the "splendid panorama of Jerusalem."[59]

If, as Paul Virilio argues, "the history of battle is primarily the history of radically changing fields of perception,"[60] Prescott's narration in the *History* of the soldiers' "astonishment and rapture" (2:52) suggests the growing force of the panorama as a sophisticated imaginative device during a period in which the archival "recovery" of the Hispanic past (in which Prescott was a central figure), the appropriation of pre-Columbian material culture, and the westward expansion of the United States were historically conjoined. For although the passage cited above refers strictly to the Spanish conquest, it also suggests the symbolic core of Manifest Destiny. The panoramic fantasy of "annihilating" the distance must have been extraordinarily seductive for a nation intent on an uninterrupted march to the Pacific. Given that within a few years after Prescott published these words Mexico lost the upper half of its territory, including California, Arizona, and New Mexico, to the United States the account was also prophetic. Yet Prescott raises the imaginative stakes further by comparing the scene to the founding site of Western associations between landscape views and territorial expansion, Moses' view of the Promised Land from Pisgah. "What then," he writes,

> must have been the emotions of the Spaniards, when, after working their toil-some way into the upper air, the cloudy tabernacle parted before their eyes, and they beheld these fair scenes in all their pristine magnificence and beauty! It was like the spectacle which greeted the eyes of Moses from the summit of Pisgah, and, in the warm glow of their feelings, they cried out, "It is the promised land." (2:52–53)

Once again, the use of sources is crucial. Prescott's note tells us that his source here is not Díaz del Castillo, whom Prescott called his "great favourite,"[61] but Fray Juan de Torquemada (1557–1664), a polemical Franciscan whose *Monarquía Indiana,* first issued in 1615, synthesizes previous writers on Mexican history, including Antonio de Herrera y Tordesillas (c. 1559?–1625), Francisco López de Gómara (c. 1511–1560), and Gerónimo de Mendieta (1525–1604). Although in the *History* Prescott notes that Torquemada sometimes falls into "serious errors," he goes on to say that the student will "find few better guides . . . in tracing the stream of historic truth up to the fountain head" (1:52). It is, of course, impossible to know what the conquistadors exclaimed upon seeing the valley of Mexico for the first time, whether they compared it to medieval romance or Hebrew legend, to both or neither. Gómara, for instance, who was Cortés's private chaplain, notes simply that "es la mejor vista del mundo," i.e., it was the best view in the world.[62] We do know, however, that Franciscans associated Cortés with Moses, drawing out elaborate "similitudes" such as their "divine election," their reliance on go-betweens, and their stand against pagan oppressors, i.e., Montezuma and Pharaoh.[63]

Torquemada's ideology emerges not only in the reference to the Promised Land, but also in the unquoted remainder of the sentence following just after. Here is the Spanish original, cited from a facsimile of the second, now standard, edition of 1723: "Decian algunos Castellanos, que aquella era la Tierra, para su Buena Dicha prometida, y que mientras mas Moros, mas ganancia."[64] The Spanish soldiers, according to Torquemada, cried out that it was the Promised Land, a site they associated, by a potent idiomatic

link, with the Spanish reconquest of the Moors, who were driven out of
Spain in 1492. The orientalist idiom "a más Moros, más ganancia" means
"the greater the difficulty the greater the triumph," a variant of the English
"nothing ventured, nothing gained," itself dating from Chaucer. Yet the
saying's allusion to the wars of reconquest figures the abstract notion of
risk within a deadly calculus, with glory measured in Moorish bodies:
the more Moors arrayed against you, the greater your triumph will be.
Torquemada's account thus joins the conquest of New Spain to the reconquest of Old Spain, and both to the mandate to "go in and possess the
land which the Lord sware unto your fathers" (Deut. 3:8).[65]

Although these associations are common among seventeenth-century
Franciscan historians, their reappearance in Prescott bears further examination. In the first instance, Prescott's *History* explicitly endorsed the idea
of a divine justification for the Spanish conquest. At the end of a harrow-
ing chapter on the Aztec practice of human sacrifice, he writes: "In this
state of things, it was beneficently ordered by Providence that the land
should be delivered over to another race, who would rescue it from the
brutish superstitions that daily extended wider and wider" (1:85).[66] According to the eminent geologist Charles Lyell, "every body in London" was
reading the *Conquest of Mexico;* this included Dickens, who wrote in 1844
of being particularly impressed by Prescott's account of Aztec civilization.[67]
The thrust of that account was clear to British reviewers. A lengthy and
favorable review of the *History* in the *Times* commented that the "punishment [of the Aztecs] was as deserved as that which fell upon the san-
guinary and idolatrous Canaanites."[68] Of course, the notion of America
as Promised Land could hardly have escaped Prescott, whose residence
in Boston—the city on a hill—placed him at the very center of Puritan
consciousness. The same language that endorses the rationale for dispos-
sessing the Canaanites also figured in the campaigns waged against Native
Americans in the name of Manifest Destiny. And it is ironic that even
while Spanish narratives were rhetorically employing the trope of the promised land to justify exterminating the Aztecs, the Spanish were expelling
and killing actual Jews in the 1490s—a point surely not lost on Prescott,
who labored for nine years writing *Ferdinand and Isabella,* a history of
the monarchs responsible for these policies.[69] Second, although there is
no explicit reference to the expulsion of the Moors in Prescott's account,
the idea functions as an absent presence, carried over from *Ferdinand*

and Isabella and layered beneath the *History*'s embrace of the civilization/
barbarism, Christianity/idolatry binaries that underwrote the war of reconquest, the Mexican War, and U.S. westward expansion. The *Quarterly
Review* (London), which ran a fifty-page article on Prescott, approvingly
picked up the inference: "[The conquest] was, as Mr. Prescott calls it, a
crusade . . . one of the last, but not least, vigorous outbursts of that
same spirit which had poured Europe in arms upon the East; and in
the Peninsula had just fought out the long and implacable contest of
Christian and Moor."[70] Mexican history is once again recruited to serve
European ends; although Britain was excluded from participation in the
conquest of Mexico, its literary and visual traditions could still appropriate it for the larger cause of "civilization" with which Britain was so closely
identified during Victoria's reign. Further, during the period that Prescott
was describing Aztec civilization as rude and barbaric, both Britain and
the United States were busy removing pre-Columbian material culture to
museums and private collections in London and New York. The taking
in of landscape views and antiquities were historically and ideologically
coincident.

Thus the prewar figuration of panoramic seeing. At war's end, in the fate-
ful year of 1848, the U.S. soldier and Ohio journalist Corydon Donnavan
exhibited a 21,000-square-foot moving panorama of the Mexican war that
toured cities in the Midwest and along the eastern seaboard to great
acclaim (Figure 15). Related to the still panorama perfected by Barker and
Burford, the moving panorama was composed of a series of pictures
painted on a large canvas roll, which unspooled frame by frame behind
a proscenium. In Donnavan's case and in many others, lectures accompanied the "performance," which had a fixed duration. Unlike the still
panorama, which featured an ambulatory observer and a fixed image, the
moving panorama reversed these relations by setting the image in motion
in front of a seated audience. Donnavan's panorama skillfully capitalized
on his own experience as a prisoner in the war and on the mood of exultation that swept the country as the scope of the victory, and the territory
that came with it, became clear. Donnavan's war narrative, *Adventures in
Mexico,* first published in Cincinnati in 1847, had gone through twelve
editions by 1848, a popularity no doubt aided by the visual spectacle to
which it formed a guide. A surviving playbill declares that over 30,000
people saw the panorama in just three months,[71] and a later edition of

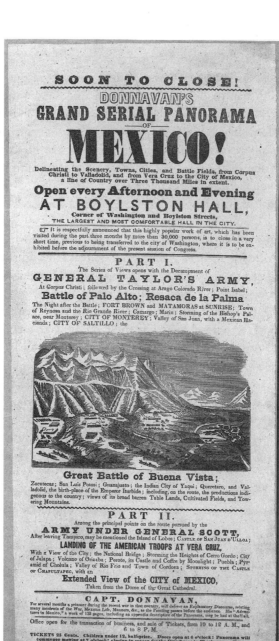

Figure 15. Poster advertising Corydon Donnavan's Grand Serial Panorama of Mexico. Courtesy of the Harvard Theatre Collection, Houghton Library.

Donnavan's narrative featured an appendix of glowing press notices from around the country.[72] An examination of Donnavan's panorama brings into focus a further stage in the form's development, in which the implicit figurations of Prescott's lapidary prose erupt in an overtly imperial rhetoric that lays bare the link between panoramic seeing and the violent expropriation of territory.

The panorama, as Donnavan described it in the appendix to his *Adventures,* did not attempt to "portray either the glories or horrors of conflict," but rather the "views of the battle-grounds, the geographical resources of the country, its natural scenery, architecture, and diversified botany" (118). Donnavan's purported aim, like Bullock's, was educational. He employed the same rhetoric of "opening" the nation to "our knowledge" (119) and betrayed a similar interest in Mexico's cultural and natural productions—its "palm, cabbage, cypress, cedar, cocoanut, ebony, banyan, calabash" (132). A review from the *New Orleans Delta* of June 12, 1847, reprinted in Donnavan's appendix, observes that the popularity of panoramas had declined since the "exhibition of Catherwood's great work," but had been revived by John Banvard's enormously successful panorama of the Mississippi, and would be further enhanced by Donnavan's, which served a similarly instructional purpose. Donnavan billed knowledge, or what he called "intelligence" (118), as a central feature of his work.

Yet Donnavan's panorama connects knowledge to power in complicated ways. For Bullock, as for Prescott, knowledge of Mexico was a prelude, a cognitive force that operated in advance of other forms of engagement. The panorama, or panoramic representations in narrative, preceded the establishment of informal economic arrangements, as in Bullock, or outright territorial aggression, as in Prescott. The panorama and its narrative analogues were proleptic ideological devices, heralding something that had not yet occurred. Even the first sight of Tenochtitlán, as narrated by the Spanish historians and endlessly recapitulated in later accounts, occurs prior to the conquest. Donnavan's panorama, coming after the successful U.S. campaign, refigures panoramic knowledge as something acquired in the aftermath, as a *fait accompli.* "Until recently," he writes, perhaps referring to Prescott's *History,* "our knowledge not only of the original half civilized proprietors of the soil, but even of the more modern race of Mexico, has been vague and unsatisfactory. Not till the traditions of the former were to be realized by the latter, were our people permitted to tread upon [the] land" (119). Here, the panorama does not make the knowledge that authorizes the second conquest, but retrospectively commemorates it.[73]

Like Prescott, Donnavan self-consciously rewrites the conquest, throwing into relief the implied binaries and racial dynamics of the *History.* Describing the route from Veracruz to Mexico City, he writes: "Almost the same route trod by the Spanish cavalier three centuries since, as a superior being, sent from a better sphere, has been retraced by the Anglo-Saxon. . . . Manifest destiny seems suddenly to have brought us in direct collision with Mexico" (119). Writing before the war, Emerson voiced a similar rhetoric in his journals:

> [I]t is very certain that the strong British race which have now overrun so much of this continent, must also overrun that tract [i.e., Texas], and Mexico and Oregon also, and it will be of small import by what particular occasions and methods it was done.[74]

Emerson foretells what Donnavan retrospectively celebrates, the triumph of the Anglo-Saxon race, which does the conquest one better: "Still paler faces have gone from the north and conquered the conquerors of the Montezumas" (119). The second conquest improves the first by further whitening Mexico's hopelessly creolized population. Aside from reflecting the language and assumptions of racial theory at midcentury, the project of ethnic cleansing and territorial expansion also produces the nation in vital ways. The *New Orleans Delta,* quoted in Donnavan's appendix, points out that the panorama is bound to "arrest the attention of a people rocked into manhood and maturity in the cradle of excitement" (122). The Mexican war, that "cradle of excitement," marks the birth of a nation—manly, invigorated, and in possession of territory "which but yesterday, as it were, was the boundary of an unexplored wilderness" (123). The war, like Prescott's panoramic vision, annihilates the boundary, pushing the known horizon westward and southward, from sea to shining sea.

TAKING (IN) THE VIEW

How did Mexicans understand the implications of panoramic representation, and the gazes of foreign travelers and historians more generally?

First, it must be reiterated here that there was no single, unified "Mexican" response, that only cultural elites had access to print culture, and that the archive as we have it is necessarily skewed to highlight the opinions of the Creole elites. That said, we can trace changes in modes of representing landscape through institutions such as the Academy of San Carlos, which, after its founding in 1785, became an important center for the refinement of art theory; and we can follow these changes in the work of Eugenio Landesio (1810–79), José María Velasco (1840–1912), and others who painted landscapes in a grand, panoramic style. Panoramic views celebrated the richness and promise of Mexico's land and were geared to larger projects of national pride. Meanwhile, an urban tradition of panoramic representation flourished in the capital, with artists such as Casimiro Castro (1826–89) producing lithographs that were widely disseminated. One may even point to the early-nineteenth-century vogue among Creoles for balloon ascents—all practices that offered the same illusion of towering command found within the British and American panoramas we have examined here.[75]

Yet there is another side of the story, one that begins with responses to Prescott's *History,* which was immediately translated and published in Mexico City in a lavishly illustrated edition that Prescott took (correctly, I think) as a high compliment to his assiduous labors. But Mexican writers mingled praise with criticism and were particularly suspicious of the civilization/barbarism opposition that structured the work's reading of Mexican history. Writing in 1845 as the conflict with the United States over Texas intensified, the eminent historian José F. Ramírez (1804–71) objected first to the work's "immoderate enthusiasm" for Cortés, second to its representation of the Aztecs. For Ramírez, the *History* ultimately purveyed a narrative

> of *barbarians;* a word that, alternating with *savages,* rampages through the whole length of the work. . . . As a result, the Mexicans *howl* and their armies, generally speaking, do not *fall back* or *retire,* they *flee.* The force in the language itself insists that their indomitable courage should be labeled *rabid fury.*[76]

Even the archconservative statesman and historian Lucas Alamán (1792–1853) took issue with Prescott's language, arguing that Prescott misapplied the term "barbarians" to the Aztecs, who had built an advanced civilization;

only the Aztec religion could properly be called "barbarous."[77] Ramírez's and Alamán's strong critique of Prescott's tropes represents the emergence of a powerful anti-imperial discourse, one capable of contesting both the motive and the means of foreign hegemony over Mexico and its past. Yet, in what is perhaps a holdover of Prescottian blindness, recent reevaluations of the *History* by scholars in the United States have ignored or overlooked the Mexican reply, even in discussions that deal explicitly with the imperial implications of Prescott's writing. Mexicans' words (yet again) have not been deemed worth hearing.[78]

The struggle over representations, however, was limited neither to events of the distant, pre-Hispanic past nor to the inevitability of a war with an expansionist United States. Ten years before the war, in the blithe heyday of British informal imperialism, Mexican intellectuals began to object to the forms of symbolic representation that had commenced with the first arrival of British travelers, those who professed, as we have seen, to be driven by "motives of curiosity only," who came "merely" to write, paint, or sketch.[79] As I showed in the previous chapter, by the 1830s Carlos María de Bustamante was already protesting against the removal of Mexican antiquities to foreign museums and private cabinets. But he also wrote presciently about visual expropriations by foreign travelers, who, driven by restless curiosity, scoured the country to examine the pre-Columbian ruins of Palenque, Uxmal, Xochicalco, and other sites. For Bustamante, it was but a short step from looking to taking, as evidenced by the loss of precious manuscripts, plans, and maps in the years just after the opening of Mexico to foreign, mainly British, travelers. Curiosity, he understood, was a fundamentally acquisitive trait. But Bustamante goes further, objecting to the travelers' incessant hunger "copiar nuestras vistas," that is, to copy our views. While it is difficult to object to mere copying, Bustamante goes on to make use of the much more potent verb *sacar* (from the medieval Latin *saccare*, to plunder or pillage), which in Spanish means not only taking a view but also understanding, inquiring, obtaining, or removing something from its proper place: "ellos han sacado vistas," i.e., they have taken, or removed, our views. Bustamante makes clear his grasp of the original Latin sense, calling the larger plunder "Este saqueo, (ó dígase mejor) esta *depredación*," i.e., this removal, or better yet, this pillaging.[80]

What is striking is Bustamante's use of *sacar* to describe the theft not only of material objects but also of landscape views, and thus his attempt to connect literal and metaphoric aspects of appropriation. Just as the verb "to sack" comes from the act of carrying away something, so too could views be painted (and later photographed) and taken away for consumption elsewhere, and the examples Bustamante provides suggest that Mexicans perceived certain kinds of viewing as particularly troubling. He mentions, for example, views taken from above Puebla. Bullock, as we saw in chapter 1, described ascending the mountains above Puebla to gain a panoramic view over it, a gesture of elevated focalization repeatedly enacted in his travel narrative and again in his Leicester Square panorama, all with the desire, as the *Literary Gazette* put it, to "set that superb country before [our] eyes."[81] Bustamante also comments on views of Popocatepetl, one of the high volcanoes that loom over Mexico City and an important mythical site for the Aztecs. As Bustamante well knew, the first Europeans to claim it were a group of Cortés's soldiers, who made the journey to its snow-covered summit to discover, as Anthony Pagden's translation has it, "the secret of the smoke, whence it came, and how."[82] Díaz del Castillo tells us that that the soldiers took advantage of the great height to survey the splendid Mexican cities they would shortly conquer.[83] Three centuries later, soldiers and the military uses of the panorama intersected again in the first British ascent of Popocatepetl, achieved in 1827 by Lt. William Glennie, an engineer in the Royal Navy.[84] Glennie was connected through marriage to Henry Aston Barker, whose father, as noted above, patented the panorama in 1786, ran the panorama in Leicester Square, and later sold it to another father and son team, the Burfords, with whom Bullock exhibited his Mexican panorama in 1826. Henry Barker, as we have seen, was particularly talented in representing military scenes, including the battle of Waterloo.

In keeping with the aims of informal imperialism, subsequent British ascents of Popocatepetl employed techniques of panoramic representation in the service of economic imperialism. In the year before Bustamante published the *Mañanas,* Daniel Thomas Egerton, a well-known British painter and illustrator who had come to Mexico in 1831, climbed the peak to make sketches for several oil paintings of the ascent, of the volcano from afar, and of the crater's interior, views that were duly transformed into panoramic entertainment for British viewers.[85] The images in Egerton's *Views in Mexico* were explicitly tied to commercial interests; their most frequent subject was the mining and processing of Mexico's silver, a theme of intense concern, as we have seen, to investors and financiers in London. Yet in ways that parallel the connections and contrasts between Bullock, Prescott, and Donnavan, the association between the aesthetic pleasure of view-taking and what Bustamante calls depredation came to striking fruition in the Mexican career of Ulysses S. Grant. As Grant describes it in his memoir, a group of U.S. soldiers celebrated the U.S. victory over Mexico by once again climbing the famous volcano, repeating in the second conquest a telling detail of the first and symbolically reinforcing their newly won territorial mastery.[86] Grant's ascent thus stands at the end of a series of gazes in travel narratives, paintings, panoramas, and museum exhibitions that fueled the drive to depredate Mexico's resources and history: the conquerors' first sight of Mexico established a pattern for subsequent sights; the visual representation of monuments led to the influx of travelers seeking new specimens to remove; the depiction of silver mining led to the arrival of further miners and speculators; the enfolding of Mexico into European conventions of landscape aesthetics suggested its availability for control and exploitation from afar. The "sacking" of Mexico's views was only a prelude to more crippling depredations and conquests.

chapter 3

AGENCIES OF THE LETTER

*The British Museum, the Foreign Office,
and the Ruins of Central America*

We call those objects valuable that resist our desire to possess them.
—GEORG SIMMEL, *The Philosophy of Money*

In our cultures "paper shuffling" is the source of an essential power that
constantly escapes attention since its materiality is ignored.
—BRUNO LATOUR, "Drawing Things Together"

On 17 July 1851 the British foreign secretary, Lord Palmerston (1784–1865), sent a dispatch to his *chargé d'affaires* in Guatemala, Frederick Chatfield, informing him that the government desired a collection of Mayan ruins for the British Museum. Thus was set in motion a secret, fourteen-year plot whose full reach, remarkably, has gone unnoticed.[1] This is partly because the plot ultimately failed to achieve its object; in the end, no monuments were obtained. It is also a result, however, of the rigid logic of imperial record keeping; the bulk of the relevant documents, some sixty dispatches, memoranda, reports, and letters, lie not in the British Museum, among other correspondence about antiquities, but in the Foreign and Colonial Office archives—not the first place one might look for archaeological material. They ended up there because the scheme was directed not from Bloomsbury but from Downing Street. This curiosity of archival organization is not incidental but constitutive, inviting us to consider how the plunder of Mesoamerican ruins came under the administrative and ideological control of political officials, and how therefore the imperial archive functions not merely as a repository of information but as a form of knowledge and a structure of power, one that was both enormously enabling and fatally flawed. Tucked between memoranda on mahogany exports, naval maneuvers, and canal and railway routes across the Central American isthmus, the letters about pre-Columbian ruins provide an opportunity to test the claim that while the "'cracy' of bureaucracy is mysterious," the "'bureau' is something that can be empirically studied," perhaps even to the point of explaining how power may be accrued "just by looking at files."[2] The files in question here, however, constitute a particularly complex form of "inscription": the dispatch, a mode of writing whose exchange across an intricate communications network enabled that quintessential trait of global empires, the ability to manipulate persons and things from afar.

Palmerston's dispatch provides a useful gateway to these issues, even as it crystallizes more specific questions about the plot itself. Given the otherness of Mayan ruins, their distance from received canons of aesthetic value, how was a notion of their desirability arrived at? What arguments were employed to justify their removal, and how were these arguments organized into a plan of action and an imperial quest rivaling any found in the pages of adventure fiction? How did diplomatic writing—its protocols and procedures, its iteration in systems of storage and retrieval, its function as the bearer of imperial will, its very style—figure in the attempted appropriation of the monuments? And in what ways did Britain's larger relationship to Central America shape the motives and means of the plot? Here is the beginning of Palmerston's dispatch:

> I enclose herewith a copy of a letter [24 Jun. 1851] which I have received from Viscount Mahon suggesting that it would be desirable to obtain for the British Museum some specimens of the sculptures from the ruined cities of Central America, and stating that the principal sculptures to which he refers are to be found at a place called Copan, upon a River of that name, at the bottom of the Bay of Honduras, and to the south of the British settlement of Belize.
>
> I have accordingly to instruct you to make inquiries [into] the practicability of obtaining specimens of the sculptures referred to in L[ord] Mahon's letter to me and to report the result, together with any additional information which you may be able to collect respecting those sculptures. The sculptures are described

Figure 16. Frederick Catherwood, stone statue, Copán, from John Lloyd
Stephens, *Incidents of Travel in Central America, Chiapas, and Yucatan* (1841).

Figure 17. Frederick Catherwood, stone statue, Copán, from John Lloyd Stephens, *Incidents of Travel in Central America, Chiapas, and Yucatan* (1841).

Figure 18. Frederick Catherwood, Altar Q, Copán, from John Lloyd Stephens, *Incidents of Travel in Central America, Chiapas, and Yucatan* (1841).

in pages 134 to 144 of the first volume of an account of travels in Central America by Mr Stephens, a citizen of the United States who visited those ruins in 1839–1840.[3] (see Figures 16–18)

As Palmerston makes clear, a request had come to him from Viscount Mahon (Philip Henry Stanhope, 1805–1875), British Museum trustee, president of the Society of Antiquaries of London, and later founder of the National Portrait Gallery. Mahon's letter linked the Central American ruins to Britain's archaeological exploits in the East, and thus to a tradition of orientalist adventuring that, as we have already seen with respect to Bullock, had secured the place of antiquities in the imperialist imaginary. Should the British Museum succeed in removing the Mayan ruins, Mahon wrote, the sculptures would form "a noble pendant to those we have lately obtained from Nineveh" (FO15/75, f. 40)—precious jewels to adorn the nation's cabinet of antiquities at Bloomsbury, a prize to illustrate its command over East and West.[4]

Mahon drew his knowledge of the ruins from *Incidents of Travel in Central America, Chiapas, and Yucatan,* published in 1841 by the American travel writer and lawyer John Lloyd Stephens with illustrations by the British architect Frederick Catherwood.[5] Although Stephens and Catherwood were not the first to describe the ruins, they had enlarged their fame. Edgar Allen Poe, who had already praised Stephens's earlier travel narratives about the Near East, called the new material on Central America "perhaps the most interesting book of travel ever published"; Prescott, writing to Stephens in 1841, predicted that the work would furnish "a sort of *carte du pays* for the future traveller"; and Wilkie Collins drew on Stephens for the Central American material in "The Perils of Certain English Prisoners" (1857), co-authored with Charles Dickens, and *The Woman in White* (1860).[6] Indeed, *Incidents* quickly became one of the century's best-selling works of travel and is still considered a classic of archaeological narrative. But within his narrative Stephens also fashioned a compelling tale of desire and plunder, explaining how, equipped with a diplomatic passport from the United States, he purchased the land on which the ruins of Copán lay (in present-day Honduras) for a mere fifty dollars. His aim was to "remove the monuments of a by-gone people from the desolate region in which they were buried, set them up in the 'great commercial emporium,' and found an institution to be the nucleus of a great national museum of American antiquities!"[7] Should he fail to remove an entire city, he proposed to "exhibit by sample: to cut one up and remove it in pieces, and make casts of the others" (2:115), thus destroying the integrity of monuments built for a specific landscape and fashioned with materials from it. If European museums could lay claim to the treasures of Egypt, Greece, and Rome, many of which fell into this same category of being rooted in the land, those in the United States would acquire the monuments of the Western hemisphere's great civilizations and display them in the same, synecdochic way: a collection of dismembered parts standing for complex wholes, small pieces whose contrast with the monumentality of the museums in which they are exhibited expresses a primary differential of imperial power. New York and Washington would join London and Paris at the top rank of museum capitals, bolstering U.S. prestige abroad and securing its cultural confidence at home.

Stephens justified his cupidity by means of a powerful argument: since the ruins lay unclaimed in a "desolate" and sparsely populated region where Central American officials were few, the monuments could not be said to belong to any government. And since the local people were not acquainted with their history, they, too, had no claim to them. Stephens believed that the ruins "belonged by right to us," and "I resolved that ours they should be" (1:115–16). Stephens viewed the civil war then raging in Central America as evidence for his thesis, allowing him to abrogate the laws of a sovereign nation by claiming that Central America possessed no viable government while simultaneously reinforcing the civilization/barbarism dichotomy examined in the previous chapter by contrasting the austere grandeur of the ruins with the anarchy and violence of contemporary Central Americans. The charge of Central American lawlessness was insistently repeated in nineteenth-century British and American accounts. In 1850, for example, Dickens's *Household Words* described Central America as a "thinly-peopled and poverty-stricken region, [where] there was *neither law nor government.*"[8] This view continues to have its adherents, and Stephens and Catherwood's justification for taking what they "found" continues to be celebrated. Lincoln S. Bates, for example, writes that although the Mexican government had prohibited the export of antiquities, Stephens and Catherwood "with typical pluck defied the ban," and more recently, Larzer Ziff, in his well-received study of American travel writing, uncritically takes Stephens at his word: "there was no Central American government and the local population was uninterested in exposing the ruins and incapable of preserving them."[9] I shall return both to the question of legality and to whether the natives were "uninterested" in their ruins, but suffice it to say here that Stephens's arguments, as well as their reiteration in studies of American travel writing, justify the dispossession of Creoles and indigenes alike and trivialize the legal traditions that sought to protect cultural property.

Informed by but also enriching Stephens's formulations, Palmerston centers his discussion squarely on the question of "value":

> It appears from Mr. Stephens's account that these ruins are overgrown with trees and other vegetation and are held in little or no *estimation* by the natives of the country, and it seems probable therefore that the chief difficulty to be encountered in removing specimens of the sculptures would consist in providing means for transporting them to any place of embarkation. You will be careful therefore that in making any inquiries in pursuance of this instruction you don't lead the people of the country to attach any *imaginary value* to things which they consider at present as *having no value at all.* (FO15/69, f. 53; my emphasis)

While assuming the significance of the ruins for Britain—a later dispatch would refer to the plan as "one to which HM's Govt. attaches great importance" (FO15/82, f. 24)—Palmerston deftly questions the capacity of the "natives" to esteem their own past and thus to assert any ownership of the relics that were its most enduring emblem. For Palmerston, as for nearly every archaeological traveler of the period, the natives (a catch-all word that applies both to indigenes and Creole elites) had sealed their disregard for that past by allowing the ruins to become overgrown. For these travelers and officials, ruins "reclaimed" by nature ceased in any real or legal sense to belong to anyone, and thus the issue of their possession was detached from the complex legal and political issues pertaining to foreign relations and property rights and reduced simply to a problem of logistics, an area in which the British excelled. The only quality of estimation permitted the natives is base cash value, while the British willingness to go through the trouble of finding the ruins—to say nothing of shipping them halfway across the globe—signifies a refined appreciation of the past characteristic of advanced cultures. Dismissing the sovereignty of nations in question could also be justified on the grounds of cultural superiority; in 1848 Palmerston declared that Britain stands "at the head of moral, social and political civilization. Our task is to lead the way and direct the march of other nations."[10] For Palmerston, the acquisition of cultural treasures was the prerogative of the civilized, a moral privilege reflected in the very style of his writing, with its studied use of the passive voice ("the ruins are held"); its fine discriminations ("little or no estimation"); its elaborate qualifications ("it seems probable"); and firm but gentle imperatives ("you will be careful therefore"). Although by 1851 the ideologies and literary forms of this kind of long-distance archaeological raid had become axiomatic in the British discourse of Mexico and Central America, Palmerston's dispatch crystallized and enshrined them in official policy.

Yet if Palmerston was convinced, like Stephens before him, that the local people were unworthy to inherit their past, he also feared their "estimation" of the ruins (and the price for which they would sell them) would soar once they caught wind of the British government's interest, hence his warning to Chatfield to avoid any mention of it. His term for this sort of esteem is "imaginary value," an appreciation based solely on the knowledge of competitive desire. Yet, as Mahon's and Palmerston's letters suggest, the ruins were already enmeshed in a competitive dynamic. British interest in the ruins, like its larger relation to the Spanish empire that went before it, was belated; Spain, not England, introduced pre-Columbian material into Europe; Spain, not England, had conquered Mexico and Central America.[11] Here, however, the immediate precursor was not Spain or Portugal, but Britain's own colonial stepchild, the newly emboldened United States, seeking cultural dominance in advance of what would subsequently become its territorial dominance in the region. Conspicuously absent from these imperial rivalries, of course, are Central Americans themselves, who, because they hold only simple notions of value, are placed outside the structure of competitive desire.

The plot to take the sculptures, which are located in present-day Guatemala and Honduras, occupied the attention of British officials from 1841, ten years before Palmerston's note to Chatfield, to 1855, when the scheme was finally abandoned. As such, it marks a significant case of direct government involvement in the quest for pre-Columbian antiquities, showing that British antiquarian research in the Americas relied not only on the efforts of singular individuals, as Elizabeth Williams has argued, but also on the vast administrative machinery of the Colonial Office, the Foreign Office, and the Royal Navy.[12] The scheme, moreover, exemplifies particularly well the cultural dimension of British informal imperialism in Latin America, which formed a symbolic counterpart to the extraction of resources (minerals, mahogany, and later oil) and the movement of capital and goods across the Atlantic stressed by theorists of economic dependency. Several contexts shape this plot, particularly the sharp, frequently acrimonious rivalry between Britain and the United States over the strategically important Central American isthmus. From the 1840s onward, the Royal Geographical Society, responding to demands from its Pacific colonies for an extension of steam mail service, actively supported various British efforts to establish a route across the isthmus.[13] Despite a formal agreement with the United States to cooperate in the building of any canal, several of these efforts were undertaken with the aim of thwarting U.S. plans in the region. The rivalry between the two nations was sharpened by the U.S. acquisition of Oregon, its triumph in the Mexican war of 1846–48, and British fears that the United States would extend its territory south to Panama. The Americans were equally suspicious. When Ephraim George Squier was appointed to a diplomatic post in Nicaragua, Charles Eliot Norton wrote to ask: "Shall you be safe there in that nation made up of Chatfields and Palmerstons or worse men than they,—all anxious and eager to plunge their daggers in the hearts of every American?"[14] Competitive tensions were fueled by the discovery of gold in California and the sudden demand for transit across the isthmus, putting Central America "at the center of world attention."[15] Despite the Clayton-Bulwer Treaty of 1850, which prohibited Britain and the United States from acquiring further territory in Central America, tensions ran high, leading at times to violent conflict. In 1856, for example, in a well-known episode, the American adventurer William Walker, after setting himself up as a dictator in Nicaragua, seized the British-controlled settlement of Greytown along the Mosquito Coast. Palmerston wanted the British navy to impose a blockade on Greytown, an act that would have plunged Britain into deeper conflict with the United States. Only Clarendon's cool head and Washington's disavowal of Walker prevented the conflict.[16] The contest for control over Central America's antiquities (and hence its past) intersected with these flare-ups. The emergence of the United States as an expansionist territorial and cultural power extended the familiar dynamic of imperial rivalry across the Atlantic, with New World resources and antiquities the desired spoils.

Just as the British obsession with Mexican antiquities in the 1820s was bound up with the changing forms of the museum and the panorama, the desire to possess Central American ruins was embodied in an equally complex mode of signification: the dispatch, a word whose various meanings (to send off or out; to put an end to; to remove impediments; to complete with efficient speed; an official letter) captures both the Latourian notion of the flat package as well as the complex relations between agency and epistolarity, writing and imperial governance. The relevant documents fall into three broad groups: dispatches exchanged between the Foreign and Colonial Secretaries and their respective diplomatic subordinates in Guatemala and British Honduras; letters passed between the British Museum and government officials; and still more letters sent between the aforementioned officials and Karl Ritter von Scherzer (1821–1903) and Moritz Wagner (1813–1887), the Swiss and German scientists whom the British Museum eventually hired to explore the ruins. Aside from being stored in places where one would not immediately expect to find them, many of these documents are difficult to access, even for experienced and persistent researchers.[17] One of my aims here, therefore, is to make these documents available *as* history, to use them to tell a little-known story about the mobilization of British antiquarian research in Central America. But rather than approaching these documents as transparent lenses through which we can view a knowable historical reality, I want to treat them, following Dominick LaCapra, as "texts that supplement or rework 'reality'"[18]—or, as I shall argue, texts whose defining feature is their status as *writing*, texts whose extraordinary power and crippling limitations inhere as much in their form as in any putative content.

REDISCOVERING THE MAYA

The British Museum's midcentury interest in the ruins of Copán, Quiriguá, and Tikal partook of a broader shift in British antiquarian attention from the Aztecs to the Maya, corresponding in turn to a shift in territorial interest from Mexico to Central America, whose strategic importance was bolstered by international competition to find a short route between the Atlantic and Pacific Oceans.[19] Although the British presence along the eastern coast of Central America dates from the mid-seventeenth century, little light had been cast on pre-Hispanic cultures, nor was much known of the region's interior, which remained *terra incognita* on European maps and charts.[20] As the Royal Geographical Society put it in 1836, there are "few parts of the habitable globe, with which we are still so little acquainted

as with the interior, as well as the shores, of Central America." The society expressed its belief, however, that the creation of the "grand oceanic
canal" would transform Central America into a "highway of nations."[21]

Searching for buried cities, archaeological travelers mapped the topo-
graphical and demographic terrain of Central America, fulfilling the Hum-
boldtian project of charting the interiors as well as the coasts of America.
Though travelers visited Mayan ruins from as early as the sixteenth century,
archaeological inquiry proper dates from the Spanish Enlightenment;
during the 1780s Creole travelers and antiquarians explored and studied
a variety of sites across Southern Mexico and Central America.[22] This
knowledge, familiar to a small number of officials and scholars, became
widely disseminated after independence (1821), when several pieces of the
archaeological puzzle were assembled. In 1822, two years before Bullock's
exhibit, a volume appeared in London entitled *Description of the Ruins
of an Ancient City, Discovered near Palenque.* This was a translation of a
report written in 1787 by Captain Antonio del Río, made at the request of
José Estachería, president of the Audencia of Guatemala. Palenque, located
in the southern Mexican state of Chiapas, was overgrown with vegetation,
but the intricate bas-relief carvings that decorated its exterior walls were
remarkably well preserved.[23] Del Río's work had a wide circulation during the nineteenth century; it was reviewed in Britain and America, cited
in Bullock's travel narrative, and discussed by Stephens and Catherwood.
In a formulation frequently encountered throughout British discourse
on Central America, the "Prefatory Address" appended to the English
translation of the report argued that the Spanish government concealed
knowledge of its antiquities in the hope of "burying in total oblivion, any
circumstance that might conduce to awaken the curiosity, or excite the
cupidity of more scientific and enterprising nations."[24] Del Río's report,
which began as a document of Central American nationalism, was now
translated into the familiar idiom of the Black Legend.

The outstanding figure in the 1830s was Juan Galindo, an Irishman
of Spanish descent who later became a naturalized citizen of the Central
American Federation. Described as the "first archaeologist in the Maya
field," Galindo combined a complex political career as a Central American patriot with an interest in antiquarian research, the fruits of which
he published in the annals of British, American, and French learned societies and in the popular press.[25] Like the Creole elites in Mexico, Galindo

yoked archaeological research to nationalism, hoping to raise his nation's esteem abroad while deepening the people's reverence for their past. His political activities on behalf of the federation brought him into contact with Foreign Secretary Palmerston, who met with Galindo in 1835 and 1836 during the latter's diplomatic journey on behalf of the federation. In January 1836, hoping to secure a favorable resolution to a boundary dispute, Galindo offered the British government full information "relative to the surveys and projects for opening a canal through the American Isthmus," warning that the United States was moving ahead with its own plans (FO15/18, f. 199). But Galindo's archaeological publications also express the ambivalence of Creole and British writing on pre-Columbian culture, a mix of praise and denigration, desire and repulsion perhaps intensified by Galindo's own political and cultural hybridity. Influenced by but alienated from a Britishness which as an Irishman he could never fully own nor, paradoxically, escape, a Central American by choice, not birth, Galindo was a liminal figure; his writings evince both cultural pride in the pre-Columbian achievements of his adopted land as well as the disdain for the "Indian" frequently encountered in European scientific discourse.[26] In an early notice published in the *Literary Gazette* Galindo claims—with Robertson and De Pauw evidently in mind—that an understanding of the ruins of Palenque will "rescue ancient America from a charge of barbarism" for it was the center of a "civilised, commercial, and extended nation." Yet he also described the "wild" Indians as "an uncivilised and timid tribe," and the "subdued" Indians as "equally in a low scale of improvement." Galindo reports that when asked who built the ruins, the indigenous betray an alienation from their past no less shocking than that noticed by Bullock at Teotihuacán. There, the indigenous had offered St. Francis as the probable builder; here, they nominate "The devil."[27] As I discuss at the end of this chapter, however, it may be a mistake to read that response too literally.

Seeking to elevate the pre-Columbian cultures of Central America above those of Mexico, Galindo argues that the Maya regions were the "most civilized portion of America," a comment that reflects both the larger nineteenth-century shift toward the Maya and Galindo's pride as a Central American.[28] He had been appointed to inspect the ruins of Copán by Mariano Gálvez, the Guatemalan chief of state.[29] As he points out elsewhere: "Now that the rulers of these regions have a direct and affectionate interest in [the ruins'] fame, we dedicate ourselves to [their] study."[30] Yet in an article for the Royal Geographical Society, of which he was a foreign corresponding member, Galindo expresses wholesale disregard for the local people. Of the Usumacinta River, the subject of his article, he wrote that the indigenous remain in "almost total ignorance," knowing little about the river's course, branches, and relative position.[31] Privately, Galindo could be even more scathing. In an unpublished letter to Thomas Winthrop, the president of the American Antiquarian Society, he reports finding the indigenous "almost in the uttermost verge of barbarism"; they are "despicably stupid" and have "no idea of who were the architects of these remains."[32]

After Galindo, the most important figures in the nineteenth-century rediscovery of Mayan cities are, as already mentioned, Stephens and Catherwood, whose researches in the late 1830s have been popularly understood as having "invented" the field. This is not only factually in-correct, ignoring the work of important Central American precursors such as Del Río, Galindo, and others cited by Stephens himself, but also a symptom of the hagiographic tendencies of archaeological history, which continues to highlight the exploits of intrepid Victorian adventurers cut-ting through the jungle to "discover" and "bring to light" buried cities and lost civilizations.[33] Recently, scholars in literary and cultural studies such as Bruce Harvey, David E. Johnson, and Jennifer L. Roberts have brought a fresh perspective to the study of Stephens and Catherwood, focusing on the ideological implications of salvage ethnography (Roberts) and the implications of U.S. imperialism in the region (Johnson and Harvey), and in the process demystifying the "great man" theory of archaeological work, itself a product of the nineteenth century.[34]

What requires further emphasis, however, is the contest over archaeo-logical discovery and possession in which Stephens's journey was situated, and which Palmerston's dispatch so clearly names. Stephens described Quiriguá, for example, as "unvisited, unsought, and utterly unknown," and his interest in the ruins as a merely "personal affair" (2:123–24)—com-monplaces of archaeological travel that date from Bullock's journeys. Yet he was compelled to acknowledge the competitive context in which his desire occurred. Narcisso Payes, the Central American on whose land the ruins were located, stubbornly rejected Stephens's attempts to detach himself from the interests of the government that had sent him. This was a clever move, for not only was Stephens sent to Central America on a diplomatic mission, but also, as noted above, he linked his quest for the ruins to a plan to found a national museum in the United States. Much to Stephens's dismay, Payes was well informed about the international market in antiquities; according to Stephens, he "consulted with the French consul general, who put an exaggerated value upon the ruins, referring him to the expenditure of several hundred thousand dollars by the French government in transporting one of the obelisks of Luxor from Thebes to Paris." Stephens, who had hoped for a price closer to a "few thousand dollars," apparently made Payes an offer, and he expressed his confidence that by the time his pages "reach the hands of the reader, two of the largest monuments will be on their way to this city [New York]" (2:124). The production of his text was thus explicitly conjoined to his ability to deliver the objects it described. *Incidents* wove nation, narration, and appropriation into one seamless fabric.[35]

Stephens's rhetoric of "speculating scheme[s]" and "exaggerated value" (2:124) makes clear how the international marketplace in antiquities shaped archaeological inquiry. And his tactic of presenting himself as a mere searcher after knowledge, divorced from any national interest, recalls successive British efforts from Bullock to Palmerston to cloak appropriative schemes under the disinterested cause of "science." Stephens goes a step further and attributes such sentiments to the locals themselves. Payes, Stephens writes, believed that the ruins "were not appreciated" in his own country, and would "be happy to contribute to the cause of science in ours"—i.e., the United States (2:124). On other occasions Stephens took advantage of his diplomatic mission to smooth the path of his archaeological work. At Palenque, he notes that "respect for my official character, the special tenour of my passport, and letters from Mexican authorities, gave me every facility," persuading the local authorities to believe that he was sent by the U.S. government "expressly to explore the ruins" (2:305), whereas, in fact, this was an expedient fiction tailored to the demands of the moment. As he states in the preface to *Incidents,* he was "at liberty to travel" only once his diplomatic mission was "fulfilled" (1:1). Such shifts between "personal" and "official" identities were central to the practice of the archaeological traveler, masking the larger projects of national self-fashioning that archaeological inquiry served.

An intriguing episode in the international quest for the ruins began when Stephens and Catherwood arrived in British Honduras on 30 October 1839 to undertake their journey through Central America. Upon landing in Belize, Stephens and Catherwood discussed their plans with the British superintendent, Col. Alexander MacDonald, indicating their intention to visit the ruins of Palenque, but only after traveling south to Honduras to investigate the Mayan city of Copán. Acting on his own initiative to preserve British scientific prestige and extend British colonial dominion in British Honduras to cultural dominion in neighboring Central America, MacDonald sent a dispatch (after the fact) to Colonial Secretary Lord John Russell, on 9 November, informing him that he had organized a small expedition to beat the Americans to Palenque. The ruins, he wrote, "form now a great object of interest among the enlightened in the United States, and I am led to understand that similar sentiments pervade the curious in Europe"; the settlement's weekly newspaper, the *Belize Advertiser,* affirmed the journey's patriotic purpose, noting that the "design of Mr. Catherwood has roused the jealousy of our Settlement."[36] The men tapped for the expedition, Patrick Walker and John Caddy, did reach Palenque before Stephens (Walker later played a key role in establishing the British protectorate over Mosquito, discussed above [FO53/44; 28 Apr. 1845]). They filed an official report, completed late in 1840, which after some delay came to Russell's attention. But Stephens and Catherwood, though second to the ruins, were first to print. The 1841 publication of *Incidents of Travel,* embellished by Catherwood's splendid drawings, both rendered Walker and Caddy's report moot and sparked another round of competition to obtain the monuments for foreign governments.

While *Incidents* was appearing in New York, John Baily, a British engineer and naval officer stationed in Guatemala, initiated a second attempt to wrest the ruins from impending U.S. control. Baily energetically promoted British interests in Central America in ways that suggest the synergy between Britain's formal rule in British Honduras and its informal sway in neighboring countries: he translated an important work on Guatemalan history into English; produced several maps; surveyed possible canal routes; wrote articles for the Royal Geographical Society; published a book on Central America, which featured a call for British immigration to the region; and sought to remove Maya ruins to London.[37] In a four-page letter written to George Ure Skinner, a Scottish merchant and orchid collector residing in Guatemala City, Baily described Quiriguá's monuments in detail. The letter, which included sketches of some monuments,[38] depicted the sculptures as having been wrought with "a much greater degree of skill in execution and a more intimate acquaintance with cultivated art" than comparable Mexican antiquities. His rhetoric of international interest closely paralleled MacDonald's: Their publication would "excite a great share of scientific attention" in Europe (CA 21 May 1841). The following month, Baily wrote to James Bateman, the celebrated orchidist of Knypersley Hall, Staffordshire, whose collaboration with Skinner in search of Central American orchids produced the largest if not also the greatest flower book of the century. The mammoth size and ravishing prints of *The Orchidaceae of Mexico and Guatemala* (1837–43) testifies to that related midcentury craze, the hunt for tropical orchids, which like ruins were sought throughout Central America by zealous collectors.[39] The parallels are suggestive. Before the arrival of the orchid hunters Guatemala was, according to Bateman, an "unwrought mine of natural history," but afterwards, one could find vast tracts of forest that had been felled in the quest for orchid species that thrived only on the upper branches of the forest canopy.[40] George Cruickshank, who drew some of the vignettes for Bateman's work, pointed up the connection himself, wryly depicting the *Orchidaceae* hoisted by block and tackle, as if it were an oversized monument or part of a ruin (Figure 19).[41]

Baily had met Stephens in Central America and warned, using Stephens's own terms, that in the United States the ruins had already occasioned "much speculation" (CA 30 Jun. 1841). In 1854, Chatfield affirmed that the ruins were also sought by French and Belgian learned societies (FO15/84, f. 33). Though Baily asserted the now-familiar claim of "promoting general knowledge," his mention of speculation links the commodity value of the ruins to the wider contest between Britain and the United States over territory, resources, and political influence in Central America. Indeed, in the same letter, Baily mentions seeing Stephens "in Nicaragua last year, near the probable site of the much talked of Canal"—a site both Baily and Stephens had surveyed on behalf of their respective governments.[42] Portable, rare, suitable for illustration and display, ruins, like orchids, served as symbolic markers of the larger influence sought by competing empires in the region, but as products of human culture they were also much more important, suggesting both the grandeur and fragility of the ancient past, and, because many of them were inscribed with figures, the cultures of writing and history.

These first unofficial letters, passing among a loose, informal network of naval officers, orchid collectors, businessmen, and travelers, were quickly translated into the forms and language of official discourse. In 1842 Skinner appealed directly to the British Museum trustees to purchase the ruins and bring them to London (CA 12 Feb. 1842).[43] He pointed out that the ruins lay close to the Motagua River, which, according to admiralty charts, was navigable, and that the work of removing and transporting the monuments could be done by the Caribs, who could ship them down the river like so much cut mahogany—long a mainstay of the extractive economy in nearby British Honduras. Skinner also noted that George Ackermann (son of Rudolph, the publisher of fine art prints in London) had been authorized by Narcisso Payes, who still owned the land on which Quiriguá lay, to act on his behalf to sell the entire city.[44] Skinner believed that eight to nine hundred pounds would suffice for the whole, including

Figure 19. George Cruickshank, "Monumental Orchids," from *Vignettes from Mr. Bateman's "Orchidaceae of Mexico and Guatemala"* (1844). Courtesy of Harry Elkins Widener Collection, Houghton Library of the Harvard College Library, HEW 3.1.18.

the right to excavate and remove anything found to be of value. Finally, Skinner revealed that he had already discussed the matter with Lord Aberdeen, a figure who typifies the permeable boundary between British antiquarian and political spheres. A classicist of some ability, Aberdeen played a key role in purchasing the Parthenon statues for the British Museum, a move that earned him the scorn of none other than Lord Byron, his cousin. In *English Bards and Scotch Reviewers* (1809) Byron labeled him (vituperatively in this context) "traveled Thane, Athenian Aberdeen," and in *Childe Harold's Pilgrimage* (1812) grouped him with Elgin himself, "The last, the worst, dull despoiler" of Greek antiquity.[45] Aberdeen had been president of the Society of Antiquaries and a British Museum trustee since 1812; from 1841 to 1846, he was foreign secretary, and from 1852 to 1855 prime minister.[46] The British Museum trustees, convinced the government would deny the request for funds, declined Skinner's offer. Despite Skinner's further appeals to Aberdeen, the matter appeared to end there; after Aberdeen resigned the presidency of the Society of Antiquaries in 1846, Lord Mahon became his successor, and for five years, nothing more was heard of the ruins.[47]

AGENCIES OF THE LETTER

In testimony before a House of Lords Select Committee on India in 1852, John Stuart Mill argued for the absolute centrality of writing to the imperial project: not only is "the whole government of India . . . carried out in writing," but "there is not a single act done in India, the whole of the reasons for which are not placed on record." For Mill, the disciplines of writing and recording assured a "greater security for good government than exists in almost any other government in the world, because no other has a system of recordation so complete."[48] This view was widely held. Henry Taylor, a senior clerk in the mid-nineteenth-century Colonial Office, put it this way, crystallizing the rationale behind the British empire's meticulously kept archives: "Few questions are well considered till they are largely written about."[49] In Latour's terms, what Mill and Taylor describe is not the state per se but an embodiment of it through the "construction of long networks in which numerous faithful records circulate in both directions, records which are, in turn, summarized and displayed to convince."[50] The plot examined here is an excellent example of this paper-mediated entity. At once executed by and preserved in writing, it was inconceivable apart from the special technology of the dispatch and the bureaucracies (British Museum, Foreign and Colonial Offices) that relied on it as the primary means of doing imperial business. Yet governance by and through writing, despite Mill's claim, was frequently a vexing matter. Because dispatches had to be sent, they could be delayed, lost, misplaced, or stolen; because they had to be interpreted, they were subject to willful or accidental misreading. The systems of distribution and interpretation on which they depended introduced error and inhibited action. This fundamental instability was compounded during the period examined here when a proliferation of dispatches undermined the empire's ability to govern from afar. The plot—and its cultural technology—thus suggests an empire at its territorial, communicative, and conceptual limits, an imperial overreach that would eventually contribute to the weakening of Britain's control over the independent nations of Latin America.

Because I am interested here in how letter writing connects to plotting, and beyond that to desire of various kinds, I want to consider briefly the letter both as literary genre and diplomatic instrument. Studies of the epistolary novel rightly underscore the crucial role of the letter in constructing middle-class subjectivity and negotiating women's entry into print culture.[51] Yet as Amanda Gilroy and Will Verhoeven have pointed out, the focus on the bourgeois novel, and its attendant values of privacy, interiority, and domesticity, obscures the "male epistolary subject," and along with it the agency of the letter in the work of empire.[52] Here, it may be useful to consider what Harold Love calls "scribal" communities: "groups of like-minded individuals [bound] into a community, sect or political faction, with the exchange of texts in manuscript serving to nourish a shared set of values and to enrich personal allegiances."[53] For imperial administrators, the "texts in manuscript" are that special form of letter, the dispatch, whose writing, answering, and recordation not only comprised their principal work, but also, as Mill claimed, the warp and woof of imperial governance. During the nineteenth century, the empire's growth severely stretched this fabric. Like the imperial archive described by Thomas Richards,[54] information—in the form of dispatches, reports, memoranda—poured in more rapidly than it could be processed; the well-kept files threatened to break down; the archive nearly collapsed under its own massive weight. As historians of the nineteenth-century Foreign and Colonial Offices note, new systems of storage, indexing, docketing, and retrieval had to be installed to handle the glut.[55] Since the empire's ability to act at a distance was dependent on the exchange of dispatches, the problem of information management became a central preoccupation of imperial bureaucracy.

Yet the problems facing administrators only magnified the instability of all epistolary communication. Like letters, dispatches implied the physical absence of the receiver, and the distances they had to travel created a temporal lag between writing and reply. The uncertainty and fragility of epistolary exchange slowed imperial governance, bogging it down, blunting its effectiveness. As the empire grew, so did the problem—more dispatches from ever more places. At the far peripheries, dispatches could take months to arrive from London, by which time the circumstances they described might have changed altogether. Once in hand, new orders still had to be put into "action," which often meant the writing of more letters, addressed to local officials, business concerns, heads of state, and one's superiors back in London. Meanwhile, new dispatches with new instructions arrived with each mail packet. The government's reliance on acting *by* dispatch paradoxically impeded its ability to act *with* dispatch, even as it permitted the "man on the spot" to act independently from his superiors at home.

Palmerston, who held the Foreign Office "seals" (the bureaucratic trope is significant) from 1830 to 1834, from 1835 to 1841, and again from 1846 to 1851, saw the problem with great clarity, and his responses capture not only the centrality of writing in the imperial mind but more radically the desire to impose, through the centralized *control* of writing, a grand, totalizing order, a regime of power exercised through many hands acting as one, and one hand controlling the many—an image of imperial governance itself. Palmerston labored like Hercules to master every remote corner of British policy, which meant, as a practical matter, casting his panoramic eye over each piece of incoming and outgoing mail. His passion for work was legendary; Kenneth Bourne notes that "he reckoned on having to read most of the incoming political correspondence and on drafting or at least outlining all the replies and memoranda himself."[56] Out-of-town ministers were to be provided with abstracts and bulletins of important correspondence (all of which were copied by hand); when asked whether a certain dispatch was to be copied for the minister at Paris, he replied, "Everything should go to Lord Granville unless I give a special direction to the contrary."[57] All this occurred, moreover, during an unprecedented increase in the volume of dispatches sent and received at the Foreign Office; the dispatches sent along by one undersecretary "rose from 200 in 1829 to over 700 in 1831 and more than 1,500 in 1832."[58] Clerks and undersecretaries were pushed to their limits, leading one, the younger son of Walter Scott, to complain to Maria Edgeworth that Palmerston was "disliked by all under him—each under unbearable discord crying out against him as loud as they dare and cursing deep."[59] If all this seems now a bit perverse, it fits perfectly with the cult of duty of an aristocratic class convinced of its own superiority and influenced by what Linda Colley has called "an exhilarating sense of expanding British power in the world."[60]

The most revealing account of Palmerston's rage for order comes from a late Victorian archivist at the Foreign Office, Edward Hertslet. Hertslet observes dryly that Palmerston was "very particular about Handwriting,"[61] and goes on to provide a case history of obsession in which the fate of empire seemed at moments to hang on the proper use of the semicolon. "Protocol Palmerston," as the FO clerks called him, returned illegible or poorly written dispatches to consuls abroad with instructions for resubmission—Frederick Chatfield, the British consul in Guatemala, was one of those thus chastened. On several occasions Palmerston "sent circulars to ministers and consuls abroad, desiring them to write large, round, legible hands, and to use black ink" (77). Dispatches he deemed "Readable Copy" were given to clerks to rewrite in the "approved style." On one poorly written dispatch he scribbled: "Tell Mr. W____, in a 'Separate,' that the person who copies out his despatches should form his letters by connecting his slanting down strokes by visible lines at top or bottom according to the letters which he intends his parallel lines to represent" (78). According to Hertslet, all FO "hands" were urged to "take more pains to form their letters distinctly" (79), and were railed against for pompous diction and overwrought sentences. Palmerston's regime included lectures on proper word order: "Sentences should be constructed to begin with the nominative, to go on with the verb, and to end with the accusative" (82). In 1851, an infuriated Palmerston wrote:

> Write to the Stationery Office for a sufficient supply of Full Stops, Semi-colons, and Commas; but more especially Semi-Colons, for the use of the copying

clerks of the office; I furnish these things out of my own private stores when I
have time to look over despatches for signature, but I am not always sufficiently
at leisure to supply deficiencies. (81)

No jot or iota was beneath his notice.

These are not merely the ravings of a work-obsessed, detail-oriented
man, but rather a grasping and ultimately futile attempt to exercise control
over something that was ultimately beyond control—events at a distance,
which Foreign Secretary Palmerston's work obliged him to know and influence through the fragile instrument of correspondence, the writing and
reading of dispatches sent through and along a dispersed and far-flung
communications network. The difficulty of standardizing that enterprise
was increased by the sheer variability of human hands, the hands that
composed and copied the incoming and outgoing dispatches, that slipped
into the passive voice, and formed each letter in their own, idiosyncratic
way. Hence Palmerston's buried reference to the technology of printing,
imagining himself as the compositor who keeps extra supplies of movable
type on hand in the hope of holding it all together. Palmerston's trope,
moreover, accurately reflects a moment in imperial administration when
the standardization promised by print in its various forms—Parliamentary
Blue Books, confidential correspondence edited and drawn up for Parliament, and Hertslet's *State Papers*—was making inroads on but had yet to
supplant the irregular but traditional culture of handwriting that had long
prevailed in the Foreign and Colonial Offices. By the 1840s the Foreign
Office was issuing confidential print; by the 1860s the growth of printed
material in the Colonial Office necessitated elaborate dockets to keep
track of it; by 1870 Hertslet's printed *State Papers* and *Treaties* had grown
to thirty-seven and eleven volumes respectively. The gradual dominance
of print promised not only to standardize but also to conserve the historical record; Hertslet notes that Palmerston was particularly concerned to
construct an archive in which dispatches would "be preserved for all time"
(77). "My view of the records of the Foreign Office," Palmerston wrote
in 1849, "is that they should contain as full a record of all that passes and
of the real motives and grounds of events."[62] Palmerston knew firsthand
the importance of preservation: Hertslet reports that during an attack on
his foreign policy in the House of Commons Palmerston sent the librarian and his staff searching all night through 3,000 manuscript volumes for

precedents (72). It is almost as if Palmerston had studied his Latour, or Latour his Palmerston: "a man whose eye dominates records through which some sort of connections are established with millions of others may be said to *dominate*."[63] That domination was effected through control over the dispatch, which was both instrument and repository of institutional memory, an irreplaceable artifact in the imperial archive.

The much-fetishized dispatch, however, was also situated at a critical juncture of male intimacy, hierarchy, and power. The Foreign and Colonial Offices, it must be remembered, were comprised solely of *men* writing to other men: men of the same class, educated at the same schools, many from the same few families, bound together in a tightly knit world of entitlement, favoritism, patronage, nepotism, mentoring, and rivalry—in short, a world of carefully cultivated homosocial bonds. As Bourne points out, "More than one Rolleston, Staveley and Hammond turned up in the nineteenth-century F.O., and numerous Bidwells and Hertslets."[64] During the nineteenth century, most Foreign Office recruits were younger sons of the aristocracy; some began their careers as early as sixteen or seventeen, most a year or two later. The new recruits were quickly infantilized; a special room, set aside to alleviate the drudgery of the copying desk, was known derisively as the "nursery."[65] The members of this all-male club also specialized, not surprisingly, in the emasculating put-down. Hertslet recounts that Palmerston once inveighed against the office procedure of fastening papers together with pins by requesting that "all the Pins in this Office be immediately made over to the Female Branch of the Establishment"(82). The language of homosocial hierarchy, rivalry, and intimacy was common coin in the centers of power, and it served the important ideological function of reinforcing the world of imperial adventure as a male domain against the domestic, feminized space of the home.

Just how incestuous that world could be can be glimpsed by a brief survey of some key interlocking relationships. Mahon, as already pointed out, succeeded Aberdeen as president of the Society of Antiquaries in 1846, to which he had been elected a fellow in 1841. Like Aberdeen, he was also a British Museum trustee, and thus linked to the project of the "national repository" (FO15/84, f. 69); in 1834–35 he also served the Duke of Wellington as under-secretary in the Foreign Office, where he crossed paths with Palmerston, who was between appointments as foreign secretary. Lord John Russell was the colonial secretary in Robert Peel's administration when the ruins first came to the government's attention in 1839, and prime minister from 1846 to 1852, when the issue was taken up again. At times, moves in and out of the cabinet took on the elegant symmetry of chiasmus: Aberdeen succeeded Palmerston as foreign secretary, while Palmerston succeeded Aberdeen as prime minister. The same few individuals circled in and out of the cabinet. The British Museum was equally inbred; when Mahon wrote Palmerston to lay out his plan for taking the ruins, he noted that the idea had been hatched in conversation among two or three "brother Trustees" (FO15/75, f. 40). The intimacies nurtured by ruling class society extended, moreover, to the colonial periphery. Palmerston, to take one example, was at Harrow with Aberdeen and also Edmond Wodehouse, MP from Norfolk, and father of Philip Edmond Wodehouse, the superintendent of British Honduras from 1851 to 1854. Shortly after arriving at his new post, Wodehouse *fils* wrote his father requesting that he use his friendship with Palmerston to further the son's career abroad by assigning him an important role in the plot to take the ruins; as I discuss in greater detail below, Palmerston's favor to his schoolboy friend shaped events in significant ways. Another network of affiliations between metropole and colony united Baily the naval officer and surveyor, Skinner the orchid collector and businessman in Guatemala, Bateman the orchidist in Staffordshire, Ackermann his publisher, and Aberdeen the antiquary and politician.

Like secret agents lurking in the London fog, these figures joined together in a plot, both in the sense of a complex story and in the sense suggested by the French *complot,* a covert design or action, a machination or intrigue. Indeed, concealment was central from Walker and Caddy's visit to Palenque through Palmerston's warning to Chatfield to say nothing of the British government's interest in the ruins.[66] Yet, like the wider culture of diplomatic writing sketched above, the plot should also be understood as gendered. First, its structure of desire paralleled the male nineteenth-century quest narrative, which as outlined by Peter Brooks, entails both a highly charged, libidinous pursuit of a valued object (usually a woman), and resisting or frustrating forces that defer, if only to heighten, its consummation.[67] Second, the plot, with its elements of secrecy, exoticism, and plunder, enabled its participants to act out a certain kind of adventure story that had deep roots in the masculine imaginary, one that, as Martin Green argues, "prepared the young men of England to go out to the colonies, to rule, and their families to rejoice in their fates out there"; Joseph Bristow's term for these players is apt: "Empire Boys."[68] They wrote the stories and lived them out through the imperial adventure abroad. Third, in addition to a male rhythm of arousal, consummation, and quiescence, the conspiracy was also informed by complex erotics of rivalry, both internal and external, that shaped the identities of its participants as well as its outcome. Here again, the novel provides a useful model in the erotic structure of the double-suitor convention, where two men vie for the hand of a woman. In such triangles, according to René Girard, the bond coupling the rivals is as potent, perhaps more so, as any bond joining the rivals to the desired love object; as Eve Sedgwick puts it, the structure of "emulation and identification" may usefully describe "*any* relation of rivalry," whether the "entities occupying the corners of the triangle be heroes, heroines, gods, books, or whatever." I follow Sedgwick's lead that "desire" names an "affective or social force . . . even when its manifestation is hostility or hatred or something less emotively charged, that shapes an important relationship."[69] This expanded definition of erotic rivalry makes it possible to see the many sides of struggles such as the one examined here, where the quest for objects and territories produced enmity as well as emulation. Stephens formed his notions of the national museum in imitation of the British Museum; the British Museum, in turn, sought to foil the Americans by taking the ruins Stephens had publicized. Once again, however, we should note that these erotic structures exclude the Central Americans, who remain invisible, out of place, shunted aside.

For all its constructive power in the Anglo-American contest, homosocial rivalry also functioned *within* and *among* the agencies recruited to pursue the ruins for Britain, mirroring internally the erotics of competition, aggression, and desire that were played out at the edges of empire. In reply to Mahon's initial letter, Palmerston sent instructions in July 1851 both to Frederick Chatfield, his agent in Guatemala, and the Colonial Office, with a request that similar instructions be addressed to the superintendent at Belize (CO123/84, f. 335). This was good strategy, and it shows how informal imperialism of the sort we are examining here meshed with and at times depended on outright colonial rule. The settlement at Belize was a key British possession in Central America, and given its proximity to the ruins, would be necessary to the success of any plan in Central America. Yet Palmerston's move spurred competition, not cooperation. As noted above, Philip Edmond Wodehouse, newly arrived at his post in Belize, seized the opportunity to write privately to his father in hopes of advancing his diplomatic career, which also meant obstructing Chatfield, his FO counterpart in Central America (FO15/75, f. 115; 19 Sep. 1851). The day after the orders arrived from the Colonial Office, he wrote his father. But he delayed a month before acknowledging the receipt of those instructions to Governor Charles E. Grey, who was his immediate Colonial Office superior at Jamaica (CO123/83; 15 Oct. 1851). Meanwhile, more than a month passed before Chatfield had the opportunity to reply to Palmerston's dispatch—mail arriving in Guatemala City a month later than in Belize (FO15/72, f. 142; 24 Oct. 1851).[70] Wodehouse's delay shrewdly exploited the uncertainties of colonial mail, allowing him to plot his own self-advancement before answering his superiors at the Colonial Office.

In a further effort to undermine Chatfield's authority, Wodehouse took advantage of the uncertainties of Central American geography. Palmerston's instructions to Chatfield (FO15/69, f. 53)—copied to Wodehouse (CO123/84, f. 335)—placed the Copán ruins upon a river of the same name, located near the "bottom of the bay of Honduras, to the south of the British settlement of Belize." This vague identification left the exact location up in the air, as the Copán river flowed through both Honduras and Guatemala, an indeterminacy Wodehouse immediately exploited by evoking the conflict between the states and by pointing out that Chatfield, who was stationed in Guatemala, "is, as Lord Palmerston must well know, looked upon in a very unfriendly light" by Honduras. As an aside, Wodehouse also mentioned that Chatfield was evidently "hurt at" his initial contacts with the Central American governments because he told Wodehouse to communicate "only through him." Returning to the subject of the ruins, Wodehouse went on to say that though he doubted Honduras would undertake a negotiation as a "National affair," his own good relations with the government of Honduras would facilitate a visit to Copán if he were to "apply for it as a personal affair," just as Stephens had attempted a decade before. Such a strategy would be all the more likely to succeed because it would move outside "the regular diplomatic channel"— i.e., Chatfield. Wodehouse concluded by asking that Palmerston suggest this course of action to the Colonial Office, thus concealing that the request initiated with him, was channeled to his father, and passed on to Palmerston. On one level, the strategy succeeded brilliantly, as Palmerston asked the Colonial Office to appoint Wodehouse while Chatfield's own dispatch was crossing the Atlantic—three months after Palmerston first wrote to him. But Wodehouse was not ultimately sent to inspect the ruins, because the Colonial Office would not release him from his duties in the British settlement. Colonial Secretary Earl Grey requested that someone else be sent, and what's more, that the Foreign Office pay the bill. A summary of the discussions was sent to Governor Charles E. Grey at Jamaica in December 1851, and copies of the relevant dispatches sent the next month to Mahon. The trustees decided against further action until the person sent to the ruins from Belize filed his report (FO97/89, f. 4). Seven months had now elapsed since Palmerston's initial dispatch. No significant progress had been made; the plot was stalled; the museum's desire unfulfilled.

DISCOVERY BY PROXY

The mid-Victorian empire was both efficient and bungling, capable of reaching across vast distances yet given to myopic obsessions over commas and inkwells. Internal rivalry posed a constant threat to the smooth co-ordination among government branches. Paper, in which Mill placed such great faith, piled up at terrifying rates, encumbering the empire's ability to act with dispatch. Thus while Latour's notion of acting at a distance through the exchange of immutable mobiles (dispatches) provides a useful rubric, it is important to recognize the enormous problems created by the sheer accumulation of paper. This is well illustrated in the next stage of the Mayan plot, which culminated in the hiring of two foreign scientists who happened to be traveling through Central America. Nothing less than mobile eyes, extensions of the British Museum abroad, Karl Ritter von Scherzer and Moritz Wagner acted as proxies, personifying the reliance on mediation that had been central to the plot from the start.[71] Though their letters to the British Museum trustees were suffused with the honeyed tones and intimate phrases of homosocial discourse, they never actually met any of the trustees with whom they corresponded. They existed, in some sense, as epistolary, even virtual, subjects, typifying Britain's often-slender knowledge of and hold over the territories it sought to control. Scherzer and Wagner did, however, finally accomplish the desired mission—reaching a ruin and reporting on it—but in doing so they heralded the plot's demise; their account of the difficulty and expense of obtaining the Mayan ruins, along with their dismissal of the ruins' artistic worth, persuaded the trustees to scrap the plan. Decades would pass before the British Museum realized the dream of adding Mayan ruins to the national repository.

In the months immediately prior to the hiring of Scherzer and Wagner, the plot appeared to have died another kind of death, vanishing amidst the Foreign and Colonial Office files (war in the Crimea also drained away enthusiasm). On 14 February 1854, two and one half years after the plot first began, Henry Ellis, the British Museum's librarian, wrote the Foreign Office to inquire whether any report had yet been received on the ruins of Copán (FO15/84). Wodehouse, formerly superintendent at Belize, was now back in London awaiting his next overseas appointment (he went on to serve in British Guiana, South Africa, and India). When queried by the Colonial Office—to whom the request for an update had also gone— he explained why no report had been filed, reminding his superiors that he had received no funds and that the colonial secretary had forbidden him to go himself (FO15/84, f. 7). But this was only half true. As noted above, and as corroborated by a Foreign Office clerk who searched through the records (FO15/84, f. 5), the Foreign Office had consented to defray the expenses of a traveler, only not Wodehouse, because he was needed at Belize. This, then, raises a question: did resentment over the failure of his scheme for self-advancement cause Wodehouse to bury the whole matter rather than appoint someone else as instructed? Or was there simple mis-communication? We cannot know, but in explaining these missed chances to the British Museum the Foreign Office performed an exquisite bureau-cratic burial: "His Lordship [Clarendon] has ascertained, on inquiry at the Colonial Office, that *difficulties were interposed* to the projected mission of some person from Belize to Copan" (FO15/84, f. 9; my emphasis). Lost amidst the passives, individual subjects fade away. Plots, which require agents, stand still. Action loses its name.

Two months later, an exasperated Mahon wrote again to the Foreign Office, noting the three years that had passed since his first letter to Palmerston. Though he saw the morass into which his request had sunk, he retained a blithe though ill-advised faith in writing as a means of get-ting things done. Noting that Chatfield was now back in London at the conclusion of his appointment in Guatemala, he asked that the Foreign

Office request him to draw up a memo, to "be put on record both in the Foreign and Colonial Offices (for the question is in some measure suspended between the two)" (FO15/84, f. 21). The plot had gone awry from a mixture of ineptitude and homosocial rivalry. The solution, as always, was more writing: more memoranda, letters, and reports—all logged, duly noted, and "put on record." So complete was the addiction to memoranda that no one could seem to imagine a way out of it, though "recordation" was as much the problem as the solution. The British Museum, no less than the Foreign and Colonial Offices, was in thrall to writing and the preservation of bureaucratic structures. After retaining Scherzer and Wagner, the trustees reminded them that they should observe a strict chain of command: the museum would write to the Foreign Office, which would communicate with the consul in Guatemala, Charles L. Wyke; Scherzer and Wagner, in turn, were to deal with Wyke, who would then report back to the Foreign Office, which would then report back to the British Museum. No wonder George Ure Skinner, the orchid collector and sometime antiquarian, referred to Bloomsbury as the "Red Tape Museum."[72]

With Chatfield's memo (FO15/84, f. 33), the plot lurched forward, returning to the same issues that had preoccupied officials from the start. Quiriguá and Copán once more surfaced as the most promising sites, though yet again, British officials realized they would have to contend with the desire of other nations. In this context, Chatfield revived Palmerston's trope of "imaginary value," referring to international competition as nothing but mere "rumor" cooked up to raise the price (f. 35). Once more the local people, when mentioned at all, appear not as inheritors or owners of their past, but only as mute laborers. The ruins, Chatfield pointed out, could be carried on their heads, much like "carriages, pianos" and other "bulky merchandise" (f. 36). The only thing new is the mention of Tikal, a magnificent Mayan city located in the remote northern regions of Guatemala, due west of the border with British Honduras. As Chatfield was writing his memo to the Foreign Office, Mahon presented to the Society of Antiquaries a translated extract of a report written about that site in 1848 by Modesto Méndez, a Guatemalan magistrate in the region of Petén, where the ruined city lay. Chatfield had supplied Mahon with the report, as well as with several drawings, which are still in the society's library.[73] Méndez, a notable patriot in the struggle for independence from Spain, originally published the report in the official newspaper *Gaceta de Guatemala,* a testament to the site's importance in shaping the nation's sense of its past.[74] Yet like Del Río's report, discussed above, Méndez's was quickly co-opted by British interests, who used it to identify the ruins they sought to remove to London. Local knowledge once again became imperial knowledge.

Over the next several months, the British Museum and the Foreign Office bickered over who should appoint a person to survey the ruins and revisited the reasons why no one had been sent before. The museum reasserted its desire to have the Foreign Office choose someone; the Foreign Office thought the museum should do so. In the end, Mahon interceded again, drafting a letter for the trustees that was sent to the Foreign Office under Ellis's signature summarizing events to date and suggesting a way forward (FO15/84, f. 69; 15 Aug. 1854). After three fruitless years and over forty letters and dispatches, the plot again resumed. The empire once more geared itself to act; yet again, its agency was enacted through writing. The reformulated plot now fixed on Copán as the best site. The firmness of its stone made it easier to cart away, the other sites (Quiriguá and Tikal) apparently made up of "some friable composition rendering them ill adapted either for removal or preservation" (f. 69). Once again, the trustees proposed that the Foreign Office refer the matter to its legation in Guatemala, recalling that at an earlier date the superintendent at Honduras had offered to visit the ruins himself. The trustees, however, tactfully set aside the issue of responsibility, attributing previous failures to the retirement of Lord Grey from office and "other subsidiary causes" (f. 70).

But in recommending that the selection of a proxy traveler be left to the Foreign Office, the trustees also reasserted an important ideological tenet: the inferiority of Mesoamerican antiquities to classical ones, which meant that the appointed person need have no special "literary accomplishment," whereas for Greek or Roman antiquities a "full and clear preliminary knowledge would be requisite" (f. 70). In 1845 the watercolorist James Stephanoff gave powerful visual expression to these ideas, showing a hierarchy of sculptural styles rising from an apparently primitive origin in Mayan arts to the acknowledged superiority of the Parthenon marbles (Figure 20). When exhibited at the Old Watercolour Society in 1845, the painting was glossed as follows:

> At the base of the picture are specimens of Hindu and Javanese sculpture, and on either side are the colossal figures and bas-reliefs from Copan and Palenque;

Figure 20. James Stephanoff, *An Assemblage of Works of Art, from the Earliest Period to the Time of Phydias, a Watercolor* (1845). Copyright The British Museum.

those above them are from Persepolis and Babylon, followed by the Egyptian, Etruscan, and early Greek remains, and surmounted by the pediment from Aegina . . . and terminating in a portion of the equestrian bas-relief of the Panathenaic procession to the Temple of Minerva.[75]

The placement of the Copán and Palenque sculptures at the bottom of this hierarchy did not mean, of course, that they were undesirable; they were pursued, as we have seen, with great energy. It meant, rather, that desire for them was expressed within a precise ideology of value, indexed to standards that ensured the preeminence of the European and classical traditions. The larger context of cultural hierarchy (of which aesthetic hierarchy was a feature) sustained the justifications that were invoked to wrest the ruins from their rightful owners. European and classical standards of beauty, which the British Museum imagined itself to represent, were closely correlated to notions of cultural value and thus to logics of cultural difference that underwrote the imperial project.[76] Finally, Stephanoff's painting, executed sometime before 1845, proleptically imagines the removal of objects to Britain that had only been made known to the wider European public in 1841 and that were actively pursued by the British Museum in 1851. The museum already possessed other objects in the painting, including most famously the Parthenon marbles, and the painting suggests that it will only be a matter of time before the Copán and Palenque sculptures join the collection.

Since the object in Central America was "merely to acquire and to secure from further injury some of the only records of an extinct race of men and a wholly separate sphere of civilization" (FO15/84, f. 70), no special aesthetic qualifications were deemed necessary, only a knowledge of Spanish (always considered a less-sophisticated language), and that only for the purpose of carrying out negotiations with the locals. The museum was willing to pay five to six hundred pounds for the sculptures, but cautioned the Foreign Office to instruct its agents to act with "great caution and judgment," lest the price rise artificially once word got around that a foreign government was interested in the ruins. The museum reaffirmed its mission of archaeological salvage: preserving and protecting, storing and keeping safe, making valuable information available for the study of other cultures. Yet it admitted no contradiction in recommending, as an efficiency, the technique practiced at Nineveh by Layard, who, finding the sculptures carved on one side only, found a means to "chip away . . . large pieces from the other side and reduce them as it were from rocks to slabs (f. 71). This practice of selective reduction from whole to part, already employed by Stephens and Catherwood in removing lintels from Kabah and Uxmal, became popular among British travelers and archaeologists— though no more than among present-day looters, who shorten the work through the use of chainsaws.[77] In each case, the integrity of the cultural site is destroyed, writing is effaced, figuration reduced to decoration, signs to designs.

With the hiring of Scherzer and Wagner in late October 1854, the trustees placed the quest for ruins within the frame of midcentury racial theory, a subject I explore at greater length in the next chapter. Rooted in the gathering of cranial data and the conviction of European cultural and racial superiority, ethnology looked to archaeology for further proof of cultural hierarchy, while asserting its own centrality to the new science of archaeology. Scherzer, who traveled under the patronage of the Imperial Academy of Sciences in Vienna, was one of Europe's leading ethnologists and scientific travelers (the Royal Geographical Society's obituary referred glowingly to the "great value" of his researches in Central America).[78] After completing his work for the British Museum, he sailed round the globe as the lead scientist on the *Novara* expedition (1857–59), for which he drew up an influential ethnological manual: *On Measurements as a Diagnostic Means for Distinguishing the Human Races*. Scherzer's manual, part of an ambitious scheme to form an ethnological data bank "on a larger scale than has ever been done before," called for seventy-nine individual measurements of each human subject, as a "principal means of comparing the *Normal* Caucasian with the *Normal* Malay, Mongol, Papuan, New Zealander, Indian, &c."[79] Among those who praised this elaborate plan were Alexander von Humboldt and the British ethnologist Joseph Barnard Davis. Yet while the racial imperatives of Scherzer's reports for the British Museum are clear, they merely threw into relief ideas about race and culture already implicit in the British view of Central American peoples.

Within a month of their appointment Scherzer and Wagner submitted the first of several substantial reports on the value and practicability of removing the ruins.[80] Copán, they wrote, was impossible to visit owing to a war between Guatemala and Honduras. A visit to Tikal, likewise, would have to be postponed to the following year, after the rainy season. The prospects were better at Quiriguá, partly because Wyke had secured official permission to excavate (FO15/84, 29 Oct. 1854). Yet after an extensive survey of the site, all Scherzer and Wagner could find were three "portable idols" of value. To obtain them without inflating the price, Scherzer advised the usual tactic, urging Wyke not to deal directly with the Payes family, who still owned the land, but to employ a third person—in effect another proxy—one "not suspected to negotiate for a Foreign Royal Institution" (FO15/82, f. 374). Employing a popular cultural stereotype, he also warned of the "difficulty and great length of time till Spanish people are brought to a decision" (FO15/82, f. 374), a trait he later named the "mania of the Neo-Spaniards for hesitation and mistrust" (CA 10 Dec. 1854). It is, of course, partly thanks to that mistrust that the ruins remain today in Guatemala.

Scherzer revisits the issue of value set forth so vividly by Palmerston in 1851, but instead of restating the distinction between Britain's estimation of the ruins and that of the natives, he turns to a more complex issue: the difference between aesthetic and ethnographic value. This difference, crucial in general terms to the nineteenth-century conjoining of museums and anthropology,[81] is also central to the ideological frame in which the meaning of Central American antiquities was constructed and perceived. For Scherzer contends that while the sculptures at Quiriguá merit the attention of the "archaeologist and Ethnographer," they are much less interesting from an "artistic point of view," "the taste and the ability of the artists" indicating a "low state of culture" and a "barbarous state of art."[82] Hence a pivotal separation, endlessly rehearsed in national and provincial museums: the segregation of works deemed aesthetic (elevated, transcendent, transhistorical) from those considered merely ethnographic (contingent, primitive, inextricably tied to race). The British Museum's pre-Columbian collections, to take a ready example, fall under the purview of the Department of Ethnography, a division of the museum that during the nineteenth century repeatedly staved off critics who wanted to dissolve it and during the twentieth was exiled from the main museum site in Bloomsbury to a building across town in Piccadilly.

With regard to African art, Annie Coombes argues that by the end of the nineteenth century an ideological consensus had formed around the "effectivity" of ethnological displays in Britain. The museum establishment promoted the material culture in its custody as "simultaneously: fodder for purportedly disinterested scientific and comparative study of culture; as 'proof' of racial inferiority (and therefore as justification of colonial intervention), but also in their capacity as objects of exotic delectation; aesthetic pleasure and, more frequently . . . spectacle."[83] The inklings of this museum ideology are already apparent in Bullock's division between "Ancient" and "Modern" Mexico; here Scherzer takes it one step further by correlating racial and cultural advancement. Scherzer believed that all the Central American monuments were created by "the same race," and were probably from the "same period."[84] None of the monuments, he argued, "is worked finer or with more aptness than the others. Nothing indicates in these sculptures a sense for beauty, refined or improved by [its] own perfection or foreign models" (CA 18 Dec. 1854, f. 27). Scherzer thus reminds us that a desire to possess Mayan ruins was not incompatible with an equally powerful desire to put them in their place, below the ancient cultures of the Old World.

So what became of the British Museum's plot to take the ruins of Copán, Quiriguá, and perhaps even Tikal? There are several possible endings from which to choose. The most direct, though in some ways the least satisfying, comes in 1855, when Superintendent William Stevenson, at Belize, writes the last official dispatch on the matter, informing his immediate supervisor, Governor Henry Barkly, at Jamaica, that he will do all he can to forward the aims of the British Museum (FO15/87, f. 180). Two years later, Stevenson donated a collection of ninety objects from British Honduras to the British Museum—a sizable and significant collection, but not the "noble pendant" Mahon and the trustees had desired. The great monuments of Copán, Quiriguá, and Tikal remained in place.[85] A second possible ending occurs in 1875, when the British traveler John Boddam-Whetham, while traveling in the Petén region, purchased two wooden lintels taken from Tikal; these went first to the South Kensington Museum and subsequently to Bloomsbury.[86] A third conclusion, and the most important, concerns a group of Maya artifacts that came to the British Museum through Alfred P. Maudslay, whose work in the Maya region during the 1880s is acknowledged to have brought modern scientific rigor to the discipline. Introduced to Central America by the naturalist Osbert Salvin, whose stereographic photos of Copán were published in 1863,[87] Maudslay amassed an extraordinary collection during several years' work in the Maya region, including a stunning carved bust from Copán that the modernist art critic Roger Fry compared to the "greatest sculpture of Europe,"[88] the Yaxchilán bas-relief lintels, and over 400 plaster casts of other objects. All these are now in Bloomsbury; the Yaxchilán lintels, because they fall within Mexico's current border, are displayed in the museum's Mexican Gallery. Maudslay's archaeological work was not funded by the British government, nor is there any evidence that it was inspired or influenced by the plot examined here. Yet the ideologies of value that I have tracked here reverberate throughout his work. In his popular travel narrative, *A Glimpse at Guatemala,* we read the following:

> The ordinances issued from time to time by the Government [of Guatemala] prohibiting excavations and the removal of sculptures and pottery have confirmed both Indians and Ladinos in the belief that the mounds contain hidden treasure, and the result may easily be disastrous, for it is as likely as not that the Indians may themselves begin rummaging amongst the ruins in search of treasure which does not exist, and will destroy in the process much that, although it is valueless to them, is of the highest importance to the archaeologist.[89]

For Maudslay, as for Stephens and Palmerston and the nineteenth-century museum establishment, neither the indigenous nor the Ladinos are capable of properly valuing the ruins. This is a privilege reserved for foreign archaeologists and museum keepers.[90]

REVERENCE AND RETICENCE

But what of the Creole elites and even more the indigenous, deemed by Scherzer, in a letter to the trustees, to be a "lazy sort of people" who care more for the "tune of the Marimba, their favorite instrument" than the "sound of the hammer or the hatchet" (CA 10 Dec. 1854)? While post-colonial theory has rightly argued that it is impossible to speak for the Other, the British emphasis on writing and recordation begs the question of the connection between the monuments and the local people, who are consistently represented as lawless and devoid of writing and historical consciousness. In order to see the full complexity of the imperial encounter, we need to fill in as best we can the gaps and silences in the archival record, remembering that the archive is itself a construct, shaped as much by what it excludes as what it preserves. First the Creole elites:

despite British travelers and government officials who claimed that Central America was lawless and ungoverned, Guatemalan and Honduran elites used the law as a primary means of protecting their nations' cultural heritage. Such laws had roots in Spanish jurisprudence going back to the sixteenth-century period of colonial settlement and were continually updated throughout the post-independence period. They derived from the principle that the legal power of a state rests on its authority over its people and its territory, an authority that is internally authenticated and thus not subject to validation by other states, though by the time the British become interested in the monuments they had formally recognized the sovereignty of Guatemala and Honduras and hence their internal laws. On 4 October 1831 Mariano Gálvez, the Guatemalan chief of state, announced the formation of a museum "that might be the depository of the curiosities in which the Guatemalan soil abounds, and that to form it is of great interest and very proper for a civilized country"; over the next few years Gálvez also sent expeditions to gather information about Guatemala's archaeological sites.[91] Galindo, as we have seen, was also active throughout the 1830s. Honduras passed legislation in 1845 explicitly protecting the monuments that lay in the valley of Copán, most likely as a result of Stephens's attempt to carry away the ruins and the fear that other governments might follow suit; according to the 1874 legislation that extended the earlier law, "esos monumentos se declaran propiedad de la Nación."[92] In a wonderful example of the force of words, the law declares monuments found in Honduras to be the nation's property, enacting what it proclaims. When the legislation was extended later in the century to establish a national museum, it spoke directly to the problem of precious monuments leaving the country "to enrich foreign museums"—an unmistakable reference to decades of foreign depredation in the name of European and U.S. archaeological and museological "rescue work."[93] Although the Creole elites who comprised Central American officialdom held contradictory ideas about the indigenous past, they clearly sought to protect it, especially from foreign travelers and the consular agents who assisted them. That they failed in many instances to do so, sometimes even selling out their own cultural heritage, owes more to persistent economic and political asymmetries than to any disregard for the past.

The indigenous response to imperial plunder is more difficult to ascertain, for the archive as we have it is, not surprisingly, skewed to emphasize their passivity and silence—that is, when it notices them at all. The inscrutable "Indian" (the nomenclature is itself a misrepresentation) is a constitutive feature of European discourse on the Americas, and we must be careful, as Sara Suleri warns, that in focusing on the idea of "intransigence" we do not simply "replicate what in the context of imperialist discourse was the familiar category of the exotic."[94] Yet to understand the power and limitations of that discourse we must examine those moments within it when the voice of the indigenous, however muted and ventriloquized, can be heard. Even within the imperial machinery of letters and dispatches that sought to rob the indigenous of their history, traces of reverence for the past lie preserved. Two such moments stand out, one at the beginning of the plot, one near its end. In Chatfield's first response to Palmerston's directive (FO15/72, f. 142), he obediently reports the steps he has taken to secure the ruins for the British Museum, along the way noting, as I have emphasized throughout this account, that the ruins "are held in little or no estimation by the Natives of the country." This repeats almost verbatim the language of Palmerston's dispatch, in turn derived from Mahon's first letter and beyond that Stephens's travel narrative. This, in other words, is the official line, a concise formulation of the way European discourse comprehends the indigenous Other. But a few paragraphs later, from within the margins of Chatfield's text, a countervailing notion emerges, an acknowledgment of indigenous affect that not even his scrupulous obedience to British cultural ideologies can fully repress: "It may not be uninteresting to mention, that in Nicaragua the local people usually make a deep reverence in passing any of these sculptures, and that they are very reluctant to assist at their removal; they have no doubt deep traditions respecting them, but it is difficult to get them to speak on the subject." On one level this is a classic illustration of the differential relations of power in the imperial context, contrasting the official who writes with the subalterns who remain silent. But the refusal of the local people to speak or assist also suggests their respect for history as something alive in the present, their opposition to the imperialist plot that would remove the remnants of their cultural heritage, and their refusal to reveal themselves to their imperial masters. They have that within which passes show, which cannot be appropriated, removed, or displayed in a foreign museum. Reluctance and silence can be read as techniques of resistance, weapons of the oppressed.

Chatfield's remark recalls Bullock's comments in his travel narrative about the effect of disinterring the statue of the *Coatlicue,* comments that, because they give rare voice to indigenous sentiment, may serve as a useful gloss on Chatfield's account of indigenous reverence and reticence. Bullock reports that during the time the *Coatlicue* was exposed he paid special attention to the demeanor of the "Indians":

> I attentively marked their countenances; not a smile escaped them, or even a word—all was silence and attention. In reply to a joke of one of the students, an old Indian remarked, "It is true we have three very good Spanish gods, but we might still have been allowed to keep a few of those of our ancestors!" and I was informed that chaplets of flowers had been placed on the figure by natives who had stolen thither, unseen, in the evening for that purpose.[95]

Bullock goes on to give a rather conventional reading of what he has reported, arguing that it shows that despite 300 years of Spanish Catholicism "there remains some taint of heathen superstition among the descendants of the original inhabitants."[96] But coming after the powerful description, this explanation rings hollow. Clearly what catches Bullock's attention is not a spectacle of pagan belief but the power of an object to re-awaken the connection between contemporary Mexican indigenes and the "original inhabitants," a connection not even the ruthlessness of Spanish colonialism could fully suppress. Resistance to colonial oppression, like the *Coatlicue* itself, lies just under the surface, waiting to erupt.

The indigenous ambivalence toward strangers' interest in the monuments—what I have called in previous chapters the colonial unconscious—wells up frequently in the British discourse of Central America, competing against the normative view that the local people are incapable of valuing or understanding the past and its embodiment in artifacts. At the end of his climactic report on Quiriguá (CA 18 Nov. 1854), Scherzer also notes the indigenous resistance to foreign designs on their ruins (this passage is among those omitted from the version published in 1936):

> It is with hesitation that Indians are serving as guides through the forests, where such remains exist, which they much more prefer to hide than to show. Their look becomes mournful whenever they see a *white* man copying the mysterious signs of such rocks. (f. 41; emphasis in original)

Not only do the local people dislike the interest in the ruins stirred by these travelers, but also their attempts to copy the signs themselves. Like Bustamante's comments about the copying of views discussed in chapter 2, the indigenous discomfort with copying may suggest a realization that when Europeans come with pencil and paper, the packing crates cannot be far behind, crates that will carry off the figured stones, the ancestors' recorded history, for display elsewhere. They may also have feared the defacement of the signs on the monuments themselves. Boddam-Whetham reports that when he visited Copán in the 1870s he found the words "J. Higgins" carved on the monuments in "bold characters";[97] similar accounts of disfiguration abound in nineteenth-century travel writing. In such contexts, writing and looking are frequently inseparable from desire, despoliation, and appropriation. That the juxtaposition of indigenous silence and Western writing is itself recorded in an inscription can be read as a strategy of containment, but also as a sign of the way in which official writing undoes its own best efforts to cast the local people as incapable of expressing their evaluation of the ruins aside from mere cash price, or "imaginary value." Figuring as the counterpart to the "mysterious signs" of the ultimately immobile sculptures, the unreadable silences of the indigenous—irreducible, stubborn, and resistant to appropriation—argue for a quality of reverence the dispatch cannot contain.

chapter 4

FREAK SHOW

The Aztec Children and the Ruins of Race

that love for shows,
Which stamps us as the "Staring Nation"
—BULWER LYTTON, *The Siamese Twins*

Now, the half-breed is a calamity. For why? He is neither one thing nor another, he is divided against himself. His blood of one race tells him one thing, his blood of another race tells him another. He is an unfortunate, a calamity to himself. And it is hopeless.
—D. H. LAWRENCE, *The Plumed Serpent*

In 1853, while the British government plotted to carry off Mayan ruins from Central America, a related drama of desire and appropriation was being played out in London. The principal attraction: Máximo and Bartola, two young children taken from El Salvador who, though from the Maya region, appeared on the London stage as the "Aztec Children" (Figure 21). Queen Victoria received the children in chambers and donated twenty-five pounds to the exhibit;[1] scientists measured their small heads (they were microcephalics); daguerreotypists burned their image into a still-novel medium.[2] The public thronged to glimpse what a handbill called "The only Aztecs yet introduced to civilized white people!"; those unable to attend the "live" show could find the children sculpted in wax at Reimer's Anatomical and Ethnological Museum in

Figure 21. Poster advertising the Aztec Lilliputians as they appeared before Queen Victoria. Courtesy of the Harvard Theatre Collection, Houghton Library.

Leicester Square.[3] Colonial officials wrote from abroad to shed light on
the children's possible origin; similar exhibits sprang up in their wake.[4]
The press gave the affair extensive coverage: the *Times* proclaimed them
"a new type of humanity only three feet high," while *Household Words*
admitted that they were "extremely interesting—as a cancer may be interesting to the physiologist."[5] The relationship between pre-Columbian
archaeology and racial science, already suggested by the British Museum's
hiring of Karl Ritter von Scherzer to explore the ruins of Central America, now became deeply entangled.

The children's progress from sensation to specimen marks a crucial
stage in the uses of freakery; to grasp its significance, however, requires
a deeper examination of the global traffic in freaks than that offered by
studies such as Richard Altick's *Shows of London* or Erin O'Connor's *Raw
Material,* which largely emphasize the meaning of freakery *within* the
nation.[6] To be sure, the children's theatrical career illuminates the vigorous afterlife of Regency spectacle—its thirst for displays of human anomaly, its fascination with the irregular, the misshapen, the gigantic, and the
miniature. We can easily imagine the children within the carnival-like
interior of the Egyptian Hall along with the Polish Dwarf, General Tom
Thumb, and other examples of Lilliputian humanity. As I discussed in
chapter 1, William Bullock's display of a native of Mexico, José Cayetano
Ponce de Leon, was carried out under the sign of cultural reciprocity.
Bullock allowed José the freedom to speak with visitors to the exhibition
and also suggested that José's journey to London was as likely to be
charged with ethnographic wonder as his own to Mexico—for his "friends
looked upon [us] in little better light than we do on the Esquimaux."[7]
Bullock's vision of cultural reciprocity functioned in the service of British
capital; José's presence reassured British investors that they could count
on a docile, cooperative workforce.

The Regency's fascination with Mexico, driven by economic oppor-
tunism and the ideal of cultural exchange, bears only passing resemblance
to the "scientific" racism that prevailed in midcentury exhibitions, with its
calipers and grids, its connection to medical discourses on abnormality
and to the imperial project abroad.[8] While British science had already sub-
jected Africans to racial measurement, it took longer and struggled harder
to theorize the racial composition of Latin American peoples, particularly
the *mestizo,* whose hybridity confounded the binary models that upheld

most racial theory. This theorization, however much delayed, was a key part of Britain's informal strategy in Latin America. As I have argued in previous chapters, it was a strategy that spurned the establishment of formal colonies for a more flexible mode of influence from afar, in which the symbolic and material appropriation of cultural artifacts intersected at key moments with an imperialism of free trade. The removal and display of medically and racially enfreaked subjects from the region, along with their subsequent absorption into anthropological theory, was a significant component of this larger ensemble of representations. Benjamin Brodie, in his presidential address of 1853 to the Ethnological Society of London, argued that because the "British empire extends over the whole globe," it was incumbent on colonial administrators to acquire ethnological information; James Hunt, his counterpart at the Anthropological Society of London, agreed: "Does not the success of our colonization depend on the deductions of our science?"[9]

If freak discourse is "reflective of our collective transformation into modernity,"[10] we still know very little about freaks themselves, what projects they served, and what controversies they provoked. The histories of Tom Thumb, the Elephant Man, Chang and Eng, the Hilton sisters, and a few others mark the horizon of our knowledge. The archive of printed ephemera on which this knowledge depends has not been thoroughly studied. Moreover, freakery, like the panoramas I discussed in chapter 2, continues to suffer from a methodological bias toward synoptic overviews, making the freak's most definitive characteristic—idiosyncratic particularity—fade from view.[11] In this chapter, I want to examine a particular freak show, tracking it through Victorian discourses of the theater, journalism, pathology, and ethnology. My aim is to show how Victorian freakery served Britain's relationship to Latin America: formulating ideologies of race and cultural difference, assisting in the project of removing cultural property for display in the metropolis, and opening up the ethnological implications of archaeology—which, as a result of Stephens's journeys to Central America and Layard's to the Near East, had now emerged as a central discipline in the human sciences. In particular, I want to show how ethnological spectacle laid the foundation for an important ideology already at work in other areas of inquiry and in official government policy: vilifying indigenous peoples while stripping away their "sculptured remains" for exhibition abroad. As we saw in the previous chapter, the plot to take Mayan ruins from Central America, which was ongoing during the children's appearance in London, rhetorically voided any claim the local people might have to their own monuments. The plot was driven by a distinctive formulation of imperial desire, in which monuments were both desired as trophies yet deemed worthy of only ethnographic, not aesthetic, appreciation. In Máximo and Bartola, we find the formulation's perverse anthropological corollary: the extension of imperial desire from things to persons, debased human subjects who are sought after and fetishized as human spectacle only to be transformed into proofs of racial degeneracy.[12]

FROM ARCHAEOLOGY TO ETHNOLOGY

To contextualize this argument, I want to lay out a necessarily uneven convergence of enabling developments—in language, disciplinary organization, techniques of display, and geographical interest—that helped account for the children's extraordinary power as a cultural phenomenon: the surge of British travelers to Latin America after 1821 and along with it the collection of new ethnological data from the area;[13] the commingling of travel with ethnology after 1839 through the distribution of ethnological questionnaires for gathering racial data from abroad;[14] an increasing emphasis, from about 1840, on measurement in the natural and physical sciences;[15] the split in 1843 of the Ethnological Society of London from the Aborigines Protection Society, which hardened the division between "ethnological research" and "humanitarian purpose";[16] the emergence, after about 1840, of professionalized archaeology from the hobby world of antiquarianism; the opening of the British Museum's "Ethnographical" room in 1845 and the formalization of new taxonomies of display in the study of non-European culture; the recognition in 1846 of ethnology as a discrete section within the British Association for the Advancement of Science; the first appearance in 1847 of the term "freak" to mean an anomalous human body (OED);[17] the wide dissemination in mid-Victorian Britain of racial discourses, such as Thomas Carlyle's "Occasional Discourse on the Nigger Question" and Charles Dickens's "Noble Savage";[18] the emergence after midcentury of an anthropology defined as a "science of the visible, physical body";[19] the 1853 re-exhibition of Burford's 1826 panorama of Mexico City in Leicester Square;[20] and the 1851 Great Exhibition in Hyde Park, a spectacle whose chief anthropological lesson, according to

George Stocking, was that "not all men had advanced at the same pace, or arrived at the same point."[21]

By 1853 enfreakment, pathology, racial theory, and New World archaeology had become intertwined. The global itineraries of British travelers, along with a network of showmen and promoters, mobilized a steady stream of exotic freaks for display in the metropolis. In 1855 the noted physician John Conolly, president of the Ethnological Society of London, took the Aztec Children's return to London (after a two-year tour abroad) as an occasion to address the important, though he felt deplorable, traffic in ethnological spectacle. He noted that "there is scarcely a year in which, among the miscellaneous attractions of a London season, we do not find some exhibition illustrative of the varieties of mankind," which meant that "no country should be expected to prosecute the study of Ethnology with more success" than Britain.[22] Mid-Victorian London was witness, indeed, to many racially inflected shows—among them Eskimos, "Earthmen," Zulus, Algerian Arabs, and Plains Indians. Those who captured the attention of ethnologists were caught up in a circular chain, with stage and examination table, playbill and medical treatise, comprising a mutually interdependent structure. Freak shows depended on a supply of curiosities from abroad, which in turn provided racial theorists with new specimens to analyze, new data to be transformed into inscriptions. Racial characterizations were then funneled back into the materials purveyed by freak show promoters, lending them an air of respectability and further strengthening the bond between scientific and mass culture. Ethnology gained access to rare specimens, and racial ideology was disseminated to a broad public. The display of freaks in London thus lends credence to the notion advanced in recent historiography that empire was not "a phenomenon 'out there'" but a palpable presence "everywhere in European culture *at home*."[23]

In *Orientalism*, Edward Said analyzed the power of "citationary authority," "a set of references, a congeries of characteristics, that seems to have its origin in a quotation, or a fragment of a text, or a citation from someone's work . . . or some bit of previous imagining, or an amalgam of all these."[24] A system of citationary authority also functioned in Britain's relations with Latin America, but it was complicated, as I have been arguing, by a busy traffic in appropriated objects—raw goods, cultural artifacts dug from the earth, and human specimens. Although Máximo and Bartola circulated in print through a variety of pamphlets, playbills, posters, and articles in newspapers and scientific journals, they had a corporeal reality that was fundamental to their significance as well as a powerful link to the sculptured objects that museum keepers and government officials tried so desperately to obtain. Thus it is significant that the text from which their first discursive traces emerge was the century's most important work of archaeological travel: Stephens and Catherwood's *Incidents of Travel in Central America, Chiapas, and the Yucatan* (1841), a text whose ideological entanglement with imperial acquisitiveness I examined in the previous chapter. Late in the second volume, Stephens recounts hearing a Spanish padre tell of a city deep in the Central American jungle that had never been conquered by the Spanish:

> The thing that roused us was the assertion by the padre that, four days on the road to Mexico, on the other side of the great sierra, was a living city, large and populous, occupied by Indians, precisely in the same state as before the discovery of America. . . . [M]any years before . . . he looked over an immense plain extending to Yucatan and the Gulf of Mexico, and saw at a great distance a large city spread over a great space, and with turrets white and glittering in the sun. The traditionary account of the Indians . . . is, that no white man has ever reached this city; that the inhabitants speak the Maya language, are aware that a race of strangers has conquered the whole country around, and murder any white man who attempts to enter their territory.[25]

Despite the alluring panoramic vista, Stephens did not search for the city; it remained a road not taken, a blank patch on the map of archeological discovery.

But the gap in Stephens's work spawned further narratives. In 1850, a thirty-five-page pamphlet was published in New York, purportedly the true account of one Pedro Velásquez, who with two other travelers had discovered the lost city and come away with two remarkable children. By 1853, the pamphlet and its human subjects had crossed the Atlantic to London. The pamphlet's full title is worth quoting: *Memoir of an Eventful Expedition into Central America, Resulting in the Discovery of the Idolatrous City of Iximaya, in an Unexplored Region; and the Possession of Two Remarkable Aztec Children, Máximo (the Man) and Bartola (the Girl), Descendants and Specimens of the Sacerdotal Caste (Now Nearly Extinct), of the Ancient*

Aztec Founders of the Ruined Temples of That Country.[26] Stephens's geographical lacunae—the "unexplored region," the city never reached—were
now filled in; archaeology—"the ruined temples"—was now wedded to
ethnological curiosity; and the desire to mobilize objects for possession and
study, heretofore focused on shaped blocks of stone, was now extended
to persons.

At once advertisement, viewing manual, souvenir (price one shilling),
and Latourian "inscription," the pamphlet capitalized on the growing prestige of Central American archaeology, which by 1850 enjoyed an influence
reaching from North America to Western Europe and Russia. The pamphlet's North American travelers—the American Huertis and the Canadian Hammond—closely resemble Stephens and his British illustrator
Frederick Catherwood. The former, like Stephens, had traveled in the
Near East; the latter, like Catherwood, was an expert surveyor.[27] Like their
precursors, Huertis and Hammond embarked on a well-funded journey
from New Orleans to British Honduras and then on to the ruins of
Central America. Driven by an "emulous passion" (4), the second set of
travelers literally walks the path of the first. Their journey also mirrors
British interest in Central America, which, as we have seen, was spurred
by the various schemes for an interoceanic canal, the establishment of
British trading houses, plans for settlement and colonization, the findings
of travelers and archaeologists, the craze for orchids, and the steady growth
of the British Museum's pre-Columbian collections. Yet the exhibit's references to a received archaeological "source" work to mask its exploitation
of what was still largely unknown—the vast interior of Central America.
Although the Royal Geographical Society and the British government had
promoted Central American geography since the 1830s, midcentury maps
were still far less precise about the interior than the coastlines. The pamphlet suggests, coyly, that in reference to Central America "that which
we do not know surpasses that which is known" (1), but some reviewers
were not easily taken in. Dickens's *Household Words,* for example, urged
that a "deputation from the Royal Geographical Society . . . exact from the
showman a strict account of [the city's] latitudes and longitudes," and
Richard Cull, secretary of the Ethnological Society, announced that "High
geographical authorities remain unconvinced."[28] Yet Charles L. Wyke, the
British consul in Guatemala, was sufficiently concerned that he sent a dispatch to the foreign secretary on the subject, promising to report further

with more information on the city (FO15/79, f. 29; 30 Aug. 1853), and the distinguished ethnologist R. G. Latham reminded the Ethnological Society of London that "the existence of Casas Grandes [i.e., temples] in the locality to which the Astecs [sic] are attributed is likely."[29] Clearly at some level the ploy was successful.

In a way that illustrates Derrida's notion of the "supplement,"[30] the exhibit added to, altered, and replaced its source, not merely by its revision of a prior archaeological project, but through its claim to have discovered a living ethnological archive. That claim, it turns out, intersected in compelling ways with calls for the centralization of ethnological data in London. In 1839, the British Association for the Advancement of Science (BAAS) formed a committee, including Charles Darwin, James Cowles Prichard, and Thomas Hodgkin, to draw up a list of questions to distribute to travelers going abroad.[31] It reported in 1841 that copies of the seven-page questionnaire had been sent to the British Museum, the Royal Geographical Society, and to other "scientific bodies, foreign as well as British," and that "considerable pains" had been taken to place it "in the hands of intelligent travellers about to visit those quarters in which natives exist"—i.e., the colonial periphery. The BAAS report emphasized the humanitarian project of gathering information from the "feeble and perishing branches of the human family," who were not only "changing character, but rapidly disappearing."[32] This motivation was shared by Prichard, the leading ethnologist of the day, who at the 1839 meeting that sparked the initiative read a paper on the subject of human extinction.[33] Although driven by a humanitarian impulse, Prichard argued that "science, as well as humanity, is interested in the efforts which are made to rescue [the perishing races], and to preserve from oblivion many important details connected with them."[34]

Prichard's latter point suggests how the scientific, data-gathering emphasis that flourished in racial thought after midcentury emerged not apart from but within humanitarian origins of an earlier ethnological tradition; it was present from the very beginning of the Ethnological Society of London, the inaugural meeting of which called for a "museum illustrative of the varieties of mankind, and of the arts of uncivilized life."[35] Chief among the "details" Prichard requested were cranial measurements, which served no apparent humanitarian purpose; "the head," he wrote, "is so important as distinctive of race, that particular attention must be paid to it."[36] Hodgkin went further, urging travelers to help form the equivalent of a human museum by securing "well-selected aboriginal youths" to transport to London as a "practical means for advancing the cause of Ethnological investigation."[37] Over the next few decades, the humanitarian impulse gradually weakened as racial science, exploiting the traffic in bodies created by Britain's "extensive colonial possessions and commerce," converted ethnological data into theories of racial dominance fundamental to the colonial project.[38] In an oft-cited piece published three weeks before the children's arrival in London (though after their New York appearance had been reviewed in *Household Words*) Dickens explained the link between racial theory and colonial expansion. Referring to ethnological shows such as the Bushmen, the Zulu Kaffirs, and George Catlin's American Indians, Dickens prophesies the extinction of the "savage" before the march of European progress: "he passes away before an immeasurably better and higher power than ever ran wild in any earthly woods, and the world will be all the better when his place knows him no more." Celebrating what Prichard laments, Dickens urges that the "savage" be "civilized off the face of the earth."[39]

By the mid-1850s data for racial theory was coming not only, as Prichard and Hodgkin had imagined, from scientific travelers, but from ethnological exhibitions, which transported indigenous peoples from their native haunts to the metropolitan centers of examination. The Aztec Children perfectly matched the ethnological community's desire for examples of vanishing peoples; the pamphlet describes them as "members of a race kept preserved in rocky fastnesses, and now discovered on the eve of physical decline and disappearance" (28). The pamphlet also suggests that the discovery of a lost race—like a Rosetta Stone—might unlock further mysteries. Who built the monuments of Mexico and Central America? Did their builders originate in the Old World, perhaps, as some had suggested, among the Assyrians, the Egyptians, or even the ancient tribes of Israel? Against such questions the pamphlet urges the evidentiary weight of "human beings, of flesh and blood": "HERE THEY ARE! LIVING!"—"the most remarkable and intensely interesting objects that were ever presented to the European public" (35–36).

The racial implications of the exhibit were heightened by the images that accompanied the London editions of the pamphlet, images that represented the children to a wider public beyond those able to attend the "live" show. These illustrations referred to but significantly revised Catherwood's widely reproduced depictions of Central American monuments, which, circulating in the several editions of Stephens's work and through the reviews in British periodicals, formed the public's knowledge of pre-Columbian civilization. Like the panorama, Catherwood's images rendered up Central America to be viewed, "exposing" the hidden mysteries of lost civilizations, peeling back the jungle so that the monuments could be revealed to the curious eye. The clearing of the vegetation necessary for the taking of Catherwood's views functioned as a material analogue to the exposure imaged in the published views. Hence was born not only a new subject but also a new visual vocabulary, a way of looking at Mesoamerican antiquity from a particular angle and with certain ideologically specific assumptions. This way of seeing would subsequently inform a series of nineteenth-century photographers who depicted Maya ruins, among them Claude Désiré Charnay, Osbert Salvin, Alfred P. Maudslay, and Frans Blom.[40] Catherwood's depictions of Copán (see Figures 16 and 17), for example, are adopted as the archaeological background for the frontispiece to one edition of the pamphlet (Figure 22), in which the children perch atop columns set in the middle distance between two rows of stelae. The setting not only locates the children within the visual register of archaeological narrative but also reinforces the trope of "anachronistic space," in which "colonized people . . . do not inhabit history proper but exist in a permanently anterior time within the geographic space of the modern empire as anachronistic humans, atavistic, irrational, bereft of human agency."[41] The stelae frame and enclose the children, associating them with a stony, lifeless past while dissociating them from the technological modernity of the viewer. Indeed the *London Times,* in its first piece on the exhibit, noted that "the children bear the strongest resemblance to sculptured figures which are unquestionably of Aztec origin"; the *Times* sealed the children's displacement from the present by observing that when an "ancient Mexican idol" that had been brought to them was accidentally broken, the children "burst into an agony of grief at the calamity."[42] What had served as a sign of indigenous belief in Bullock's account of the disinterred *Coatlicue* (chapter 3) is here used to lend credence to an obvious fraud, turning reverence into a commoditized spectacle.

A related set of images (Figure 23), again derived from Catherwood, shows four profiles depicted at Palenque, in southern Mexico. These

Figure 22. The Aztec Lilliputians among the ruins, from Pedro Velásquez, *Memoir of an Eventful Expedition into Central America* (c. 1853). Courtesy of the John Carter Brown Library at Brown University.

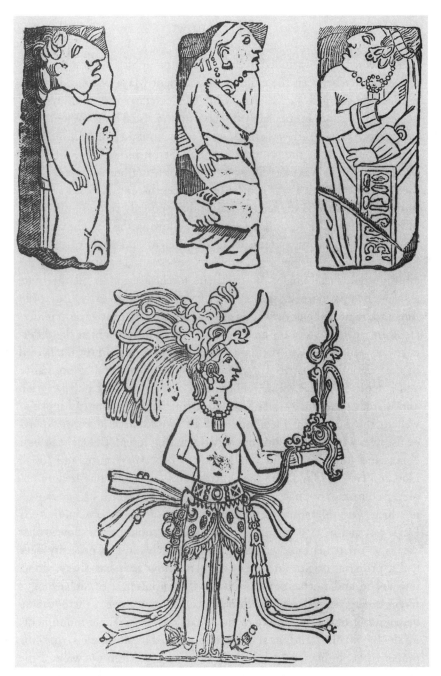

Figure 23. Archaeological figures from Palenque, from Pedro Velásquez, *Memoir of an Eventful Expedition into Central America* (c. 1853). Courtesy of the John Carter Brown Library at Brown University.

images, which were included in the publicity pamphlet, suggest the physical similarity between the children and ancient Maya peoples, but in a particularly charged way. Richard Cull, the secretary of the Ethnological Society of London, immediately understood the visual hint: "When I first saw these Aztecs . . . I was struck with their similarity of head to those figures copied from the sculptures in . . . Stephens' valuable works."[43] What struck him was a certain style of representing human figures, profile illustration, which was central to nineteenth-century racial imaging in that it accentuated the anatomical, and supposedly cultural, difference of human "races." Prichard, for example, following the Dutchman Peter Camper, requested measurements of the "height and angle of the forehead."[44] As we see in Figure 24, profiles were essential to highlighting the all-important facial angle; the children's foreheads appear all the more sloped when juxtaposed against a nearly vertical (and massive) European forehead, reinforcing deviance not as an absolute but a relative term understood by reference to a norm. The use of profiles to heighten the difference between an implicit standard and its deviation was, in turn, reflected in the relationship between a viewing subject understood as normative and a depicted object whose rendering in profile was a sign of deviation and therefore deviance—racial, sexual, criminal.[45] The strategy spoke as well to the theoretical inclinations of an important midcentury, polygenist school of physical anthropology (including Joseph B. Davis, Robert Knox, and John Beddoe in England, Paul Broca in France, and Josiah Nott and George Gliddon in the United States), which emphasized phrenology, comparative anatomy, and particularly the study of crania—all of which were influential in the examinations of the Aztec Children. As Davis asserted in 1856, the evidence of ancient monuments showed that race is a "permanent and enduring entity, which must of necessity have had a primeval origin, and exists the same now as it has always done, unchanged and unchangeable." Hence the importance of archaeology's recent emergence as a serious discipline. As Davis argued, there was no better proof of the durability of race than the "remarkable monuments [of the Egyptians]," and the startling fact, noticed by all travelers, that "the proper rural population look as if they had stepped from the walls of the temples as animated images of their far-off ancestors."[46] The persistence of racial traits into the present, in which latter-day descendants appear as "animated images" of their ancestors, personifies the archaeological

Figure 24. Racial profiling, c. 1853, from *Illustrated Magazine of Art*. Courtesy of Research Library, Getty Research Institute, Los Angeles.

record, constructing a museum of living subjects to match those figured in stone.

The Aztec Children gave the union of archaeology and ethnology an added charge. In his 1855 address Conolly called for a centralized effort to join the study of human curiosities with the collecting and display of ethnographic objects. What spurred him on was, fittingly in this context, a display by Charles Bedford Young of a collection of "numerous and highly curious" Aztec antiquities in Pall Mall, collected in Mexico and later sold to the British Museum and installed in its newly opened Ethnographical Room.[47] With Young's exhibit in mind, Conolly appealed for a closer relationship between the study of both human beings and cultural artifacts: "A centralization of some of the objects in these various collections, and the arrangement of portions of them, with a view to the particular illustration of different branches of ethnological inquiry, would greatly facilitate the progress of this science."[48] Conolly hoped to use ethnographic curiosities from the British Museum's growing pre-Columbian archive to illuminate the living curiosities produced by freak shows. And within a year of Conolly's address Davis was referring to archaeology and ethnology as "twin sisters, intimately connected, and mutually supporting each other"; later, quoting Ernest Dieffenbach, he urged that it was "necessary to collect everything that will throw light on this subject" of ethnology, and not just crania but "whole skeletons" as well.[49] Each discipline extended Britain's imperial reach, enabling the study of data gathered at the colonial periphery.

FROM FREAK TO SPECIMEN

The display of human beings with extraordinary bodies dates from antiquity and has a long history in Europe's relation to the Americas: the first Amerindians to reach Europe were sent by Columbus; Newfoundlanders exhibited in London in 1501 were said to be "clothid in bestys skinnys" and to behave as "bruyt bestis."[50] But it was only during the nineteenth century that science "officially enunciated teratology as the study, classification, and manipulation of monstrous bodies," a disciplinary change that for Rosemarie Garland Thomson signifies the broader movement of our "collective cultural transformation into modernity," one most evident in the fascination with deviance, both as phenomenon itself and sign of its other: normalcy.[51] Yet we cannot explain the enduring power of freakery simply in these terms, as if the freak's alterity was displayed only to consolidate our own identities as nonfreaks, i.e., humans. Freakery is a glass through which we see darkly. The most compelling freaks are at once self and other, familiar and strange. Freakishness, as Robert Bogdan puts it, is "not a quality that belongs to the person on display. It is something we created: a perspective, a set of practices—a social construction."[52] Freaks captivate us because they are both like and unlike us, reflecting our needs for kinship and estrangement.

During the nineteenth century, these tensions were inscribed in two related forms of spectacle: the freak show and the medical/ethnological examination. Both served as theaters of intimate contact between subject and object, zones where self and other explored and entered into play with each other. The *Athenaeum* pointed up the freak show's familiar, indeed familial, quality, reporting that Máximo and Bartola "exhibited the behavior of intelligent *English* children at two or three years of age."[53] This point was accentuated by the children's visit to Queen Victoria, national exemplar of the cult of domesticity. The embosoming by the nation received an added charge from the children's status as orphans, miraculously rescued from paganism and brought to civilization in Britain: few cultures have sentimentalized the orphan more thoroughly than the Victorians; few have been more invested in the salvific mission of imperialism. The children's smallness also worked to enfold them within a broader maternal erotics based on the formal property of diminution, which, as Lori Merish argues, was associated with a larger "problematic of identification" centering on "the child's body" and demanding, therefore, a "maternal response."[54]

The focus on the smallness of the children reinforced the structural equivalence of child and freak as figures uneasily suspended between subject and object, occupying bodies not entirely their own, subject to unwanted—and frequently proprietary—touches. No wonder *Household Words* reported that, "next to kissing [the children], the chief pleasure [of the public] seemed to consist in feeling their heads"; the heads in question, the article added, were like "dolls' heads, and so of course it is agreeable to feel them."[55] These touches, both caresses and reminders of the children's powerlessness, were enabled by the way in which the children were staged. Rather than being separated from the audience, the children were exhibited in ways that encouraged mutual interaction. They mingled and spoke with the public; the public touched, and was touched by, the children. Even in their appearance before the Ethnological Society of London, Máximo and Bartola "ran about the room without any evident alarm," and "began to play with the President's (Sir Benjamin Brodie) pen, ink, and paper."[56] They *played*, not as actors but as children, and in so doing collapsed the boundary between audience and performer, self and other. Their play made it that much harder to see them as monsters, and that much easier to imagine them as forsaken representatives of the enfeebled "branches of the human family" scattered across Britain's vast imperial field, peoples humanitarian ethnologists sought to analyze and missionaries to save.

If these gestures of intimacy suggested a salvific imperialism, medical and ethnological discourse refused, or at least problematized, the desire for identification. Here, the touch becomes a probe; the stare a sign of alienation. In a widely cited examination performed in Boston, Jonathan Mason Warren of the Harvard Medical School introduced his findings by emphasizing that he was interested only in "simple matters of fact," and would not indulge in "any speculations" concerning the children (3)—a jab at the inflated claims of the show's promoters.[57] Employing calipers and measuring rule, Warren gauged the children's limbs, skulls, and teeth; employing the rhetorical device of citationary authority, he quoted works on pathology, teratology, and sexuality, including the *Histoire générale et particulière des anomalies* (1838) of Isidore Geoffroy Saint-Hilaire (1805–61), a leading teratologist, which gave him a catalogue of other dwarfs against which to compare the children. He noted, drawing on Camper again, that the "line of the nostril is oblique, instead of being longitudinal, as in the Caucasian race" (4), and remarked that other facial characteristics combined to give the children an "unintelligent expression" (5). Warren was particularly eager to compare the children to animals: their posture reminded him of the "Simian tribe" (5), their language skills the "canine race" (8).[58] He compared the circumference of their skulls with measurements of chimpanzees, orangutans, and the skull of an idiot boy preserved in J. G. Spurzheim's famous collection of crania (10–11). If the freak show collapsed the boundary between self and other, the comparisons of the ethnologist pushed the other way by dissolving the opposition between human and beast, sane and insane, hence enforcing an ever-greater distance between the scientist who examined and the less-than-human, less-than-rational subject of his examination. In an age in which numerical data had become the *sine qua non* of science, Warren's preference for quantitative measurements of "fact" over narrative "speculation" lends the paper scientific weight. But Warren's uses of numbers and grids are also rhetorical strategies, tabular signs of the scientist's investment in categories over and against the freak show's interest in narrative particularity. The freak show economy was predicated on novelty, and thus produced highly individualized subjects, each carefully differentiated from the last. By midcentury, many freaks were accompanied by the kind of background story we have seen here: autobiographical accounts, memoirs, life histories, and other narrative forms that individuated freaks by giving them interiority, a biography. Although freak shows accentuated physical anomaly, they were grounded in the concept of the individual, a quality that emerged from the *character* of the freak, from psychology, and from narrative.

When the children arrived in London, among the first to examine them was Richard Owen, the celebrated naturalist and comparative anatomist known popularly as the "British Cuvier." Owen updated Warren's measurements of the children's limbs, teeth, and heads; he concluded that the children were "hemi-cephalic monsters" (134), a point he sealed by appending an engraving comparing Máximo's profile to the skull of an idiot preserved in St. Bartholomew's Hospital (Figure 25).[59] This distorted image mirrors those used in nineteenth-century racial theory. Stephen Jay Gould points out that in Samuel Morton's *Crania Americana* (1839), the lithographer tilted back a Native American skull to suggest that it was less "vaulted" and therefore "smaller and more 'primitive'" than the skull of a white male to which it was contrasted.[60] An apparently "objective" image thus reinforces Morton's thesis that Indians "for the most part are incapable of a continued process of reasoning on abstract subjects."[61] The Native American skull, however, only appears less vaulted when placed next to the European skull, which is oriented conventionally. Race, as Nancy Stepan puts it, was a "contrastive concept";[62] just as the abnormal body was measured against its healthy counterpart—vividly and familiarly delineated in Henry Gray's *Anatomy* (1858)—any one race could only be understood by contrast to another. Yet Owen's illustration, like a stereoscopic image, also draws Máximo and the idiot boy together. By placing him next to a drawing of a skull, grossly enlarged to emphasize the boy's microcephaly, Owen's image transforms him into a specimen case, mere data. He has been reduced, quite literally, to an illustration, a figure of and for death. The grinning skull mocks, prophesying Máximo's physical death and the symbolic annihilation of his subject-hood.

MONSTROUS MESTIZOS

As we have seen, mid-Victorian medicine combined with ethnology and teratology in complex ways to produce the Aztec Children as dehumanized specimens, stripped of particularity and reduced to types. This process was in direct reply to the exorbitant claims of the freak show economy itself, a way of putting distance between those claims and a scientific reality that could be verified and measured. This was true even though, as Conolly and others admitted, the scientific community depended on the freak show economy for its supply of medical and ethnological subjects.

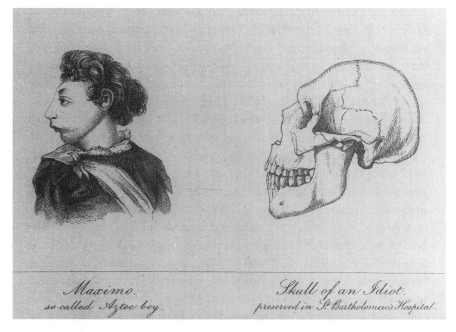

Máximo.
so-called Aztec boy.

Skull of an Idiot.
preserved in St Bartholomew's Hospital.

Figure 25. "Máximo and the Skull of an Idiot," from *Journal of the Ethnological Society of London* (1856). Courtesy of the Tozzer Library of the Harvard College Library.

Having poked and prodded the children, science pronounced them re-markable only in the low degree of their intelligence. Yet this was hardly the limit of ethnological curiosity; beyond the subject of idiocy was the more pressing and complicated subject of race. Here, the ethnologists were concerned to counter the claim that the Aztec Children represented a pure, sacerdotal caste. While we may smile at the audacity of such claims, the question of lost, undiscovered, or undefiled races was not an idle one in the nineteenth century. Indeed, as we saw above, it animated the fervent attempt to gather ethnological data from around the globe and provided the plot for many a late Victorian novel (e.g., H. Rider Haggard's *Heart of the World* and Arthur Conan Doyle's *Lost World*). Latin America's vast, unmapped regions, the detachment of its landmass from the Old World, and its luxuriant biological life made it a likely candidate for the discovery of such races. But it was also a site where, much to the horror of racial theorists in Britain, races had long commingled through love and conquest, producing a bewildering muddle of blended peoples whose impurity challenged basic tenets of racial theory. So prevalent was this tendency that one ethnologist described the region as "the great laboratory of the modern mixed breeds or hybrid nations."[63] To understand the extent of the public's fascination with the Aztec Children, we must exam-ine how demographers, ethnologists, and travelers portrayed the phenom-enon of racial mixture in Latin America.

The question of the children's race was explicit from the beginning, not only in the elaborate narrative that described their origin, but also in the first medical examinations they endured. After noting the children's age, height, and weight, Jonathan Mason Warren described their skin color: "a dark yellowish cast, lighter than what is generally attributed to the Indian in this part of the country" (3). In a lengthy footnote appended to the end his examination, Warren explained the origins of this "lightness":

> In order to explain some observations in the preceding paper which would otherwise appear obscure, it should be remarked that the children who are the subjects of it were exhibited in Boston as belonging to a race of dwarfs, the descendants of priests from a hitherto undiscovered city in Central America. . . . It is now pretty well understood, that they belong to some of the mixed tribes of Indians inhabiting Central America, and we hope hereafter to procure some exact details as to the peculiarities of their parents. (17)

Warren supported these findings with a colored drawing executed by John C. Dalton (1825–1889), the noted American physiologist (Figure 26).[64] Starkly representing its subject against props (to show size), in profile (to show facial angle), and in exotic dress (to show cultural otherness), the Dalton drawing employs the contrastive logic of racial imaging to suggest the vast difference in civilization between the "savage" boy and his gentlemanly examiners, visually troped by the top hat and white gloves. Here, the temples and stelae, which figure prominently in the *Illustrated Memoir*, have been stripped away, allowing the viewer to focus more clearly on racial difference and the machinery of enfreakment.

Richard Owen, like Warren, reserved comment on the children's racial origin until the end of his examination, but he displaced the issue from the children to their documentary sources. He pointed out that those wishing to settle the matter had to rely on "conflicting evidence" (136). On one side was the story purveyed by Velásquez of the lost city with its sacerdotal caste; on the other, the story of Inocente Burgos, a native of San Salvador, that he "himself was the father of the two children" (137). The problem with these accounts, according to Owen, was that in each case the evidence was "afforded by Mexicans of Spanish origin" (136). More disturbing than Owen's geographical ignorance—San Salvador is in El Salvador, not Mexico—is his cultural arrogance toward the *mestizo*, i.e., "Mexicans of Spanish origin." According to Owen, such people—because they are mixed—cannot be trusted; the traditional British suspicion toward the Spaniard merges here with the disgust at the mixed races of Latin America. Yet if Owen's examination displaced the question of race onto the reliability of *mestizo* informants, it also displaced it onto the question of sexuality. First, Owen notes, apparently with surprise, that on inspecting Máximo's genitals "a slight erection ensued" (133). Second, when describing Bartola, he observes that "other gestures in playing with the girl seemed to indicate a precocious dawning of the venereal appetite," and that her "clitoris was somewhat larger than in most children of that age" (133). Such comments, coupled with a diagnosis of idiocy, recall an earlier generation's fervid interest in Saartjie Baartman's genitalia, and suggest the contours of a familiar racialized figure: the dark-skinned female whose heightened sexuality corresponds to her stunted intelligence. The stereotype was common in nineteenth-century culture; perhaps its most compact expression is in Charlotte Brontë's *Jane Eyre* (1847), when Mr.

Figure 26. John C. Dalton, "Aztec Dwarf," from Jonathan Mason Warren, *An Account of Two Remarkable Indian Dwarfs Exhibited in Boston under the Name of Aztec Children* (1851). Courtesy of the Harvard Theatre Collection, Houghton Library.

Rochester remarks of Bertha Mason, his West Indian bride: "what a pygmy intellect . . . and what giant propensities."[65]

Racial and medical discourses spectacularly merged in Robert Knox's essay "Some Remarks on the Aztecque [sic] and Bosjieman Children" (1855), which, appearing in the prestigious British medical journal, *The Lancet*, transforms Owen's conclusions into a set of generalized traits applicable to all Latin Americans. Knox, who studied medicine at Edinburgh and Paris, was one of the "key figures in the general Western movement toward a dogmatic pseudo-scientific racism."[66] *The Races of Men* (1850) insists, famously, that "race is everything: literature, science, art—in a word, civilization, depends on it."[67] These views accorded with the school of polygenist anthropology that rose to prominence in the 1850s and found its institutional base in the Anthropological Society of London, established by James Hunt, Knox's disciple. Like J. B. Davis, Knox emphasized the value of archaeological research, especially in proving the pertinacity of racial traits. His examination of the children points up the "unmistakable resemblance" between their profiles and images of ancient Central American peoples inscribed on monuments.[68] Were it not for the "rude" sculptures and paintings archaeologists have brought to light, he argues, the "existence of a *race,* with such a configuration of features and head, would have been questioned and the possibility denied" (358). For Knox, archaeological evidence suggests that the ancient Central Americans "bear a marked resemblance to the form of idiotic head, which occasionally appears in all the races of men; it consists in a remarkably convex outline of face, small cranium, and retreating chin" (358). These conclusions comport with the European vilification of American indigenes from the eighteenth century forward, but Knox breaks new ground in his theory of "interrupted descent," whereby he is able to explain the survival of the children's race into the mid-nineteenth century: "a race of men or animals may be so reduced," he argues, "as to be thought extinct; still some remain, and such as do are of course the direct descendants of the ancient race" (358). This is so because of the permanence of racial traits, which are carried in the blood itself. Knox calls attention to racial intermingling, and turns for his data to the traveler's on-the-spot testimony, thus rejoining the circle drawn by the BAAS ethnological questionnaire of 1839. His chosen eyewitness: the young Charles Darwin. Knox quotes a passage from the *Journal of Researches* describing the inhabitants of Lima as "a depraved, drunken set of people, [that] present every imaginable shade of mixture between European, Negro, and Indian blood" (359).[69] As repulsed by this confusion as Darwin, Knox develops a general rule: "Jewish, Negro, or Gipsy blood, once mingled with another race, never seems to disappear" (359). Writing two years later and specifically about Salvadorans such as Máximo and Bartola, Scherzer described the population of "mixed Indian and Negro blood" as "small, undersized, but strongly made men, with reserved, ugly, and brutal-looking faces. The mixture of two races so degenerate as the Indian and Ethiopian is not likely to have a beneficial effect on the descendants, but it is a mixture unfortunately very common."[70] Other ethnologists followed suit, marshaling what evidence they could find—from specific information about the children themselves to general accounts of Latin American racial mixture—to discredit the children's supposed racial purity and to put them in their place as nothing more than garden variety *mestizos,* offspring of once-great but now hopelessly mixed races. Scherzer's summation is characteristic: "The two mulatto children, which a speculative Yankee actually imposed on the credulous in Europe, as the last scions of the almost extinct priestly caste of the Aztecs, are nothing more than two remarkably undeveloped individuals of this mixed descent."[71] An 1867 article in the *Anthropological Review* echoed the claim: "The mother of these children is a vigorous Mulatto, the father is a Mulatto; as to the children being Aztecs it is a fable. They are idiots; they were known in the country as monitos, or little monkeys."[72] The *mestizo* has now become its degenerate relative, the mulatto, which in turn provides a neat explanation for the children's coloration, precocious venereal appetites, and low intelligence.

This "solution" to the children's origin is connected to what Robert J. C. Young has called the central issue of nineteenth-century anthropological thought, the question of hybridity, bound up in turn with "*the* dominant motif" of British fiction, "the uncertain crossing and invasion of identities."[73] These issues animated nearly all ethnological writing on Latin America, in part because Spanish colonialism had been so effective in wiping out the so-called pure Indian, in part because mid-nineteenth-century anthropological thought regarded the commingling of races with unrivaled fear and loathing. Ephraim George Squier, the most important anthropological thinker in the antebellum United States, spent several years studying the peoples and cultures of Central America as U.S. Consul to

Nicaragua, an appointment, like Stephens's to Central America, that permitted him also to conduct archaeological research. In his 1855 *Notes on Central America,* he wrote of *mestizos:*

> there can be no admixture of widely separated families, or of superior with
> inferior races, which can be harmonious, or otherwise than disastrous in its
> consequences. . . . In Central and South America, and Mexico, we find a people
> not only demoralized from the unrestrained association of different races, but
> also the superior stocks becoming gradually absorbed in the lower, and their
> institutions disappearing under the relative barbarism of which the latter are
> the exponents.[74]

The prejudice against racial mixture in the Americas extended not only to the mixture of Spanish and Indian stock, but also to the commingling of *mestizos* with blacks. For race theorists, each admixture yielded a further degradation. The detrimental political consequences of intermixture were formulated by such thinkers as Herbert Spencer. In *The Principles of Sociology* (1876), Spencer argued that the

> half-caste, inheriting from one line of ancestry proclivities adapted to one set of
> institutions, and from the other line of ancestry proclivities adapted to another
> set of institutions, is not fitted for either. He is a unit whose nature has not been
> moulded by any social type, and therefore cannot, with others like himself,
> evolve any social type. Modern Mexico and the South American Republics,
> with their perpetual revolutions, show us the result.[75]

Whether from an anthropological or political viewpoint, Latin America epitomized all that was wrong with hybridity.

But polygenist racial theory also held that the children of mixed-race parents were unlikely to be prolific—the crossing of races produces infertile young. This theory was drawn from the ideas of the Comte de Buffon in France and John Hunter in Britain and was a centerpiece of the racial theory espoused throughout the 1850s and 1860s by J. B. Davis, Robert Knox, William Bollaert, James Hunt, and other members of the "anthropologicals," who in turn showed so much interest in the Aztec Children. Davis suggested that "any mixture of breeds among the families of man can only be effected so as to produce fruitful and permanent results, when the original families are very similar, or belong to tribes nearly allied."[76] Knox wrote in the second edition of *The Races of Men* that "if an animal be the product of two distinct species, the hybrid . . . was sure to perish or to become extinct."[77] William Bollaert, an important traveler and ethnologist associated with the leading scientific societies, authored several noteworthy papers on Latin American antiquity as well as a seminal demographic study of New World races, in which he argued that the precipitous decline in the population of Spanish America stemmed from the "morally and physically" detrimental habit of mixing races: "I conceive that the mixture of the three species of White, Indian, and Negro has been unsatisfactory to a healthy strong population, or even of a prolific character." Racial commingling resulted in "arrested prolificness" and produced "at times repugnant varieties among the Zamboes, and especially from the Indian and negress. The *in and in* breeding of the Mulatto variety [i.e., mulattos with mulattos] seems soon to approach sterility." He grants that the *mestizo* is a better mixture, but "even here it may be a question how long prolific character would have been persistent."[78] Demonstrating the polygenist contention that the infertility of mules served as a warning against the interbreeding of distinct human races, he cited his own study of the breeding characteristics of the South American family of mammals, "The Llama, Alpaco, Huanacu, Vicuña," published in *The Sporting Review*.[79] A few years later, in the first number of his new journal, Hunt praised Bollaert's findings, noting with satisfaction that the decline in the reproductive powers of the "strange confusion of races" demonstrated the universal law that "the native races everywhere should diminish before the advent of the white man." Hunt used Bollaert to emphasize a key point: the superiority of European races not only over aboriginal peoples, but also over the "the mixed breeds of South America." The white man, Hunt proclaimed, was "destined to be the renovator of the world."[80]

We thus return to the discourse of inevitable, if gradual, extinction. Here, what must vanish are not the inhabitants of an undiscovered city, or a few enfeebled branches of the human family, but the population of an entire continent, which will recede before the colonizing force of what Scherzer calls the "bold, energetic, and active" white races.[81] In a reprise of the formulations examined in chapter 2, Scherzer looked to the Mexican War of 1846–48 for evidence that the *mestizo* populations could not withstand the advance of conquering whites from the North, while Hunt imagined in the gradual sterility and extinction of Latin American *mestizos* an opportunity for the further extension of British power. In either case, racial theory, drawing on travel and ethnological spectacle, combined to produce a monstrous *mestizo*—feeble, unintelligent, unprolific, destined to recede before the onslaught of conquering whites. The move from archaeology to ethnology, with its associated methods and mechanisms, sweeps the land clean, making visible the larger racial imperative of British cultural work in Central America. As we saw in the previous chapter, British discourse and government policy, as a preface to the looting of antiquities, performed similar cultural work, maligning indigenes and Creole elites alike, representing them as ignorant about and uncaring toward their own monuments. Here, people themselves are removed, put on display elsewhere, and transformed into proofs of racial decline and sterility. Once the land is represented as empty, colonization and settlement can begin. Again I quote Scherzer, the British government's chosen eyes in Central America. In the preface to his popular work of travel, written at the conclusion of his work for the British Museum, Scherzer noted that his aim was simply to "point out the great advantages offered by these magnificent countries to trade and emigration, and to show that there exist in Central America tracts of measureless extent, in which prudent and industrious European settlers may not only secure a prosperous and healthy material existence, but maintain their nationality, and remain in commercial and political relation with the land of their birth."[82] Thus could Central America, even in 1860, still be imagined as newfound land.

PERFORMING RESISTANCE

After their initial London appearance, Máximo and Bartola continued their career for several more decades; there are traces of their journeys to Prussia, Bavaria, Holland, Denmark, and Russia, where royals and ethnological doctors alike continued to express interest in them. They returned for a time to the United States, where they found employment at Barnum's American Museum. A Currier and Ives lithograph advertising the children's appearance at Barnum's features a quotation from Alexander von Humboldt in which he names the children a "worthy study to those who seriously occupy themselves with types of human organization and with the laws respecting them."[83] In 1867 the children, by then adults, appeared again in Britain, exchanging vows in a marriage ceremony in London—clearly an attempt to revive the curiosity of a fickle public ever eager for new amusements. Circus route books and photographs bear witness to them into the 1890s, but eventually they fade from view, leaving in their wake a host of imitators.[84]

Máximo and Bartola's longevity is a sign both of the continuing power of freakery as a cultural apparatus for reinforcing difference, and a marker of their own extraordinary ability to find a niche within it, one that enabled them to thrive, perhaps even to prosper. But since the archive on which we must rely imposes an almost total silence on them, we shall never know how they understood their role in the European culture of spectacle, whether they remained entirely subject to others, or as some early accounts suggest, found ways to temper that subjection through the very vehicle of performance. Temper, not subvert, for given the radical asymmetries of power that constructed the children's "career" as freaks, it is impossible that they could have criticized their condition. The primitive, Marianna Torgovnick reminds us, "does what we ask it to do. Voiceless, it lets us speak for it."[85] No wonder, then, that the *Illustrated London News* was moved to ask, "Can the Aztecs Speak?"[86]

To grasp the power of intercultural performance to subvert the gaze, I turn here to the protests, rallies, and artworks staged in 1992–93 that, in offering alternative perspectives on the quincentennial celebrations of Columbus's landing, critiqued the victimization of American indigenes by European and U.S. imperialism. A powerful and disturbing example was a collaborative piece by the internationally acclaimed Latino/a performance artists Guillermo Gómez-Peña and Coco Fusco. Entitled "Two Undiscovered Amerindians Visit . . . ," it was mounted in the Plaza Colón in Madrid, Covent Garden, and the Smithsonian, sites associated with the forced removal, oppression, and objectification of non-Western peoples (Figure 27). Gómez-Peña and Fusco offered an extraordinary critique of the tradition and tools of ethnological spectacle I have been examining here by making themselves into both the objects and subjects of the gaze. Dressed in "native" costume, equipped with a falsified but authentic-looking map of their invented "homeland" Guatinaui (an imaginary island in the Caribbean), and acting the parts of peoples only recently "discovered" by science, Gómez-Peña and Fusco sardonically played on the classic tropes of racialized freakery to question an entire tradition of viewing and dissecting the Other. The performance took place within a large steel cage in which they had imprisoned themselves, though passersby were invited to look at them, to have their photos taken with them, to request a native dance or song—in short, to act out and recapitulate the structures of "containment" that have underpinned the culture of exhibiting Amerindians from Columbus's first voyages to the Aztec Children and beyond. In an ironic commentary on the lengths to which most nineteenth-century spectacle went to prove the authenticity of their subjects, "a substantial portion of the public," according to Fusco, "believed that our fictional identities were real ones," one even claiming to have "remembered [the] island from *National Geographic.*"[87] One effect of this verisimilitude was to demonstrate the *ongoing* processes of subjectification that shape Latino/a identities in the present.

Later reworked into a video, *The Couple in a Cage,* the performance intervened synchronically and diachronically, thwarting the celebration of Columbus's "discovery" by enacting the practices of racial enfreakment

Figure 27. Coco Fusco and Guillermo Gómez-Peña, *Two Undiscovered Amerindians Visit Madrid.* Photograph by Peter Barker.

that had arisen in its wake and come to a high degree of refinement during the nineteenth century. In *English Is Broken Here* Fusco recalls that "a chronology with highlights from the history of exhibiting non-Western peoples was on one didactic panel" to the side of the cage (39); it included the Aztec Children and Julia Pastrana, the Mexican "Bear Woman," and other famous nineteenth-century freaks. The cage evoked the museums, stages, and show halls that were the clean, well-lighted places for exhibiting ethnological curiosities, and sites such as Covent Garden were selected because of their historical association with theatre and racial display. Fusco notes with some irony that when the "curator of the Amerindian collection at the British Museum came to look at us," she conceded that "she felt very guilty. Her museum had already declined to give us permission to be displayed" (54); this was just two years before the opening of the Mexican Gallery. Ethnology and archaeology continued on their strangely intertwined paths. For his part, Gómez-Peña also makes reference to late-eighteenth- and early-nineteenth-century technologies, comparing the performance to "living dioramas," in which "'Authentic Primitives' were exhibited as human artifacts and mythical specimens in cages, taverns, gardens, salons, and fairs, as well as in museums of ethnography and natural history."[88] Such practices, he writes, resulted in the perpetuation of stereotypes "still evident in contemporary mass media and pop cultural depictions of the Latino 'other.'"[89] But Gómez-Peña's and Fusco's focus on the "construction of ethnic Otherness as essentially *performative*" reverses the gaze,[90] upsetting the invisibility and neutrality that has been the presumed privilege of the dominant culture in its voyeuristic fantasies about the Other, whether activated through panoramas, photography, freak shows, or museum exhibits. As Gómez-Peña puts it, the performances encourage spectators to "actually replace us. They get to display themselves in our place for a short period of time and experience how it feels to be looked at. We exchange identities with the audience, so to speak."[91] Spectators are thus themselves put under examination, their ignorance parodied, their faith in the mechanisms of science called into question, their willing participation in the dehumanizing spectacle of otherness critiqued, thus bearing out in unexpected ways Foucault's observation that in modernity "man appears in his ambiguous position as an object of knowledge and as a subject that knows: enslaved sovereign, observed spectator."[92] What is also striking is the performers' strategy to wage a subversive campaign not from outside but within the cage, from within the grimly efficient machinery of racial objectification itself. Only by looking at them looking at us, and thus seeing ourselves anew, will it be possible to mitigate the cold logic of the gaze and the vast architecture of oppression it supports.

This analysis of the problematics of looking, however, needs to be extended to cultural criticism itself, where it is all too easy to create intellectual capital by recycling racialized and sexualized images from the gallery of colonial atrocities in the name of critique. There is a real danger that in examining the evils of the past we may feed a hidden voyeurism of our own, a prurient need to peer into history's dark places masked ever so thinly by a commitment to high theory or historical rigor. The ocular bias of our work is buried deep within the customary terms we use to define it—to "examine," "scrutinize," "inquire," "inspect," or simply "look at"— and is thus inseparable from the structures we seek to understand. But as Gómez-Peña and Fusco suggest, the desire to stand outside these structures is illusory, a product of Western notions of an all-seeing, perhaps even panoramic subject. Therefore, only by figuratively inhabiting the cage (self-consciously, with an acute awareness of its historicity, perhaps parodically), can one hope to undermine it. The critique of colonial discourse, contained within the structures it opposes (description, analysis, "examination"), must become itself an object of investigation, must be willing to look at itself looking, without abandoning its ethical imperative: to dismantle Western practices of othering.

H. RIDER HAGGARD AND IMPERIAL NOSTALGIA

> I hold [a relic] as I write.
>> —H. Rider Haggard, *Days of My Life*

By way of conclusion, I want to examine H. Rider Haggard's Mexican novel, *Montezuma's Daughter* (1894), the relationship between material culture and the novel, and the consolations of revisionist imperial history. To begin, let us revisit a theme explored at length in this book: the individual surrounded by his accumulated collections. According to his daughter Lilias, Haggard

> loved collecting things . . . so his family were obligated when accompanying him about the world to keep up a constant chant, "It won't go in—it won't go in!" . . . He always said that looking back on life, what he regretted were not his extravagances but his economies.[1]

Despite the family's pleas about overstuffed trunks and suitcases, Haggard's object fever knew no bounds; he stuffed his red brick estate in Norfolk with "things" acquired on journeys abroad, making it, even by Victorian standards of clutter, a "treasure house for curios."[2] Haggard, who "loved ruins as a bee loves honey,"[3] collected Greek vases, Arabian shields, coins, spearheads, and Zulu battle-axes; "gongs, stuffed animals and birds, heavy earthen vases, and ugly crescent knives"; "a cedar rod believed similar to the one Moses cast before the Pharaoh" and a "green jade Mexican idol."[4] The heterogeneity and scope of his collection accurately reflected the institutions to which the study formed a domestic analogue (Figure 28), returning us to the relationship explored in previous chapters between personal and national acquisitiveness.[5] Like his contemporary Sigmund Freud, who surrounded himself with upwards of 3,000 Greek, Roman, and Etruscan antiquities,[6] Haggard used his collections to prod his imagination. Arrayed around him, objects evoked the worlds represented in his fiction, serving as an aid to memory by figuring the vast project of imaginative archaeology his *oeuvre* represents: its collection and recollection of far-flung peoples and objects, its exploration of the past, its vivid encounter with the power of things. The fiction itself is frequently organized around or prompted by talismans—from the crumpled treasure map in *King Solomon's Mines* to the "shard of Amenartas" that begins *She* (a photographically reproduced "facsimile" of which served as the novel's frontispiece)—things that anchor Haggard's narratives in the material

Figure 28. Donald Macbeth, *One of the Ethnography Galleries, a Photograph* (1908). Copyright The British Museum.

world, lending them weight and authenticity. Like the Victorian museum, Haggard's novels celebrate the power of talismanic things, especially ancient ones, to awaken individual and collective pasts, to stimulate memory and reflection.

Haggard himself shared the adventure novelist's compulsion "to live out something of an adventure,"[7] to mesh life and work by traveling to the outlying regions he wrote about. Like so many Victorian disinherited sons, Haggard lived the formative stage of that adventure at the colonial periphery, where, at age nineteen, he was sent to make a fortune and a name. His colonial adventure took him first to Natal as secretary to Henry Bulwer and later to the Transvaal, where from 1877 to 1879 he served as master of the high court, finding a sense of mission he had never felt at home. On his return to Britain he studied for the bar (1880–1884), and then turned to the work of transforming his African experiences into fiction. *King Solomon's Mines* (1885) was an immediate and huge success, its account of Africa so full of verisimilitude that for many readers it stood *for* Africa; indeed, Haggard reports that a dealer in jewels "actually sent an expedition to look for King Solomon's Mines, or at any rate talked of doing so."[8] Within a year *King Solomon's Mines* had sold 31,000 copies in Britain and gone through thirteen editions in the United States.[9] Haggard followed this success with the equally exotic African tales *She* (1887) and *Allan Quatermain* (1887), which established him as the indispensable chronicler of imperial adventure.

Appearing alongside other examples of the genre such as Robert Louis Stevenson's *Treasure Island* (1883), *Kidnapped* (1886), and *The Black Arrow* (1888), Haggard's African novels took his male readers—*King Solomon's Mines* was dedicated to the "Big and little boys who read it"—on an imaginative journey that Haggard himself had lived, and that in its romantic evocation of travel and exploration lay at the very heart of the imperial enterprise. In 1901, the writer and anthropologist Andrew Lang (1844–1912) heralded the emphasis on lived experience as central to a new kind of manly, outdoor literature that he deemed powerful precisely to the degree that it opposed the feminine spaces of domestic fiction. The new adventure writers, as Lang put it,

> have at least seen new worlds for themselves; have gone out of the streets of the overpopulated lands into the open air; have sailed and ridden, walked and

hunted; have escaped from the smoke and fog of towns. New strength has come from fresher air into their brains and blood.[10]

As cities grew crowded, so did the lure of "undiscovered" worlds—all the more because, as Marlow realizes at the beginning of *Heart of Darkness* (1899), the blank spaces on the map of adventure were rapidly being filled in.

Despite the labors of John Lloyd Stephens and the other archaeological travelers examined in chapter 3, one place that might still be called "undiscovered" was the interior of Mexico and Central America. The dense jungles were said to conceal buried cities, lost treasure, and forgotten races, such as those alluded to in the Aztec Children hoax. This was a time capsule of a place where even in an industrialized present anachronistic practices and beliefs lived on. Its monumental temples and indigenous population suggested a primitive world lurking just beneath the surface of modern life, a theme that would animate the modernist movement.[11] As I have been arguing in this book archaeology, museum exhibitions, travel literature, historical writing, and various forms of popular spectacle worked together to create a picture of this lost world, representing it in various guises and for diverse publics. The novel, too, though a relative latecomer to this subject matter, performed its part. Between 1857 and 1900, at least thirty British and American novels were set in either contemporary or pre-conquest Mexico or in the Mexican days of the Southwest.[12] Notable examples include Charles Dickens and Wilkie Collins's "Perils of Certain English Prisoners" (1857), and Collins's *Woman in White* (1860), which, as mentioned in chapter 3, drew heavily on Stephens and Catherwood's *Incidents of Travel in Central America, Chiapas and Yucatan* (1841). Less well known are works such as William Westall's *Phantom City: A Volcanic Romance* (1886), Thomas A. Janvier's *Aztec Treasure-House, a Romance of Contemporaneous Antiquity* (1890), Walter McDougall's *Hidden City* (1891), G. A. Henty's *By Right of Conquest* (1891), Kirk Munroe's *White Conquerors of Mexico: A Tale of Toltec and Aztec* (1894), and Frank Savile's *Beyond the Great South Wall: The Secret of the Antarctic* (1899), in which an explorer searches for a lost Mayan city in the Antarctic. One might take this last work as a figure for the remoteness of Southern Mexico and Central America in the popular British imagination, and hence in the novel, overshadowed as it was by travel literature and museum exhibitions.

Before D. H. Lawrence, whose *Plumed Serpent* (1926) is still the best-known British novel about Mexico, the novelist who did the most to bring Mexico into view was Haggard. Prompted by his own visit to Mexico in the early 1890s and the desire to explore new subjects in his work, Haggard wrote two novels that suggest some of the ways pre-Columbian material was absorbed into late-century British fiction: *Montezuma's Daughter* (1894) and *Heart of the World* (1895).[13] Both novels spring from actual stories of buried treasure and hidden antiquities. Both participate in the logic of imperial possession that represented Mexico and Central America as storehouses of wealth and knowledge awaiting plunder by enterprising British subjects. Both works collect, synthesize, and represent the foundational symbols and myths of pre-Columbian culture, most importantly the return of the fair god Quetzalcoatl, or plumed serpent (Lawrence's novel appeared in Britain as *Quetzalcoatl*). Finally, both works place British heroes at the center of world historical events from which the British were wholly excluded, and thus offer revisionist accounts of Britain's role in the Americas.

In what follows, I read the more successful and better-known of these works, *Montezuma's Daughter,* against three intertwined contexts: Haggard's biography, particularly his journey to Mexico and the death of his son; the late-nineteenth-century history of British and American influence in Mexico; and select features of the British discourse about Mexico and Central America examined thus far in this book. While it is hard to dispute Anne D. McClintock's suggestion in relation to Haggard that the "Victorian obsession with treasure troves and treasure maps is a vivid example of commodity fetishism—the disavowal of the origins of money in labor,"[14] the quest for buried treasure combines personal, affective implications and larger imperial ones. The story of the lost treasure allowed Haggard to bridge a chasm of grief while commenting on Britain's lost opportunities in Latin America. This is evident in the novel's narrative structure, which celebrates the heroic age of Elizabethan exploration to offset the loss of a rich empire. That consolation, in turn, is structurally connected to other related acts, from the writing of the novel itself to the wielding of talismanic symbols within it.

Haggard visited Mexico during what historians call the "Porfiriato," a period of rapid change in Mexican social and political life brought on by the policies of José de la Cruz Porfirio Díaz, who, save a four-year hiatus

from 1880 to 1884, ruled the country with an iron fist for thirty-five years
(1876–1911). Inspired by the writings of Comte, Mill, and Spencer—Díaz's
motto was "order and progress"—Díaz modernized finance, trade, industry, agriculture, communications, transportation, and mining. While he
deepened the misery of the indigenous, Díaz produced industrial growth
(and wealth for elites) the likes of which Mexico had never seen. Rail-
roads, to take a ready example, grew from only 400 miles of track in 1876
to 15,000 in 1911, and later the mining and petroleum industries also
boomed. Foreigners rushed in; already by 1894 Henry Adams was com-
plaining that Mexico was "overrun by Americans and English," many of
them clutching guidebooks and travel accounts, over sixty of which were
written between 1880 and 1900 alone.[15] And after having no diplomatic
relations with Britain between 1867 and 1884, because of tension over the
repayment of old loans, Mexico invited Britain to reopen its embassies. In
1884 the *South American Journal* wrote that with the resumption of diplomatic relations "the gates of Mexico will be opened wide to the influx of
British enterprise and capital, which have done so much for the progress
and development of other Spanish-American states."[16] A new mining
code, established in 1884, gave landowners vertical property rights to anything found below the surface of the ground, a privilege that Hispanic
jurisprudence had heretofore reserved for the nation; taxes on mining
proceeds were also relaxed, exempting some minerals altogether and low-
ering duties on others. Manuel Barriga, head of the Mexican Information
Bureau, made it a point to assure investors that "whatever other difficulties the management of Mexican companies may have to deal with, there
is certainly no labor difficulty."[17] British trade journals and the Foreign
Office disseminated this crucial information, thereby stimulating more
investment.

A major British figure was Weetman Pearson (Lord Cowdray), who
constructed a large-scale drainage system for Mexico City, built a railroad
from the Pacific to the Atlantic over the isthmus of Tehauntepec, and,
through the El Águila Company, dominated the petroleum industry
during a period when Mexico became one of the world's largest energy
producers.[18] Mexico signed new treaties of friendship, commerce, and
navigation with France, Norway, Ecuador, and Japan. Yet by far the greatest beneficiary of the Porfiriato was the United States, whose rising wealth
and power were mirrored by a corresponding decline in British influence.

Britain went from controlling about 50 percent of Mexico's import trade in the 1820s, to seeing its stake decline to 35 percent in 1876 and 11 percent in 1911. The U.S. share, meanwhile, rose from 25 percent in 1876 to over 50 percent in 1911. Likewise, by 1911, Britain was receiving only 14 percent of Mexico's exports, while the United States took in almost 75 percent.[19] Meanwhile, from the 1870s onward, U.S. cultural institutions exerted a tremendous influence in Mexico and Central America, particularly in archaeology and museum anthropology. The Peabody Museum at Harvard, the Field Museum in Chicago, and the Carnegie Institution in Washington, D.C., among others, actively promoted Mesoamerican research, sponsoring digs, sending experts, and bringing back crate loads of artifacts to fill the nation's museums. These economic and cultural shifts, coupled with U.S. territorial expansion in the region, signaled the completion of a program of hemispheric dominance begun with the announcement of the Monroe Doctrine in 1823. During the Porfiriato, the balance of power in the Atlantic moved from an East-West to a North-South axis, leading Díaz to coin the now-famous Mexican saying: "Poor Mexico: so far from God, so close to the United States."

Though these changes occurred slowly, the trend was clear by the 1890s, and Haggard's journey occurred at the crucial tipping point just prior to the Spanish-American War, when the United States consolidated its grip on the hemisphere. In some ways, Haggard's desire to visit Mexico was driven by a retrospective logic, recapitulating and renewing a pattern of British speculation and adventure-hunting established during the heyday of British interest in the 1820s. Having gotten rich from his African fiction, Haggard speculated on the London Stock Exchange and, like Disraeli and Bullock decades before, trained his eye on Mexican mining companies. In 1889, through connections in the City of London, he met J. Gladwyn Jebb, managing director of the Santa Fé Copper Mines in the southern Mexican state of Chiapas. Immediately taken with Jebb's good looks and vivid conversation, Haggard was mesmerized by his romantic tales of Mexico's "history, its legends, and many strange adventures which had befallen him there."[20] It was not long before Haggard was investing in mining stocks Jebb recommended,[21] and he soon accepted an invitation to come with his wife to Mexico City, his first visit to the New World. While researching a novel on Montezuma, he and Jebb proposed to "explore some of the ruined cities in the Palenque district, and also to make an attempt to recover Montezuma's, or rather Guatemoc's treasure," the secret of which Jebb claimed to have learned through his long residence in Mexico.[22] The tale of the lost treasure appealed to Haggard's "romantic instincts" and antiquarian impulses, and he looked forward to seeing "such relics of old Mexico as could be seen in the museum . . . and the mighty volcano of Popocatepetl" (*Days* 2:51). In Mexico, Haggard hoped to satisfy his lust for outsized adventure and his fascination with the past, while shaping both into a new historical fiction.

Just as the Mexico Haggard valued was ancient and legendary, so too was its treasure, whose existence had circulated in stories dating from the Spanish conquest. As Haggard tells it, Cortés, having occupied Tenochtitlán and imprisoned Montezuma, was forced to flee the city by an Aztec revolt during the so-called *noche triste,* or sad night, when many Spaniards were slain. Cuauhtémoc, who led the Aztec forces, gathered up and then hid the treasure the Spaniards left behind, which included

> eighteen large jars of gold, either in the form of ornaments or dust, several jars
> full of precious stones, much arms and armour, also of gold, and lastly a great
> golden head more than life-size, being a portrait of the Emperor Montezuma.
> (*Days* 2:52)

Jebb told Haggard how he had become acquainted with a Cuban geologist named Don Anselmo who had stumbled across the site where the treasure was concealed, its secret location having been handed down from Indian to Indian for generations to keep the treasure out of Spanish hands (*Days* 2:52 ff.). Anselmo's prying had caught the attention of the most recent person in the chain, and Anselmo successfully elicited the entire story from him, including maps and plans of the site. Anselmo soon entered into a partnership with his informant, trying first to raise funds to purchase the property outright and, when this failed, gaining permission from the owner to prospect for sulfur. Workers dug to a level of sixty feet, at which point they found, in accordance with the legend, a stone marked with an owl, the symbol of Cuauhtémoc. Beyond it lay a tunnel leading to a flight of stairs, terminating at a solid wall. Just at this time, however, the land changed hands again. Fearing that the new owner would discover the real object of their digging and rightfully claim what was beneath the surface of his property, Anselmo and his partner directed the workers to fill the shaft and announce that no sulfur had been found. At this point Anselmo turned for help to Jebb, who was well known for his interest in antiquities. The plan was for Jebb to approach the new owner of the land and request permission to excavate for Aztec artifacts. Haggard recalls seeing "the arrival of the formal letter of leave, but not what stipulations were made as to the disposal of any articles that might be found" (*Days* 2:53).[23]

It was precisely at this moment, when Haggard, Jebb, and Anselmo were preparing to clear the shaft, that Haggard received a terrible shock, news that his nine-year-old son, Jock, who had remained behind in England, had died suddenly from complications related to measles. While his wife returned with Mrs. Jebb to England, Haggard stayed in Mexico, making several expeditions with Jebb into the back reaches of Chiapas, looking for antiquities and treasure, hoping to cure "nerves shattered by sorrow and anxiety,"[24] but in truth having "no heart to enter upon the adventure" (*Days* 2:53). Jebb never visited the site, and when he returned to Mexico after a year away in England Anselmo had disappeared and with him the location of the treasure.

Thus the narrative of lost treasure and lost life. What did Haggard make of this material? Initially, he distracted himself by working feverishly at *Montezuma's Daughter*, completing it in three months during the summer of 1891. The novel follows the adventures of Thomas Wingfield of Ditchingham, taking us from sixteenth-century England, to Spain, and finally ancient Mexico, where we see the conquest of Mexico through Thomas's eyes. English on his father's side and Spanish on his mother's, Thomas is drawn in the classic mode of the shape-shifting hero caught between warring selves. Told by his father to "keep your heart English," lest "her blood should master mine within you," he is given the impossible task of holding one half of his identity in check, a command made more difficult because his hot Spanish blood fuels his precocious virility, making a man of him "when many a pure-bred Englishman is still nothing but a boy."[25] His cultural (and, in the novel, racial) hybridity, moreover, enables mobility denied his purebred countrymen: "I could speak Castilian so perfectly, and was so Spanish in appearance, that it was not difficult for me to pass myself off as one of their nation" (82). His heart set on marrying the virginal English heroine Lily, Thomas goes to Spain to find his mother's killer, the wicked Spaniard Juan de García. Once there he comes into an inheritance and sails for home, only to be taken prisoner on board a Spanish ship bound for the Indies captained by none other than de García. Near the coast of Mexico he is thrown overboard, but makes his way to land, where, amazed at his white skin (relative to theirs, of course), the local people receive him as a deity, the son of Quetzalcoatl. Thus except for a Spanish priest marooned earlier, Thomas, going native, becomes "the first white man who ever dwelt among the Indians" (101). His adventures in Mexico eventually bring him to Tenochtitlán just as Cortés and his men march on the capital. He becomes betrothed to Otomie, Montezuma's daughter, and on the night of the *noche triste,* helps Cuauhtémoc bury the Aztec treasure. After further adventures, and the death of his wife and children, he returns safely to England and Englishness, and marries Lily.

In giving us a hero who turns native only to return at the end to white "civilization," the novel reflects the late Victorian fascination and repulsion with primitivism whose most familiar touchstone is *Heart of Darkness,* published just six years after Haggard's novel.[26] It also employs all the stock devices and tropes of adventure fiction—love triangles, rivalry, disinheritance, exotic travel, captivity, encounters with natives, buried treasure, and military conquest—to tell a distinctively New World tale, combining the author's on-the-spot observations of the Mexican landscape and information gleaned, according to the novel's preface, from Prescott's *History of the Conquest of Mexico* and the *Historia general de las cosas de la Nueva España* by Father Bernardino de Sahagún, a vast compendium of colonial ethnography that forms the basis for much of our contemporary knowledge of Aztec civilization. Haggard also drew on Díaz del Castillo's *Historia verdadera,* and may even have imagined himself in competition with his predecessor, who turns up in the narrative as a soldier in Cortés's army. Díaz's unpretentious, earthy style, and his soldier's-eye view of the action strongly influence the narrative technique of *Montezuma's Daughter,* which is told by the equally straightforward Thomas Wingfield, a type of English Díaz who fills in the "English side" of the conquest.

In one of the few commentaries on the novel, D. S. Higgins rightly argues that in composing a novel in which the hero's children die Haggard realized a "therapeutic" benefit, working out his grief by making Wingfield undergo a similar loss.[27] But how are the consolations of fictionalized grief connected both to the larger themes of the novel and to the historical moment in which it was written, a moment, as I have argued, in which the greatest days of British influence in Mexico had already passed? How might we understand Haggard's novel as a representation of historical, as well as personal, loss? I would argue that by making Wingfield not only the eyewitness of "things that no other Englishman has seen" (2) but also a vital participant in the events he witnesses, the novel offers a clever, imaginative solution to the problem of imperial belatedness, Britain's awareness of having missed the greatest spoils in the New World. In so doing, Haggard improves on earlier British writers who turned to lament as an implicit critique of Spanish colonialism. Darwin, for example, wondered in the *Journal of Researches,* "How different would have been the aspect of this river if English colonists had by good fortune first sailed up the Plata! What noble towns would now have occupied its shores!"[28] Using the novelist's imaginative license, Haggard goes one step further by placing an Englishman at the Spanish conquest and making him a key source of historical knowledge for it. Haggard's narrative structure thus compensates for the English exclusion from the conquest by viewing it from the perspective of later English victories over Spain, thus pointing toward a providential design to history in which Britain emerges triumphant.[29] The novel's first sentence gestures in this direction: "Now glory be to God who has given us the victory!" That victory, shaped by timely storms in the English Channel, is the defeat of the Spanish Armada in 1588—a crucial moment in the narrative of English nationalism. By way of introducing the Mexican subject of the novel, the narrator casts the event in world-historical terms, arguing that the Spanish "came to conquer, to bring us to the torture and the stake—to do to us free Englishmen as Cortes did by the Indians of Anahuac" (1). This not only links the conquest with the Inquisition—a frequent trope in British imperial historiography—but also projects the Anglo-Spanish conflict from the Channel to the New World, thus globalizing the scope of adventure fiction. What is at stake here is the fate of empires, figured in the domination of the seas, with the Americas as the richest prize. The narrative frame further links nation and narration by including Wingfield's audience with Elizabeth I ten years earlier, in which she asked him to give "some particulars of the story of [his] life" (2), especially the twenty years he spent in Mexico. And while, as the narrative reveals, Montezuma's treasure remains buried in Mexico, its loss is compensated for by a potent symbol, Wingfield's gift to Elizabeth of the great emerald that had once hung around the neck of Montezuma's

daughter, a gesture of fealty that also points to England as the rightful pos-
sessor of Mexico's vast mineral wealth.

The 1588 setting of Wingfield's narration brings into focus a series of
related compensations, each underwritten by a faith in the providential
design of history. The first, following Prescott and other nineteenth-
century commentators, casts the fall of the Aztecs as punishment for prac-
ticing a bloody religion which "sacrificed the lives of thousands to their
false gods." As Wingfield relates it, the "true God" has answered them,
giving "for peace the sword of the Spaniard, for prosperity the rack and
the torment and the day of slavery" (3). Yet, as we saw in chapter 2, many
nineteenth-century writers suggested this was only a partial recompense in
the divine logic of history, for the conquerors "wrought cruelties greater
than any that were done by the benighted Aztecs" (3), thereby dooming
themselves to a short-lived imperial future. Though Wingfield could not
know the eventual outcome of Spanish rule in the New World, he imagines a day when

> the proudest of peoples of the earth [are] bereft of fame and wealth and honour,
> a starveling remnant happy in nothing save their past. What Drake began at
> Gravelines God will finish in many another place and time, till at last Spain is
> of no more account and lies as low as the empire of Montezuma lies to-day. (3)

Haggard knew, of course, as did his readers, that that day had come to pass
in the 1820s, when the Spanish crown lost its richest colonies to independence movements seemingly overnight, and watched as Britain rushed
in to fill the vacuum. Yet, less than a century later, as Haggard himself
acknowledged, the era of greatest British influence was ebbing away;
sounding very much like Corydon Donnavan and other boosters of Manifest Destiny, Haggard wrote in his autobiography that if only Mexico
"were inhabited by some righteous race, what a land it might be . . . !
For my part, I believe that it would be well for it if it should pass into the
power of the United States" (*Days* 2:64). Not Britain, which by the time
Haggard wrote these words was enervated from the Great War, but the
United States should be Mexico's new master. No wonder that Haggard
set his fiction in the distant past, at a moment when England's imperial
greatness seemed all before it, not something merely to be memorialized
in fiction and lore.

Yet if these large historical consolations speak to the waning of British power, what did the novel offer to Haggard himself, sunk in grief and self-recrimination over his child's death? For this, I want to return to Montezuma's treasure, or rather to its representation and reconstitution in narratives of various kinds, its multiple losses and permutations, its slippage through the hands first of the Aztecs, then the Spanish, and finally Haggard and Jebb. During the night the treasure was buried, Thomas tells us, one bag of jewels broke while being lowered into the pit, and "a great necklace of emeralds" chanced to fall around his neck. Cuahtémoc urged him to keep it, "in memory of this night" (201), which Thomas did, giving one stone from it to Queen Elizabeth (an act of national consolation), but keeping the rest because they reminded him of Otomie, his Aztec wife and mother of his now-deceased children. While the greater part of the treasure was interred in the earth, one part survived, becoming a token of remembrance and a symbol for memory itself.

The fictional and the historical merge yet again in Lilias Rider Haggard's account of her father in the months after his return from Mexico, when all were forbidden from speaking the dead boy's name and Rider sought refuge in his work. On 9 December 1892 another child was welcomed into the Haggard household, a little girl. Lilias writes that after this her father's health began to improve, and he took more interest in his work, writing *People of the Mist* and revising *Montezuma's Daughter*. She reports as well that Haggard's secretary Ida Hector "always said she wished the readers of that book," *Montezuma's Daughter,* could have seen Haggard comforting the new baby.[30] But Lilias adds another telling detail, one that brings us back to Haggard's study and the objects displayed within it:

> Up and down he walked, dictating as he went, the child on his shoulder, her round blue eyes wandering now to the shadow of the copper lamp which glowed like a flower on the ceiling; now to the great green chalcedony head of the Aztec god on the wall with gaping mouth and eyes, in which jewels had flashed in the days of Montezuma. Below it hung the sacrificial bowl carved with strange symbols, stained with the blood of the human hearts offered upon the altars of the gods.[31]

These objects, of course, were all collected on Haggard's trip to Mexico, reminding him of the place, evoking the ancient past, comforting and consoling him perhaps as much as the child on his shoulder. Like museum artifacts, they have been stripped of their original meanings to serve stories never imagined at their birth. At once shockingly uncanny (in the sense of *unheimlich*) and perfectly at home, they speak to the transformations that all collected and redisplayed things undergo when diverted from the uses for which they were originally intended. In this way they form a fitting conclusion to the various processes of dislocation, dismemberment, dispossession, and mobilization I have tracked in this book, from the first exhibition of Aztec antiquities in 1824 to the fitting up of private homes with blood-soaked but surprisingly consoling artifacts in the 1890s that are associated in turn with fictions of imperial belatedness and loss. If the loss is figured primarily as an *English* loss, that, too, is only fitting, reminding us that to the victors go not only the material spoils but also the privilege of making history, of writing the stories we live by, even if that means the obliteration of other makers, other stories.

NOTES

INTRODUCTION

1. Thomas Greenwood, *Museums and Art Galleries* (London, 1888), 216.

2. For the link between museum and nationhood, see Benedict Anderson, *Imagined Communities: Reflections on the Origin and Spread of Nationalism,* rev. ed. (London: Verso, 1991), 163–86.

3. Colin McEwan, *Ancient Mexico in the British Museum* (London: British Museum Press, 1994), 79.

4. Obscure, for example, is the relationship between the Mexican Gallery and the politics of national identity, in particular the way in which the focus on ancient Mexico constrains larger discussions of the Maya, who ranged beyond Mexico's current border to Belize, Guatemala, and Honduras. The nationalist thrust makes it difficult for the visitor to understand the relationship between objects in the Mexican Gallery and the museum's impressive collection of Maya artifacts, many gathered from Guatemala, Honduras, and the former colonial possession of British Honduras. A Mesoamerican, rather than simply a Mexican, gallery would have greatly enabled such discussions. On what exhibitions and world's fairs have meant historically for Mexican nationalism, see Maurcio Tenorio-Trillo, *Mexico at the World's Fairs: Crafting a Modern Nation* (Berkeley: University of California Press, 1996).

5. Craig Clunas, "China in Britain: The Imperial Collections," in *Colonialism and the Object: Empire, Material Culture and the Museum,* ed. Tim Barringer and Tom Flynn (London: Routledge, 1998), 44.

6. Throughout 2002–04 the press was awash in stories of trouble at the British Museum, including changing leadership, budget crises, layoffs, the closure of departments, poorly conceived exhibitions, and the continuing controversy over the return of the Elgin Marbles and other cultural property. See, for example, Jonathan Jones, "Dumb Witness," *Guardian Unlimited,* 6 Dec. 2001, http://www.guardian.co.uk/arts/

story/0,3604,614234,00.html [accessed 6 Dec. 2001]; Maev Kennedy and Fiachra Gibbons, "Treasures Hidden Behind Closed Doors as British Museum Pays Price for Free Entry," *Guardian Unlimited*, 17 Jan. 2002, http://www.guardian.co.uk/uk_news/story/0,3604,634683,00.html [accessed 17 Jan. 2002].

7. The literature on museums and collecting, which now touches on many diverse fields, is rapidly expanding, and I shall not attempt to summarize it here, choosing rather to specify my debts in the chapters that follow. For overviews of British interest in Mexican and Central American antiquities, consult Elizabeth Carmichael, *The British and the Maya* (London: The Trustees of the British Museum, 1973) and Adrian Locke, "Exhibitions and Collectors of Pre-Hispanic Mexican Artefacts in Britain," in *Aztecs*, ed. Eduardo Matos Moctezuma and Felipe Solis Olguin (London: Royal Academy of Arts, 2002), 80–87. For basic information about the development of the British Museum's Department of Ethnography, including some details about the pre-Columbian collections, see H. J. Braunholtz, *Sir Hans Sloane and Ethnography* (London: Trustees of the British Museum, 1970) and Marjorie Caygill and John Cherry, eds., *A. W. Franks: Nineteenth-Century Collecting and the British Museum* (London: British Museum Press, 1997). Reliable surveys of the British Museum can be found in Edward Miller, *That Noble Cabinet: A History of the British Museum* (London: Andre Deutsch, 1973) and Marjorie Caygill, *The Story of the British Museum*, 2nd ed. (London: British Museum Press, 1992). For recent discussions of the museum in Victorian culture, see Barbara J. Black, *On Exhibit: Victorians and Their Museums* (Charlottesville: University Press of Virginia, 2000) and Carla Yanni, *Nature's Museums: Victorian Science and the Architecture of Display* (Baltimore: The Johns Hopkins University Press, 2000). On the relationship between Mesoamerican and modern art, see Barbara Braun, *Pre-Columbian Art and the Post-Columbian World: Ancient American Sources of Modern Art* (Harry N. Abrams, 1993), especially chapter 1, which surveys British, French, and U.S. collecting. And for a stimulating introduction to the legal and ethical issues surrounding the return of cultural property housed in museums, see Jeanette Greenfield, *The Return of Cultural Treasures* (Cambridge: Cambridge University Press, 1989).

8. P. J. Cain and A. G. Hopkins, *British Imperialism: Innovation and Expansion, 1688–1914* (London: Longman, 1993), 283.

9. See, for example, Tim Fulford and Peter Kitson's excellent edited volume on romanticism and colonialism, which leaves Britain's relationship with Latin America to the side (*Romanticism and Colonialism: Writing and Empire, 1780–1830* [Cambridge: Cambridge University Press, 1998]). A notable exception here is Nigel Leask's *Curiosity and the Aesthetics of Travel Writing, 1770–1840: 'From an Antique Land'* (Oxford: Oxford University Press, 2002), which includes chapters on Humboldt and the early British traveler to Mexico, William Bullock. Also valuable are Joselyn M. Almeida, "Locating Romanticism's Transatlantic Song," *European Romantic Review* 10, no. 4 (1999): 401–23; Nanora Sweet, "'Hitherto Closed to British Enterprise': Trading and Writing the Hispanic World Circa 1815," *European Romantic Review* 8, no. 2 (1997): 139–47; and Charles Rzepka, "'Cortez—or Balboa, or Somebody Like That': Form,

Fact, and Forgetting in Keats's 'Chapman's Homer' Sonnet," *Keats-Shelley Journal* 51 (2002): 35–75.

10. In the late 1880s, as Wayne M. Clegern has shown, the British archaeologist Alfred Percival Maudslay performed strategically important work in British Honduras for the Foreign Office, drawing up a detailed map of the interior that he enfolded into a 7,000-word memorandum that gave information on commercial routes and railways, treaty negotiations with Guatemala, and other areas of colonial concern. Maudslay's services were valued precisely to the extent that he had an intimate knowledge of the ground, gained from his several years of archaeological research in the area. The information did indeed prove useful in subsequent dealings between Britain and Guatemala, giving the British negotiator a firmer grasp of the facts in dispute than his Guatemalan counterpart (*Maudslay's Central America; a Strategic View in 1887* [New Orleans: Middle American Research Institute Tulane University, 1962]). For a brief discussion of the symbiosis between American archaeologists in the Maya region and U.S. imperial agendas, see Quetzil E. Castañeda, *In the Museum of Maya Culture: Touring Chichén Itzá* (Minneapolis: University of Minnesota Press, 1996), 109.

11. Homi K. Bhabha, "Of Mimicry and Man: The Ambivalence of Colonial Discourse," in *The Location of Culture* (London: Routledge, 1994), 85–93.

12. Elizabeth Williams, "Collecting and Exhibiting Pre-Columbiana in France and England, 1870–1930," in *Collecting the Pre-Columbian Past,* ed. Elizabeth Hill Boone (Washington: Dumbarton Oaks, 1993), 123–40. For a political overview of the French experience in Mexico, see Nancy Nichols Barker, *The French Experience in Mexico, 1821–1861: A History of Constant Misunderstanding* (Chapel Hill: University of North Carolina Press, 1979).

13. Thomas Richards, *The Imperial Archive: Knowledge and the Fantasy of Empire* (London: Verso, 1993), 1–9. The overflow is apparent in the poor state of cataloguing in the British Museum's Department of Ethnography. Much of the pre-Columbian collection is identified only by accession slips created during the nineteenth century. A new museumwide computer database, COMPASS, promises to provide better information on the collections, though at present its coverage is quite limited.

14. J. Jorge Klor de Alva, "The Postcolonization of the (Latin) American Experience; a Reconsideration of 'Colonialism,' 'Postcolonialism' and 'Mestizaje',", in *After Colonialism: Imperial Histories and Postcolonial Displacements,* ed. Gyan Prakash (Princeton: Princeton University Press, 1995), 270. Karen Racine's work on the Spanish American community resident in London before the wars of independence also lends credence to this view ("Imagining Independence: London's Spanish American Community, 1790–1829" [Ph.D. diss., Tulane University, 1996]).

15. Robert Knox, *The Races of Men: A Fragment* (London, 1850), 43–44.

16. Martin Lynn, "Policy, Trade, and Informal Empire," in *The Oxford History of the British Empire: The Nineteenth Century,* ed. Andrew Porter (Oxford: Oxford University Press, 1999), 108.

17. Alan Knight, "Britain and Latin America," in Porter, *The Oxford History of the British Empire,* 126, 130.

18. Sam W. Haynes, "Anglophobia and the Annexation of Texas: The Quest for National Security," in *Manifest Destiny and Empire: American Antebellum Expansionism,* ed. Sam W. Haynes and Christopher Morris (College Station: Texas A&M University Press, 1997), 129.

19. D. C. M. Platt, *Finance, Trade, and Politics in British Foreign Policy, 1815–1914* (Oxford: Clarendon Press, 1968), 312.

20. Cain and Hopkins, *British Imperialism,* 276.

21. Raymond E. Dumett, ed., *Gentlemanly Capitalism and British Imperialism: The New Debate on Empire* (New York: Longman, 1999); John Gallagher and Ronald Robinson, "The Imperialism of Free Trade," *Economic History Review* 6, no. 1 (1953): 1–14; D. C. M. Platt, ed., *Business Imperialism: An Inquiry Based on British Experience in Latin America* (Oxford: Clarendon Press, 1977).

22. Gallagher and Robinson, "Imperialism," 5–8.

23. Platt, *Finance,* 308–52; Cain and Hopkins, *British Imperialism,* 276–79; and Knight, "Britain and Latin America," 124–25.

24. Knight, "Britain and Latin America," 125. For the Enlightenment view of commerce with America as a civilizing force, see Anthony Pagden, *European Encounters with the New World from Renaissance to Romanticism* (New Haven: Yale University Press, 1993), 170–71.

25. William Bullock, *Six Months' Residence and Travels in Mexico* (London, 1824), 484. Eugenia Roldán Vera has examined Ackermann's scheme to export books to Latin America in the immediate aftermath of Latin American independence. Textbooks in Spanish were sent to several cities in Mexico, Guatemala, Gran Colombia, Peru, Chile, and Argentina (Eugenia Roldán Vera, "Book Export and the Transmission of Knowledge from Britain to Early-Independent Spanish America" [Ph.D. diss., University of Cambridge, 2001]). For other examples of the dissemination of British culture in the early post-independence period, see D. C. M. Platt, *Latin America and British Trade, 1806–1914* (London: Adam and Charles Black, 1972), 39–47.

26. Knight, "Britain and Latin America," 125.

27. Racine, "Imagining Independence."

28. Frederick Cooper and Ann Laura Stoler, "Between Metropole and Colony: Rethinking a Research Agenda," in *Tensions of Empire: Colonial Cultures in a Bourgeois World,* ed. Frederick Cooper and Ann Laura Stoler (Berkeley: University of California Press, 1997), 4.

29. Alexander von Humboldt, *Personal Narrative of a Journey to the Equinoctial Regions of the New Continent,* trans. Jason Wilson (London: Penguin Books, 1996), 8.

30. Arjun Appadurai, "Introduction: Commodities and the Politics of Value," in Appadurai, ed., *The Social Life of Things: Commodities in Cultural Perspective* (Cambridge: Cambridge University Press, 1986), 15.

31. Mieke Bal, "Telling Objects: A Narrative Perspective on Collecting," in *The Cultures of Collecting,* ed. John Elsner and Roger Cardinal (Cambridge: Harvard University Press, 1994), 111.

32. Anthony Alan Shelton, "Museum Ethnography: An Imperial Science," in *Cultural Encounters: Representing Otherness,* ed. Elizabeth Hallam and Brian V. Street (London: Routledge, 2000), 158.

33. Bruno Latour, *Science in Action: How to Follow Scientists and Engineers through Society* (Cambridge: Harvard University Press, 1987), 223.

34. Bruno Latour, "Drawing Things Together," in *Representation in Scientific Practice,* ed. Michael Lynch and Steve Woolgar (Cambridge: MIT Press, 1990), 26; emphasis in original.

35. Latour, *Science,* 225.

36. Ibid., 215 ff.

37. Latour, "Drawing," 45–46.

38. Ibid., 56.

39. Clegern points out, for example, that Maudslay's map (see above) was believed lost, until it turned up later in the Foreign Office—rescued by a janitor from a trash box.

40. Nicholas Thomas, *Colonialism's Culture: Anthropology, Travel and Government* (Princeton: Princeton University Press, 1994), ix.

41. Mary Louise Pratt, *Imperial Eyes: Travel Writing and Transculturation* (New York: Routledge, 1992), 7.

42. Edward Said, *Orientalism* (New York: Vintage Books, 1979), 52.

1. "OPEN FOR INSPECTION"

1. For a survey of eighteenth-century travelers to Mexico, see Berta Flores Salinas, *México visto por algunos de sus viajeros, siglo XVIII* (Mexico City: Ediciones Botas, 1966).

2. An excellent study of the politics of recognition and banking credit is Jaime E. Rodríguez O., *The Emergence of Spanish America: Vicente Rocafuerte and Spanish Americanism, 1808–1832* (Berkeley: University of California Press, 1975), 85–128; for the larger relationship between Spanish American and British leaders see Karen Racine, "Imagining Independence: London's Spanish American Community, 1790–1829" (Ph.D. diss., Tulane University, 1996); María Teresa Berruezo León, *La lucha de Hispanoamérica por su independencia en Inglaterra, 1800–1830* (Madrid: Ediciones de Cultura Hispánica, 1989); and Estela Guadalupe Jiménez Codinach, *La Gran Bretaña y la independencia de México, 1808–1821* (Mexico City: Fondo de Cultura Económica, 1991).

3. While Humboldt published views and descriptions of several important sites, maps, and sculptures, he had a generally low opinion of Aztec antiquities, writing that "those who love to investigate American Antiquities will not find in this capital [Mexico City] those great remains of works which are to be seen in Peru," and that one should not be surprised "by the grossness of style and the incorrectness of the contours of the art of the peoples of America" (*Political Essay on the Kingdom of New*

Spain, trans. John Black, 2 vols. [New York: 1811], 2:35; *Vues des cordillères et monumens des peuples indigènes de l'Amérique* [Paris, 1810], 3). For a sympathetic treatment of Humboldt, see Eloise Quiñones Keber, "Humboldt and Aztec Art," *Colonial Latin American Review* 5, no. 2 (1996): 277–97. All translations mine unless otherwise noted.

4. Quotations from William Bullock's Mexican works are cited in the text as follows:

> *SMR: Six Months' Residence and Travels in Mexico* (London, 1824).
>
> *MM: Catalogue of the Exhibition, Called Modern Mexico* (London, 1824)
>
> *AM: A Description of the Unique Exhibition, called Ancient Mexico: Collected on the Spot in 1823 by the assistance of the Mexican Government, and now open for Public Inspection at the Egyptian Hall, Piccadilly* (London, n.d.)
>
> *AMM: A Descriptive Catalogue of the Exhibition, Entitled Ancient and Modern Mexico* (London, n.d.)

5. C. K. Webster, ed., *Britain and the Independence of Latin America, 1812–1830,* 2 vols. (London: Oxford University Press, 1938), 1:431. On Mackie, see Henry McKenzie Johnston, *Missions to Mexico: A Tale of British Diplomacy in the 1820s* (London: British Academic Press, 1992).

6. Prior to Bullock's exhibit, Aztec artifacts plundered by the conquistadors were displayed in the Spanish court, sent as part of the 20 percent of colonial profits, or "quinto," reverting to the crown. Some later entered private and royal cabinets of curiosity, where they were admired by visitors such as Albrecht Dürer, though Anthony Pagden is right, I think, in arguing that these objects were ultimately "context-less" (*European Encounters with the New World from Renaissance to Romanticism* [New Haven: Yale University Press, 1993], 33). On the history of early Mexican collections, see Rafael Garcia Granados, *Antigüedades mejicanas en Europa* (Mexico City: n.p., 1942); D. Heikamp, "American Objects in Italian Collections of the Renaissance and Baroque: A Survey," in *First Images of America: The Impact of the New World on the Old,* ed. Fredi Chiappelli, Michael J. B. Allen, and Robert Louis Benson, 2 vols. (Berkeley: University of California Press, 1976), 1:445–82; and Anthony Alan Shelton, "Cabinets of Transgression: Renaissance Collections and the Incorporation of the New World," in *The Cultures of Collecting,* ed. John Elsner and Roger Cardinal (Cambridge: Harvard University Press, 1994), 177–203. For a larger overview, see Adrian Locke, "Exhibitions and Collectors of Pre-Hispanic Mexican Artefacts in Britain," in *Aztecs,* ed. Eduardo Matos Moctezuma and Felipe Solis Olguin (London: Royal Academy of Arts, 2002), 80–87.

7. "Six Months in Mexico," *The Literary Gazette and Journal of the Belles Lettres, Arts, Sciences,* 19 June 1824, 390.

8. For readings of the exhibits' significance in the history of Mesoamerican archaeology see John B. Glass, *Mexican Indian Pictorial Mss. Historic Collections. I. William Bullock and the Old Collection of Pictorial Manuscripts in the Mexican National Museum of Anthropology, Handbook of Middle American Indians.* HMAI Working Papers: 32 (Washington: Library of Congress, 1962) and Ian Graham, "Three Early Collectors in Mesoamerica," in *Collecting the Pre-Columbian Past,* ed. Elizabeth Hill

Boone (Washington: Dumbarton Oaks, 1993), 49–80; for their place in the history of British popular spectacle, see Richard D. Altick, *The Shows of London* (Cambridge: Belknap Press, 1978), 246–48. Nigel Leask locates Bullock at the terminus of a long history of travel writing motivated by curiosity. His contrast between Humboldt's high scientific idealism and Bullock's "burlesque" embrace of worldly gain, however, minimizes Bullock's adroit handling of scientific procedures and powerful representational practices, such as plaster casting, taxidermy, the use of panoramic backgrounds, and the assembling of habitat groups. Leask also discounts the show's ethnographic dimension, which I find fundamental to the larger pre-Columbian discourse it helped engender (Nigel Leask, *Curiosity and the Aesthetics of Travel Writing, 1770–1840: 'From an Antique Land'* [Oxford: Oxford University Press, 2002], 299–314). The most complete study in Spanish of Bullock's travel narrative is by Juan A. Ortega y Medina, who places Bullock within the context of early British travelers to Mexico ("Estudio Preliminar," in *Seis meses de residencia y viajes en México* [Mexico City: Banco de México, 1983], 7–49).

9. Mary Louise Pratt, *Imperial Eyes: Travel Writing and Transculturation* (New York: Routledge, 1992), 7.

10. "Travels and Acquisitions in Mexico [by Mr. Bullock]," *London Times,* 12 January 1824, 3b.

11. Jean Franco, "A Not-So Romantic Journey: British Travelers to South America, 1818–1828," in *Critical Passions: Selected Essays,* ed. Mary Louise Pratt and Kathleen Newman (Durham: Duke University Press, 1999), 133.

12. P. J. Cain and A. G. Hopkins, *British Imperialism: Innovation and Expansion, 1688–1914* (London: Longman, 1993), 26.

13. Benjamin Disraeli and J. A. W. Gunn, *Benjamin Disraeli Letters,* 5 vols. (Toronto: University of Toronto Press, 1982), 1:194.

14. Critics are beginning to investigate how nineteenth-century writers profited from their colonial investments; see, for example, Nancy Henry, "George Eliot and the Colonies," *Victorian Literature and Culture* 29, no. 2 (2001): 413–43.

15. Disraeli, *Letters,* 1:28.

16. Benjamin Disraeli and Lucas Alamán, *The Present State of Mexico: As Detailed in a Report Presented to the General Congress, by the Secretary of State for the Home Department and Foreign Affairs, at the Opening of the Session in 1825; with Notes, and a Memoir of Don Lucas Alaman* (London, 1825), 12, 10.

17. Benjamin Disraeli, *Lawyers and Legislators; or, Notes on the American Mining Companies* (London, 1825), 24.

18. Ibid., 8, emphasis in original.

19. Harriet Martineau, George Lillie Craik, and Charles Knight, *History of the Peace: Being a History of England from 1816 to 1854. With an Introduction 1800 to 1815,* 4 vols. (Boston, 1865), 2:407; H. G. Ward, *Mexico,* 2nd ed., 2 vols. (London, 1829), v.

20. Ward, *Mexico,* 1:iii. Ward took special aim at Bullock, disparaging him as "a real enthusiast about his mine," and giving a memorable description of Bullock's return to Mexico in 1826, accompanied by his "family, fourteen Irish miners, a smelter, a

gardener, and every thing necessary for a large establishment" (2:153). Another contemporary traveler to Mexico, the British naval office and mine commissioner G. F.
Lyon, reports that by his return journey to Mexico in 1826–27, Bullock was well aware
of "how mistaken he was in the grand ideas he had formed of this country, and how
much he has misled his countrymen in regard to the fertility of Mexico" (*Journal of
Residence and Tour in the Republic of Mexico in the Year 1826,* 2 vols. [London, 1828],
2:125). The 1820s produced an extensive literature on New World mining; for a
modern synthesis, see Robert W. Randall, *Real Del Monte: A British Mining Venture
in Mexico* (Austin: University of Texas Press, 1972). For the larger context of British
investment in Latin America, see Leland Hamilton Jenks, *The Migration of British
Capital to 1875* (London: J. Cape, 1938); Rory Miller, *Britain and Latin America in
the Nineteenth and Twentieth Centuries* (London: Longman, 1993); D. C. M. Platt,
Latin America and British Trade, 1806–1914 (London: Adam and Charles Black, 1972);
and J. Fred Rippy, *British Investments in Latin America: A Case Study in the Operations of Private Enterprise in Retarded Regions* (Minneapolis: University of Minnesota
Press, 1959).

   21. David Bushnell and Neill Macaulay, *The Emergence of Latin America in the
Nineteenth Century,* 2nd ed. (New York: Oxford University Press, 1994), 39; Carlos
Marichal, *A Century of Debt Crises in Latin America, 1820–1930* (Princeton: Princeton
University Press, 1989).

   22. Barbara A. Tenenbaum and James N. McElveen, "From Speculative to Sub-
stantive Boom: The British in Mexico, 1821–1911," in *English-Speaking Communities in
Latin America,* ed. Oliver Marshall (London: Palgrave, 2000), 52, 55. As Tenenbaum
points out, by 1835 fifty-five British merchant houses were operating in Mexico, with
most having intimate ties to the diplomatic establishment and a significant influence
on British policy (52–53).

   23. William Wordsworth, *The Letters of William and Dorothy Wordsworth, The
Later Years, 1821–28,* ed. Alan G. Hill, vol. 4, pt. 1 (Oxford: Clarendon Press, 1978),
260.

   24. Roland Barthes, "The World as Object," in *A Barthes Reader,* ed. Susan Sontag
(New York: Hill and Wang, 1982), 67.

   25. The originals of these monuments can be seen today in the Museo Nacional in
Mexico City. For a discussion of Bullock's work in the development of plaster casting,
see Diana Fane, "Reproducing the Pre-Columbian Past: Casts and Models in Exhibitions of Ancient America, 1824–1935," in Boone, ed., *Collecting the Pre-Columbian
Past,* 141–76.

   26. Bruno Latour, *Science in Action: How to Follow Scientists and Engineers through
Society* (Cambridge: Harvard University Press, 1987), 223.

   27. Several objects also went to the Society of Antiquaries of Scotland, now the
Royal Museum of Scotland. A notice in the *Literary Gazette* suggested that had the
British Museum not acquired the collection, Lord Grenville was prepared to purchase
it for donation to the collections at Oxford ("Fine Arts," *Literary Gazette and Journal
of the Belles Lettres, Arts, Sciences,* 24 Dec. 1825, 828).

28. Information about the museum's pre-Columbian holdings before 1830 is sketchy, and no complete list of the many individual collections acquired since then has ever been published. In the entry on the British Museum, the *Microcosm of London* describes a room with "two mummies, various models of works of art, weapons of the ancient Britons, Mexican idols, Chinese and Indian models, &c. and the celebrated portrait of Oliver Cromwell by Cooper" (Rudolph Ackermann et al., *Microcosm of London,* 3 vols. [London: 1808–11], 1:13). The Mexican artifacts, however, were omitted from the 1814 edition of the British Museum synopsis of the collections (British Museum, *Synopsis of the Contents of the British Museum,* 7th ed. [London: 1814]). Annually issued, the *Synopsis* offers a snapshot of prominent museum holdings and how they were displayed. Most of the museum's pre-Columbian collections, alas, have never been exhibited, banished to a warehouse in north London where they sit in wooden crates. Accession records for the collections are held in the British Museum, Department of Ethnography, and original correspondence pertaining to acquisition in the museum's central archives. Other relevant documents lie scattered among the Foreign and Colonial Office archives at the Public Record Office and in the Parliamentary Papers on the British Museum. For the history of European and American collecting of Mesoamerican objects more broadly see Boone, ed., *Collecting the Pre-Columbian Past;* Anne-Marie Hocquenghem, Peter Tamasi, and Christiane Villain-Gandossi, eds., *Pre-Columbian Collections in European Museums* (Budapest: Akademiai Kiado, 1987).

29. Johannes Fabian, *Time and the Other: How Anthropology Makes Its Object* (New York: Columbia University Press, 1983), 31–32.

30. Pratt, *Imperial Eyes,* 135.

31. For short biographical treatments, see Edward P. Alexander, "William Bullock: Little-Remembered Museologist and Showman," *Curator* 28, no. 2 (1985): 117–45; Altick, *Shows of London,* 235–52; Graham, "Three Early Collectors"; Wilbur S. Shepperson, "William Bullock: An American Failure," *Bulletin of the Historical and Philosophical Society of Ohio* 19 (1961): 144–52; and Jessie M. Sweet, "William Bullock's Collection and the University of Edinburgh, 1819," *Annals of Science* 26, no. 1 (1970): 23–32.

32. Alexander, "William Bullock," 119.

33. Nicholas Thomas, "Licensed Curiosity: Cook's Pacific Voyages," in Elsner and Cardinal, eds., *The Cultures of Collecting,* 122. See also part one, section one of Edmund Burke, *A Philosophical Enquiry into the Origin of Our Ideas of the Sublime and the Beautiful,* ed. Adam Phillips (Oxford: Oxford University Press, 1990).

34. Barbara M. Benedict, *Curiosity: A Cultural History of Early Modern Inquiry* (Chicago: University of Chicago Press, 2001), 181. For Sloane's interest in ethnography, see H. J. Braunholtz, *Sir Hans Sloane and Ethnography* (London: Trustees of the British Museum, 1970) and J. C. H. King, "Ethnographic Collections; Collecting in the Context of Sloane's Catalogue of 'Miscellanies'," in *Sir Hans Sloane: Collector, Antiquary, Founding Father of the British Museum,* ed. Arthur MacGregor (London: British Museum Press, 1994).

35. William Bullock to the Earl of Liverpool, 24 April 1813, Add. MSS, 38252, f. 265, British Library.

36. William Bullock, *A Companion to Mr. Bullock's Museum, Containing a Brief Description of Upwards of Seven Thousand Natural and Foreign Curiosities, Antiquities, and Productions of the Fine Arts, Collected Principally at Liverpool, During Several Years of Arduous Research, and at an Expence of Upwards of Twenty-Two Thousand Pounds, and Now Open for Public Inspection, in the Great Room, No. 22, Piccadilly, London . . .*, 8th ed. (London, 1810).

37. William Bullock, *A Treatise on the Art of Preserving Objects of Natural History, Intended for the Use of Sportsmen, Travellers, and Others* (London, 1818), 34.

38. John Rippingham, *Natural History, According to the Linnaean System, Explained by Familiar Dialogues in Visits to the London Museum,* 4 vols. (London, 1815).

39. Bullock perfected this important representational technique a century before Carl Akeley, whom Donna Haraway credits with the idea (*Primate Visions: Gender, Race and Nature in the World of Modern Science* [New York: Routledge, 1989], 37). Bullock's use of painted backdrops also anticipates the visual techniques described by Haraway in her discussion of the American Museum of Natural History.

40. Susan M. Pearce, *On Collecting: An Investigation into Collecting in the European Tradition* (London: Routledge, 1995), 130.

41. On the path of the Rosetta Stone to Bloomsbury, see Jeanette Greenfield, *The Return of Cultural Treasures* (Cambridge: Cambridge University Press, 1989), 136–37, who also discusses the Elgin Marbles debate at some length. For the fullest treatment of the controversy, see William St. Clair, *Lord Elgin and the Marbles* (Oxford: Oxford University Press, 1998).

42. H. M. Colvin, *A Biographical Dictionary of English Architects, 1660–1840* (London: John Murray, 1954), 507. For a compact history of the Egyptian Hall, long since a victim of the wrecking ball, see volume 29 of the *Survey of London. The Parish of St. James Westminster. Part One: South of Piccadilly,* ed. F. H. W. Sheppard (London: University of London, 1960), 266–70.

43. Edward Said, *Orientalism* (New York: Vintage Books, 1979), 42.

44. For the Egyptomania craze, see James Stevens Curl, *Egyptomania: The Egyptian Revival, A Recurring Theme in the History of Taste* (Manchester: Manchester University Press, 1994) and Dominic Montserrat, *Akhenaten: History, Fantasy, and Ancient Egypt* (London: Routledge, 2000). On the broader link between collecting and imperial self-fashioning see Brian Dolan, *Exploring European Frontiers: British Travellers in the Age of Enlightenment* (New York: St. Martin's Press, 2000).

45. Jane Austen, *Jane Austen's Letters to Her Sister Cassandra and Others,* ed. R. W. Chapman, 2nd ed. (Oxford: Oxford University Press, 1952), 267.

46. James Clifford, *The Predicament of Culture: Twentieth-Century Ethnography, Literature, and Art* (Cambridge: Harvard University Press, 1988), 217.

47. Bullock, *Treatise,* 34.

48. W. Bullock and Marie Tussaud, *The Military Carriage of Napoleon Buonaparte, Taken after the Battle of Waterloo; Together with Its Superb and Curious Contents and*

Appendages: Now Exhibiting at the Bazaar, Baker Street, Portman Square; Accurately Described (London, 1843); Jean Hornn and W. Bullock, *The Narrative of Jean Hornn, Military Coachman to Napoleon Bonaparte,* 2nd ed. (London, 1816).

49. Graham, "Three Early Collectors," 56.

50. Bullock and Tussaud, *Military Carriage,* 10, 11.

51. For discussions of Baartman, see, among many others: Yvette Abrahams, "Images of Sara Bartman: Sexuality, Race, and Gender in Early-Nineteenth-Century Britain," in *Nation, Empire, Colony: Historicizing Gender and Race,* ed. Ruth Roach Pierson and Nupur Chaudhuri (Bloomington: Indiana University Press, 1998), 220–36; Sander Gilman, *Difference and Pathology: Stereotypes of Sexuality, Race and Madness* (Ithaca: Cornell University Press, 1985), 76–108; and Anca Vlasopolos, "Venus Live! Sarah Bartmann, the Hottentot Venus, Re-Membered," *Mosaic: A Journal for the Interdisciplinary Study of Literature* 33, no. 4 (2001): 129–43. Tony Bennett discusses how the fair and other forms of spectacle continued to haunt the modern museum as a "still extant embodiment of the 'irrational' and 'chaotic' disorder that had characterized the museum's precursors" (*The Birth of the Museum: History, Theory, Politics* [London: Routledge, 1995], 3).

52. See Susan M. Pearce, "Giovanni Battista Belzoni's Exhibition of the Reconstructed Tomb of Pharoah Seti I in 1821," *Journal of the History of Collections* 12, no. 1 (2000): 109–25; and Leask, *Curiosity,* 128–56.

53. Altick, *Shows of London,* 273–75.

54. Timothy Mitchell, *Colonising Egypt* (Berkeley: University of California Press, 1991), 2; Latour, *Science in Action,* 220.

55. "Some Observations Caused by the Recent Introduction by Mr. Bullock into England of Various Rare and Curious Specimens of Mexican Antiquity; Intended Shortly to Be Submitted by Him to the Inspection of the Public," *Classical Journal* 29 (1824): 186. In *The Predicament of Culture,* James Clifford describes "salvage ethnography" as a "geopolitical, historical paradigm that has organized western practices of 'art- and culture-collecting'" (121). See Clifford's related discussion in "On Ethnographic Allegory," in *Writing Culture: The Poetics and Politics of Ethnography,* ed. James Clifford and George E. Marcus (Berkeley: University of California Press, 1986), 98–121.

56. Jean Baudrillard, "The System of Collecting," in Elsner and Cardinal, eds., *The Cultures of Collecting,* 7.

57. Arjun Appadurai, "Introduction: Commodities and the Politics of Value," in *The Social Life of Things: Commodities in Cultural Perspective,* ed. Arjun Appadurai (Cambridge: Cambridge University Press, 1986), 28.

58. Susan Stewart, *On Longing: Narratives of the Miniature, the Gigantic, the Souvenir, the Collection* (Baltimore: The Johns Hopkins University Press, 1984), 156.

59. Bullock later hired Papworth to design his utopian community, Hygeia, in Kentucky, the drawings for which are preserved in the Royal Institute for British Architects.

60. The Irish peer Viscount Kingsborough was a frequent visitor to Bullock's exhibit. In 1830 he published the lavishly illustrated *Antiquities of Mexico* in nine

massive volumes, one of the most extraordinary pictorial works of the nineteenth century. Despite its improbable theory of Hebrew settlement in Mexico, the work had an enormous influence, inspiring travelers such as John Lloyd Stephens and Frederick Catherwood, whose journeys, as I discuss in chapter 3, gave popular expression for the first time to Maya culture. See Ian Graham, "Lord Kingsborough, Sir Thomas Phillipps and Obadiah Rich: Some Bibliographical Notes," in Norman Hammond, ed., *Social Process in Maya Prehistory: Studies in Honour of Sir Eric Thompson* (London: Academic Press, 1977), 45–55; and Ignacio Bernal, "Maya Antiquaries," in *Social Process in Maya Prehistory,* 19–43.

61. "Mexican Curiosities," *New Monthly Magazine* 12 (1824): 163.

62. Latour, *Science,* 220.

63. Martin Green, *Dreams of Adventure, Deeds of Empire* (New York: Basic Books, 1979), 26.

64. "Sketches of Society," *The Literary Gazette and Journal of the Belles Lettres, Arts, Sciences,* 10 Apr. 1824, 237. The emphasis on eyewitness observation distinguished Bullock's work from eighteenth-century histories of the Americas, such as William Robertson's *History of America* (1777) and Cornelius de Pauw's *Recherches philosophiques sur les Américains* (1768), which denied that New World indigenes were capable of advanced civilization. The Aztec temples, Robertson wrote, "do not seem to have been such as entitled them to the high praises bestowed upon them by many Spanish authors. . . . Such structures convey no high idea of progress in art and ingenuity; and one can hardly conceive that a form more rude and simple could have occurred to a nation, in its first efforts towards erecting any great work" (2:298).

For discussions of Robertson and de Pauw within the larger European debate about the Americas see Benjamin Keen, *The Aztec Image in Western Thought* (New Brunswick: Rutgers University Press, 1971), 260–63; and Ignacio Bernal, *A History of Mexican Archaeology: The Vanished Civilizations of Middle America,* trans. Ruth Malet (London: Thames and Hudson, 1980), 68–69.

65. [Benjamin Disraeli], *An Inquiry into the Plans, Progress, and Policy of the American Mining Companies* (London, 1825), 3. Diego Sarmiento de Acuña, conde de Gondomar (1567?–1626) was the Spanish ambassador to England during the reign of James I; he demanded Raleigh's execution in 1618.

66. Ian Cameron, *To the Farthest Ends of the Earth: The History of the Royal Geographical Society, 1830–1980* (London: Macdonald, 1980), 16; D. Graham Burnett, *Masters of All They Surveyed: Exploration, Geography, and a British El Dorado* (Chicago: University of Chicago Press, 2000), 33–44.

67. Quoted in Kate Flint, *The Victorians and the Visual Imagination* (Cambridge: Cambridge University Press, 2000), 285.

68. "Commemoration of the Reign of Queen Elizabeth," *Geographical Journal* 21, no. 6 (1903): 589–610.

69. Ibid., 603.

70. William S. Maltby, *The Black Legend in England: The Development of Anti-Spanish Sentiment, 1558–1660* (Durham: Duke University Press, 1971), 13.

71. "Some Observations," 177.

72. Bruno Latour, "Drawing Things Together," in *Representation in Scientific Practice*, ed. Michael Lynch and Steve Woolgar (Cambridge: MIT Press, 1990), 40; emphasis in original.

73. William Swainson, "A Synopsis of the Birds Discovered in Mexico by W. Bullock, F.L.S. and H.S., and Mr. William Bullock Jun.," *Philosophical Magazine* 1 (1827): 364–69; 433–42. The quote here is from 364.

74. Latour, "Drawing," 40.

75. Appadurai, "Introduction," 15, 5.

76. Bullock was not the only traveler to Mexico to combine commercial and antiquarian interests. During his visit in Mexico, George F. Lyon reports dining with Robert Manning, partner with William Marshall in a British merchant house in Mexico, where he observed his "very pretty collection of Indian antiquities"; also in attendance that evening was William Bullock (*Journal of Residence*, 2: 125). In 1836, James Vetch, superintendent of the Real del Monte mining company, sold a fine cache of Mexican antiquities to the British Museum and published a learned discussion of New World antiquities ("On the Monuments and Relics of the Ancient Inhabitants of New Spain," *Journal of the Royal Geographical Society* 7 [1837]: 1–11). Vetch pointed out that he procured the collection at a time when, because of internal strife, Mexican laws against export were not being enforced (James Vetch to British Museum Trustees, 19 August 1836, Original Papers, Central Archives, British Museum).

77. Mauricio Tenorio-Trillo, *Mexico at the World's Fairs: Crafting a Modern Nation* (Berkeley: University of California Press, 1996).

78. Clifford, "Ethnographic Allegory," 113, 112, 117.

79. Pratt, *Imperial Eyes*, 146–51.

80. [Lucas Alamán], *Memoria que el Secretario de Estado y del Despacho de Relaciones Esteriores é Interiores presenta al Soberano Congreso Constituyente sobre los negocios de la secretaria de su cargo. Leida en la sesion de 8 Noviembre de 1823* (Mexico City, 1823). On the early development of Mexican museums, see Bernal, *History*, 130–41; Luis Castillo Ledón, *El Museo Nacional de arqueología, historia y etnografía, 1825–1925: Reseña histórica escrita para la celebración de su primer centenario* (Mexico City: Museo Nacional de Arqueología, 1924); Miguel Angel Fernández, *Historia de los museos de México* (Mexico City: Promotora de Comercialización Directa, 1988); Luis Gerardo Morales Moreno, *Orígenes de la museología mexicana: Fuentes para el estudio histórico del Museo Nacional, 1780–1840* (Mexico City: Universidad Iberoamericana, 1994); idem, "History and Patriotism in the National Museum of Mexico," in *Museums and the Making of "Ourselves": The Role of Objects in National Identity*, ed. Flora E. S. Kaplan (London: Leicester University Press, 1994), 171–91. For a review of the legal and philosophical traditions behind the historical protection of Mexican monuments, see Julio César Olivé Negrete, "Reseña histórica del pensamiento legal sobre arqueología," in *Arqueología y derecho en México*, ed. Jaime Litvak King, Luis González R., and María del Refugio González (Mexico City: UNAM, 1980), 19–46.

81. William Bullock to British Museum Trustees, 8 July 1825, Original Papers, Central Archives, British Museum.

82. "Mexican Curiosities," 168.

83. Carlos María de Bustamante, *Mañanas de la alameda de México* (1835; Mexico City: Instituto de Bellas Artes, 1986), xii.

84. Ibid., xiii.

85. Isidro R. Gondra, "Esplicación de las láminas pertenecientes a la historia antigua de México . . . ," in W. H. Prescott, *Historia de la conquista de México, por W.H. Prescott,* 3 vols. (Mexico City: Ignacio Cumplido, 1844–46), 3:10. Bullock indicates that some of the codices were lent to him on condition of their return to Mexico, but when and how they were returned remains a mystery. The pamphlet issued for the 1828 New York production of Bullock's panorama of Mexico (see next chapter) states that the "picture histories" Bullock took to England "are now returned to the Archives in Mexico," perhaps, as Graham suggests, on the occasion of Bullock's later visit to Mexico in 1826 (Robert Burford, *Description of the Panorama of the Superb City of Mexico . . . Now Open for Public Inspection at the Rotunda, New-York* [New York, 1828], 3; Graham, "Three Early Collectors," 65).

86. Catalina Rodríguez Lazcano, "La interpretación nacional (1821–1854)," in *La antropología en México: Panorama histórico,* ed. Carlos García Mora and Arturo España Caballero (Mexico City: INAH, 1987), 288.

87. Octavio Paz, *Claude Lévi-Strauss o el nuevo festín de Esopo, serie de volador* (Mexico City: J. Moritz, 1967), 83. Paz's comments on the *Coatlicue* are germane here: "Our critics wax ecstatic about the statue of *Coatlicue,* an enormous block of petrified theology. Have they ever *looked* at it? Pedantry and heroism, sexual puritanism and ferocity, calculation and delirium: a people made up of warriors and priests, astrologers and immolators" (Paz, *The Other Mexico: Critique of the Pyramid,* trans. Lysander Kemp [New York: Grove, 1972], 93).

88. Anthony Alan Shelton, "Dispossessed Histories: Mexican Museums and the Institutionalization of the Past," *Cultural Dynamics* 7, no. 1 (1995): 79. Creole ambivalence is also evident in the relationship Mexican museum directors sought to forge with the British Museum. The "Book of Presents" in the British Museum's central archives records a gift, delivered through Vicente Rocafuerte in 1830, of two wax figures and a "folio volume containing descriptions and lithographic engravings of Mexican antiquities, from the Directors of the National Museum of Mexico" (2: 70–71). The folio was certainly the very rare *Colección de las antigüedades mexicanas que ecsisten en el museo nacional,* ed. Isidro Gondra and Isidro Icaza (Mexico City, 1827), the first publication of the museum, a first edition of which is preserved in the British Library (Shelfmark 557*.h.23). On the larger question of Creole attitudes toward the pre-Hispanic past, see also J. Jorge Klor de Alva, "The Postcolonization of the (Latin) American Experience; a Reconsideration of 'Colonialism,' 'Postcolonialism' and 'Mestizaje,'" in *After Colonialism: Imperial Histories and Postcolonial Displacements,* ed. Gyan Prakash (Princeton: Princeton University Press, 1995), 241–75; D. A. Brading, *The First America: The Spanish Monarchy, Creole Patriots, and the Liberal*

State, 1492–1867 (Cambridge: Cambridge University Press, 1991); and John Leddy
Phelan, "New-Aztecism in the 18th Century and the Genesis of Mexican National-
ism," in *Culture in History, Essays in Honor of Paul Radin,* ed. Stanley Diamond (New
York: Columbia University Press, 1960), 760–70.

89. H[ilarion] Romero Gil, "Dictamen presentado á la Sociedad de Geografía y
Estadística por la comision especial que suscribe con objeto de pedir al Supremo Gob-
ierno que declare propiedad nacional los monumentos arqueológicos de la República," *Boletín de la Sociedad Mexicana de Geografía y Estadística* 8, no. 9 (1862): 440.

2. BUENA VISTA

1. Bruno Latour, *Science in Action: How to Follow Scientists and Engineers through
Society* (Cambridge: Harvard University Press, 1987), 215–57.

2. Angela Miller, "The Panorama, the Cinema, and the Emergence of the Spectacular," *Wide Angle* 18, no. 2 (1996): 36.

3. William Wordsworth, *The Prelude; or Growth of a Poet's Mind,* in *Selected Poems
and Prefaces,* ed. Jack Stillinger (Boston: Houghton Mifflin, 1965), 7:241–42; John
Ruskin, *Praeterita; Outlines of Scenes and Thoughts Perhaps Worthy of Memory in My
Past Life* (London: Rupert Hart-Davis, 1949), 105. For discussions of the panorama in
The Prelude, see Ross King, "Wordsworth, Panoramas, and the Prospect of London,"
Studies in Romanticism 32 (1993): 57–73; and Philip Shaw, "'Mimic Sights': A Note
on the Panorama and Other Indoor Displays in Book 7 of *The Prelude,*" *Notes and
Queries* 40 (1993): 462–64.

4. Walter Benjamin, "Paris, Capital of the Nineteenth Century," in *Reflections:
Essays, Aphorisms, Autobiographical Writing,* trans. Edmund Jephcott (New York:
Schocken Books, 1986), 149. William Henry Fox Talbot took the first panoramic
photographs in the mid-1840s; subsequently, the technique was widely used in expe-
ditionary and colonial photography. For the case of India, see Vidya Dehejia and
Charles Allen, eds., *India through the Lens: Photography 1840–1911* (Washington: Freer
Gallery of Art and Arthur M. Sackler Gallery, 2000); for mid-nineteenth-century
Mexico, see Keith Davis, *Desire Charnay, Expeditionary Photographer* (Albuquerque:
University of New Mexico Press, 1981), 68–71. Discussions of the relationship between
the panorama and cinema can be found in Miller, "The Panorama"; Christopher
Kent, "Spectacular History as an Ocular Discipline," *Wide Angle* 18, no. 3 (1996): 1–21;
and Bernard Comment, *The Painted Panorama,* trans. Anne-Marie Glasheen (New
York: H. N. Abrams, 2000).

5. Richard D. Altick, *The Shows of London* (Cambridge: Belknap Press, 1978); and
Stephan Oettermann, *The Panorama: History of a Mass Medium,* trans. Deborah Lucas
Schneider (New York: Zone Books, 1997). Ralph Hyde, *Panoramania! The Art and
Entertainment of the 'All-Embracing' View* (London: Barbican Art Gallery, 1988); and
Peter Galassi, *Before Photography: Painting and the Invention of Photography* (New
York: Museum of Modern Art, 1981), locate the panorama, respectively, in the realm
of the fine arts and photography. In a rich discussion of the panorama's relation to the

literary that draws on Jurgen Habermas's conception of the public sphere, William H. Galperin focuses on the "conflict between a conventional aesthetic and a newer, more public desideratum, which the Panorama can be said to have both cultivated and satisfied" (*The Return of the Visible in British Romanticism* [Baltimore: The Johns Hopkins University Press, 1993], 40). See also Nigel Leask for a suggestive reading of Robert Ker Porter's panoramas in relationship to romantic exoticism, with special reference to Humboldt ("'Wandering through Eblis': Absorption and Containment in Romantic Exoticism," in *Romanticism and Colonialism: Writing and Empire, 1780–1830*, ed. Tim Fulford and Peter J. Kitson [Cambridge: Cambridge University Press, 1998], 165–88).

6. Nancy Armstrong, *Fiction in the Age of Photography: The Legacy of British Realism* (Cambridge: Harvard University Press, 1999), 30; Susan Buck-Morss, *The Dialectics of Seeing: Walter Benjamin and the Arcades Project* (Cambridge: MIT Press, 1989); Anne Friedberg, *Window Shopping: Cinema and the Postmodern* (Berkeley: University of California Press, 1993); and Walter Benjamin, *The Arcades Project,* trans. Howard Eiland and Kevin McLaughlin (Cambridge: Belknap Press, 1999).

7. Benjamin, "Paris," 160.

8. Jeremy Bentham, *Panopticon; or, The Inspection House: Containing the Idea of a New Principle of Construction Applicable to any Sort of Establishment, in which Persons of any Description are to be Kept under Inspection,* in *The Works of Jeremy Bentham,* ed. John Bowring (Edinburgh, 1843), 4:39.

9. Michel Foucault, *Discipline and Punish: The Birth of the Prison,* trans. Alan Sheridan (New York: Vintage Books, 1979), esp. 195–228.

10. Bentham, *Panopticon,* 43.

11. On the relationship of the panopticon and the prison to structures of consciousness in eighteenth-century literature, see John Bender, *Imagining the Penitentiary: Fiction and the Architecture of Mind in Eighteenth-Century England* (Chicago: University of Chicago Press, 1987). The panoptical dream (and Orwellian nightmare) of total vision still has its adherents. In 2002, U.S. Adm. John Poindexter promoted an electronic surveillance system called "Total Information Awareness"; its panoramic emblem was a human eye embedded in the peak of a pyramid; its panoptical motto was "scientia est potentia" or "knowledge is power" (John Markoff, "Poindexter's Still a Technocrat, Still a Lightning Rod," *New York Times,* 20 January 2003, http://www.nytimes.com/2003/01/20/business/20POIN.html [accessed 20 January 2003]).

12. Foucault, *Discipline,* 228.

13. David Wilson, "Millbank, the Panopticon, and Their Victorian Audiences," *Howard Journal* 41, no. 4 (2002): 369.

14. Miriam A. Williford, *Jeremy Bentham on Spanish America: An Account of His Letters and Proposals to the New World* (Baton Rouge: Louisiana State University Press, 1980), 100–101.

15. Ibid., 41, 121. See also Ricardo D. Salvatore and Carlos Aguirre, "The Birth of the Penitentiary in Latin America: Toward an Interpretive Social History of Prisons," in *The Birth of the Penitentiary in Latin America: Essays on Criminology, Prison Reform,*

and Social Control, 1830–1940, ed. Ricardo D. Salvatore and Carlos Aguirre (Austin: University of Texas Press and Institute for Latin American Studies, 1996), 1–43.

16. Mariano Egaña, *Cartas a su padre, 1824–1829* (Santiago: Sociedad de Bibliófilos Chilenos, 1948), 193–99. I am grateful to Karen Racine for this reference.

17. Foucault, *Discipline,* 202.

18. Jonathan Crary, *Techniques of the Observer: On Vision and Modernity in the Nineteenth Century* (Cambridge: MIT Press, 1990), 6, 3, 18.

19. Allan Peter Wallach, "Making a Picture of the View from Mount Holyoke," *Bulletin of the Detroit Institute of the Arts* 66 (1990): 37.

20. F. W. Fairholt, *A Dictionary of Terms in Art* (London, 1854), quoted in Martin Meisel, *Realizations: Narrative, Pictorial, and Theatrical Arts in Nineteenth-Century England* (Princeton: Princeton University Press, 1983), 61.

21. "Pompeii," *Blackwood's Edinburgh Magazine,* April 1824, 472–73.

22. Edmund Burke, *A Philosophical Enquiry into the Origin of Our Ideas of the Sublime and the Beautiful,* ed. Adam Phillips (Oxford: Oxford University Press, 1990), 59, 66.

23. Charles Dickens, *Bleak House,* ed. George Ford and Sylvère Monod (New York: W. W. Norton, 1977), 673; George Eliot, *The Mill on the Floss,* ed. Carol T. Christ (New York: W. W. Norton, 1994), 125–26. Audrey Jaffe examines this theme at greater length in *Vanishing Points: Dickens, Narrative, and the Subject of Omniscience* (Berkeley: University of California Press, 1991).

24. Wallach, "Making a Picture," 38.

25. Miller, "The Panorama," 44. Simon Schama discusses the European aesthetic of vertical ascents, including its manifestation in scrolled panoramas such as Albert Smith's ascent of Mont Blanc, which had its London premiere in 1852. Schama, however, seems unaware of the earlier staging of elevated views in stationary panoramas and mistakenly claims that the technology (and Robert Burford) emanated from America (*Landscape and Memory* [New York: Alfred A. Knopf, 1995], 447–513).

26. See Charles Dickens, "Some Account of an Extraordinary Traveller," *Household Words,* 20 April 1850, 73–77, for a memorable portrayal of the ability of a Londoner to "travel" abroad through panoramas.

27. Oettermann, *Panorama,* 110–11.

28. Gillian Russell, *The Theatres of War: Performance, Politics, and Society, 1793–1815* (Oxford: Clarendon Press, 1995), 77. Thanks to John Reed for this reference.

29. "Panoramas," *Chambers's Journal of Popular Literature, Science and Arts,* 21 January 1860, 35.

30. Edward Hertslet, *Recollections of the Old Foreign Office* (London: John Murray, 1901), 55.

31. Royal Geographical Society, "Charter," *Journal of the Royal Geographical Society* 1 (1830): vii.

32. Annie E. Coombes, *Reinventing Africa: Museums, Material Culture and Popular Imagination in Late Victorian and Edwardian England* (New Haven: Yale University Press, 1994), 3.

33. Quoted in Kevin J. Avery and Peter L. Fodera, *John Vanderlyn's Panoramic View of the Palace and Gardens of Versailles* (New York: Metropolitan Museum of Art, 1988), 30–31.

34. See the following by Robert Burford: *Description of a View of the Continent of Boothia, Discovered by Captain Ross. . . .* (London, 1834); *Description of a View of the Great Temple of Karnak . . . from Drawings Taken by Mr. F. Catherwood. . . .* (London, 1834); *Description of a View of the City of Jerusalem. . . .* (London, 1835); and *Description of a View of the City of Lima. . . .* (London, 1836). For commentary on Burford's Jerusalem panorama, see John Davis, *The Landscape of Belief: Encountering the Holy Land in Nineteenth-Century American Art and Culture* (Princeton: Princeton University Press, 1996), 56–65; and Victor W. Von Hagen, *Frederick Catherwood, Archt.* (New York: Oxford University Press, 1950), 23–37.

35. William Bullock, *Catalogue of the Exhibition, Called Modern Mexico* (London, 1824), 4.

36. Robert Burford, *Description of a View of the City of Mexico, and Surrounding Country, now Exhibiting in the Panorama, Leicester-square. Painted . . . from Drawings taken in the Summer of 1823, Brought to this Country by Mr. W. Bullock* (London, 1826), 3.

37. Ibid., 6. An 1824 review repeats the scene: "The city is . . . embosomed in a rich valley, formed by the stupendous chain of the Cordillera. The barrier which these hills form along the horizon, and the gigantic effect which they display, towering above the 'local habitations' they enclose, is admirably executed by the artists" ("Panorama of Mexico," *Repository of Arts* 7, no. 37 [1826]: 61).

38. In 1826, the same year as Bullock's panorama, George Ackermann, whose father was the book publisher Rudolph Ackermann, issued a panoramic engraving of Mexico City based on his own travels. Although drawn from a different vantage point than Bullock's, it clearly shows the panoramic style Bullock would have employed (see Ruth E. Hamilton, *México Ilustrado/Mexico Illustrated* (Chicago: Newberry Library, 1996), 48; Ted Fraser, *George Ackermann (1803–1891)* (Charlottetown, P.E.I.: Confederation Centre Art Gallery and Museum, 1999). For a modern reconstruction of Bullock's panorama, see Dante Escalante's paintings in *Viajeros europeos del siglo XIX en México* (Mexico City: Fomento Cultural Banamex, 1996), 32–35.

39. Díaz del Castillo's *Historia verdadera de la conquista de la Nueva España* (1632; ed. Joaquín Ramírez Cabañas, 3 vols. Mexico City: P. Robredo, 1939); first English version, *The True History of the Conquest of Mexico,* trans. Maurice Keatinge (London, 1800). For a study of the English translations of the Spanish narratives of encounter and conquest, see Colin Steele, *English Interpreters of the Iberian New World from Purchas to Stevens; a Bibliographical Study, 1603–1726* ([Oxford]: Dolphin Book Co., 1975).

40. Burford, *Mexico,* 6, my emphasis; cf. William Robertson, *The History of America,* 2 vols. (London, 1777), 2:50. Nigel Leask argues that nineteenth-century British travelers refigured Díaz's description of the valley of Mexico as "disappointment," citing as evidence Bullock's description in his travel narrative in which he asks, "can this, I thought to myself, be Mexico?" ("'The Ghost in Chapultepec': Fanny Calderón

De La Barca, William Prescott and Nineteenth-Century Mexican Travel Accounts," in *Voyages and Visions: Towards a Cultural History of Travel,* ed. Jas Elsner and Joan-Pau Rubies [London: Reaktion Books, 1999], 197). Leask ignores, however, how the embodiment of such views within the panorama transformed narrative description into mass spectacle, converting disappointment into collective empowerment over the image.

41. There is an enormous literature on the sublime and the picturesque; for a brisk and opinionated assessment, see Kim Ian Michasiw, "Nine Revisionist Theses on the Picturesque," *Representations* 38 (1992): 76–100.

42. Díaz del Castillo, *Historia,* 1:308. On the "marvelous" in Renaissance contact narratives with the New World, see Stephen Greenblatt, *Marvelous Possessions: The Wonder of the New World* (Chicago: University of Chicago Press, 1991), 52–85.

43. W. J. T. Mitchell, "Imperial Landscape," in *Landscape and Power,* ed. W. J. T. Mitchell (Chicago: University of Chicago Press, 1994), 9.

44. Metaphors of elevation occur throughout the early literature relating to Britain's relationship with Latin America: "Placed as England is, on the elevated political pinnacle on which she stands, it interests her to view the progress of societies in economy, legislation, and civilization, and it becomes a sacred duty, to promote the well being of a country well affected toward her" (*Interesting Official Documents Relating to the United Provinces of Venezuela* [London, 1812], xxiii).

45. Burford, *Mexico,* 5. It is important to note, however, that the history of British battle suggests that panoramic representations were complicit with territorial aggression per se, serving as an ideological counterpart to the expropriation of land from at least the Jacobite Rebellion of 1745. Michael Charlesworth has shown, for example, how the panoramic landscapes of the English landscape painter Thomas Sandby (1721–1798), taken from a high viewing platform known as the Hoober Stand, not only served the dynastic needs of the Hanoverian state, but contributed to the development of the ordnance survey, a fundamental tool in the armature of empire. Charlesworth discusses these developments in "Thomas Sandby Climbs the Hoober Stand: The Politics of Panoramic Drawing in Eighteenth-Century Britain," *Art History* 19 (1996): 247–66; and "Subverting the Command of Place: Panorama and the Romantics," in *Placing and Displacing Romanticism,* ed. Peter J. Kitson (Aldershot: Ashgate, 2001), 129–45.

46. Burford, *Mexico,* 3.

47. Ibid., 5.

48. For a related discussion of the intermingling of these forces in nineteenth-century American representations of Peru, see Deborah Poole, "Landscape and the Imperial Subject: U.S. Images of the Andes, 1859–1930," in *Close Encounters of Empire: Writing the Cultural History of U.S.–Latin American Relations,* ed. Gilbert M. Joseph, Catherine C. LeGrand, and Ricardo D. Salvatore (Durham: Duke University Press, 1998), 107–38. For American pictorial representations of South America more generally, see Katherine Emma Manthorne, *Tropical Renaissance: North American Artists Exploring Latin America, 1839–1879* (Washington: Smithsonian Institution Press, 1989).

For American landscape representation in the context of imperial politics, see Angela L. Miller, *The Empire of the Eye: Landscape Representation and American Cultural Politics, 1825–1875* (Ithaca: Cornell University Press, 1993); and Albert Boime, *The Magisterial Gaze: Manifest Destiny and American Landscape Painting, c. 1830–1865* (Washington: Smithsonian Institution Press, 1991).

49. William H. Prescott, *History of the Conquest of Mexico: with a Preliminary View of the Ancient Mexican Civilization, and the Life of the Conqueror, Hernando Cortez,* 3 vols. (Philadelphia: J. B. Lippincott, 1863). Further citations to this work are given in the text.

50. Robert Walter Johannsen, *To the Halls of the Montezumas: The Mexican War in the American Imagination* (New York: Oxford University Press, 1985), 245–48.

51. William Hickling Prescott, *The Correspondence of William Hickling Prescott,* ed. Roger Wolcott (Boston: Houghton Mifflin Company, 1925), 590.

52. Ibid., 329.

53. Recent critics of Prescott's *History* have gone to unusual lengths to defend the author against charges of imperialism. John E. Eipper argues that we must not conflate "what Prescott's writings 'did' with the historian himself" ("The Canonizer De-Canonized: The Case of William H. Prescott," *Hispania* 83, no. 3 [2000]: 421), while John Ernest claims that "Prescott worked not to promote the principles underlying the conquest but rather to situate them within a privileged sphere of detailed research" ("Reading the Romantic Past: William H. Prescott's History of the Conquest of Mexico," *American Literary History* 5, no. 2 [1993]: 233). Yet the critical issue is not what Prescott himself said or did, but how his text, which had a circulation far wider than his private statements, represented Mexico for nineteenth-century readers.

54. Mieke Bal, *Narratology: Introduction to the Theory of Narrative* (Toronto: University of Toronto Press, 1985), 104.

55. The pervasiveness of this language is attested to by a variety of contemporary sources. See, among many others: Ralph W. Kirkham, *The Mexican War: Journal and Letters of Ralph W. Kirkham,* ed. Robert Ryal Miller (College Station: Texas A & M University Press, 1991), 43; George F. Ruxton, *Adventures in Mexico* (London, 1849), 34; and Geo. S. L. Starks, "The Conqueror's First View of Mexico," *The Ladies Repository,* June 1851, 221. Most eloquent, perhaps, is the testimony of Brantz Mayer, who writes: "I have seen the Simplon—the Spluegen—the view from Rhigi—the 'wide and winding Rhine'—and the prospect from Vesuvius . . . but none of these scenes compare with the Valley of Mexico" (*Mexico as It Was and as It Is* [New York, 1844], 34).

56. Ralph Waldo Emerson, "Nature," in *Selections from Ralph Waldo Emerson: An Organic Anthology,* ed. Stephen E. Whicher (Boston: Houghton Mifflin, 1957), 23.

57. Oettermann, *Panorama,* 315.

58. Prescott, *Correspondence,* 35.

59. Von Hagen, *Catherwood,* 47–48.

60. Paul Virilio, *War and Cinema: The Logistics of Perception,* trans. Patrick Camiller (London: Verso, 1989), 7.

61. Prescott, *Correspondence,* 483.

62. Francisco López de Gómara, *Historia de la conquista de México,* ed. Jorge Gurria Lacroix (Caracas: Biblioteca Ayacucho, 1979), 106.

63. Juan de Torquemada, *Monarquía Indiana,* 5th ed., 3 vols. (Mexico City: Editorial Porrúa, 1975), 1:340–41; see also John Leddy Phelan, *The Millenial Kingdom of the Franciscans in the New World,* 2nd ed. (Berkeley: University of California Press, 1970), 29–38. On Torquemada, see José Alcina Franch, "Juan De Torquemada, 1564–1624," in *Guide to Ethnohistorical Sources,* ed. Howard F. Cline and John B. Glass, vol. 13, pt. 2, *Handbook of Middle American Indians* (Austin: University of Texas Press, 1973), 256–75; and D. A. Brading, *The First America: The Spanish Monarchy, Creole Patriots, and the Liberal State, 1492–1867* (Cambridge: Cambridge University Press, 1991), 275–92.

64. Torquemada, *Monarquía,* 1:443.

65. For the use of this trope in Columbus's writing see Tzvetan Todorov, *The Conquest of America: The Question of the Other,* trans. Richard Howard (New York: Harper and Row, 1984), 3–34, esp. 10–12.

66. Todorov, by contrast, argues that one must compare the "religious murder" of Aztec human sacrifice with the "atheistic murder" of the Spanish massacres (ibid., 144–45).

67. Quoted in William Hickling Prescott, *The Literary Memoranda of William Hickling Prescott,* ed. C. Harvey Gardiner, 2 vols. (Norman: University of Oklahoma Press, 1961), 2:116; Charles Dickens, *The Letters of Charles Dickens, Volume Four, 1844–1846,* ed. Kathleen Tillotson (Oxford: Clarendon, 1977), 4.

68. "Conquest of Mexico," *Times,* 30 Dec. 1843, 3.

69. William Hickling Prescott, *History of the Reign of Ferdinand and Isabella, the Catholic, of Spain,* 3 vols. (London, 1838).

70. Review of *History of the Conquest of Mexico, with a Preliminary View of the Ancient Mexican Civilization, and the Life of the Conqueror, Hernando Cortez,* by William H. Prescott, *Quarterly Review* 73 (1843): 299.

71. "Donnavan's Grand Serial Panorama of Mexico," undated playbill, Panorama box, Harvard Theatre Collection, Harvard College Library.

72. C. Donnavan, *Adventures in Mexico: Experienced During a Captivity of Seven Months,* 12th ed. (Boston, 1848), 124–27. Subsequent references are to this edition and are given parenthetically in the text.

73. This was also true of John Phillips's stunning pictorial work, *Mexico Illustrated* (London, 1848), which conducted the reader on a visual tour of the path of conquest, once again from Veracruz to Mexico City.

74. Ralph Waldo Emerson, *The Journals and Miscellaneous Notebooks,* 16 vols., ed. William Gilman et al. (Cambridge: Harvard University Press, 1960–82), 9:74.

75. For Landesio and Velasco, see Donald R. McCleland, "The Legacy of Mexican Landscape Painting," in *Mexico: A Landscape Revisited/Una visión de su paisaje* (Universe Publishing: New York, 1994), 13; and Justino Fernández, *El arte del siglo XIX en México* (Mexico City: Imprenta Universitaria, 1967), 80–104. A selection of lithographs from Casimiro Castro's *México y sus alrededores* (Mexico City, 1855) is reproduced in

Nación de imágines: La litografía mexicana del siglo XIX (Mexico City: Consejo Nacional para la Cultura y las Artes, 1994), 188–99. On ballooning, see Luis Reyes de la Maza, *El teatro en México durante la independencia (1810–1839)* (Mexico City: Universidad Nacional Autónoma de México, 1969), 327. The literature on foreign pictorial representations of Mexico is sizable and growing. For a good overview, see *Viajeros europeos* and Fausto Ramírez, "La visión Europa de la América tropical: Los artistas viajeros," *Historia del arte Mexicano* 7 (1982): 139–63. The later vogue for photographic representation is examined in Carole Naggar and Fred Ritchin, *Mexico through Foreign Eyes: Photographs, 1850–1990* (New York: W. W. Norton, 1993); and Olivier Debroise, *Mexican Suite: A History of Photography in Mexico,* trans. Stella de Sá Rego (Austin: University of Texas Press, 2001).

76. José F. Ramírez, "Notas y esclarecimientos a la historia de la conquista de México del Señor W. Prescott," in *Obras del. Lic. Don José Fernando Ramírez,* 3 vols. (Mexico City: Agüeros, 1898–1904), 1: 308, 312–13; emphasis in original.

77. Lucas Alamán, commentary, *Historia de la conquista de México,* ed. Juan. A. Ortega y Medina, 3rd ed. (Mexico City: Porrúa, 1985), 18.

78. In addition to Ernest and Eipper, cited above, see Eric Wertheimer, *Imagined Empires: Incas, Aztecs, and the New World of American Literature, 1771–1876* (Cambridge: Cambridge University Press, 1999), 313. For more critical approaches to Prescott as a romantic historian see David Levin, who argues that Prescott designed his work "to support a fundamental simple theme: the inevitable ruin of a rich but barbarous empire through its inherent moral faults; the triumph of 'civilization' over 'semi-civilization,' of Christianity (however imperfectly represented) over cannibalism; the triumph of Cortés' 'genius,' 'constancy,' and resourceful leadership over Montezuma's 'pusillanimity' and 'vacillation'" (*History as Romantic Art: Bancroft, Prescott, Motley, and Parkman* [Stanford: Stanford University Press, 1959], 164). Benjamin Keen's discussion attributes the *History*'s "gross historical and psychological distortions" to the "general mediocrity and conventionality of Prescott's thought" (*The Aztec Image in Western Thought* [New Brunswick: Rutgers University Press, 1971], 363); and D. A Brading to his "irredeemably liberal and Protestant" perspective (*First America,* 634).

79. William Bullock, *Six Months' Residence and Travels in Mexico* (London, 1824), 24.

80. Carlos María de Bustamante, *Mañanas de la alameda de México* (1835; Mexico City: Instituto de Bellas Artes, 1986), xii–xiii.

81. "Panorama of Mexico," *Literary Gazette and Journal of Belles Lettres, Arts, Sciences,* 17 Jun. 1825, 813.

82. Hernán Cortés, *Letters from Mexico,* trans. Anthony Pagden (New Haven: Yale University Press, 1986), 77.

83. Bernal Díaz del Castillo, *The Discovery and Conquest of Mexico, 1517–1521,* trans. A. P. Maudslay (New York: Grove Press, 1958), 159.

84. For an account of this expedition, see "Extracto del diario que escribieron los Sres. D. Guillermo y D. Federico Glennie, en su ascensión al volcán POPOCATEPETL.—Abril de 1827," *Boletín de la sociedad mexicana de geografía y estadística* 2 (1850): 215–20.

85. Brantz Mayer, who made his own journey to the summit in the early 1840s, recounts Egerton's ascent in *Mexico as It Was and as It Is* (209–16).

86. Ulysses S. Grant, *Personal Memoirs of U. S. Grant,* 2 vols. (New York, 1885), 2:180–84.

3. AGENCIES OF THE LETTER

1. Although a few historians have made passing reference to the plot, no one to my knowledge has discussed it in any detail, nor examined the huge mass of documentary evidence in British government archives. For brief notices, see John Eric Sidney Thompson, "A Note on Scherzer's Visit to Quiriguá," *Maya Research* 3, no. 3 (1936): 330–31; Frans Blom, "Explanation," *Maya Research* 3, no. 1 (1936): 92–93, which describes the plot as a "most charming and amusing incident"; Adrian Recinos, "Evocación del viaje de Scherzer y Wagner a Centroamérica, 1853–54," *Anales de la sociedad de geografía e historia de Guatemala* 27 (1953–54): 137–41; Victor Von Hagen, *Search for the Maya: The Story of Stephens and Catherwood* (Farnborough: Saxon House, 1973), 173; Edward Miller, *That Noble Cabinet: A History of the British Museum* (London: Andre Deutsch, 1973), 221–22; and Mario Rodríguez, *A Palmerstonian Diplomat in Central America: Frederick Chatfield, Esq.* (Tucson: University of Arizona Press, 1964), 361. More recently, Ian Jenkins has characterized the plot as "never more than half-hearted," and Ian Graham as merely a "trifle reprehensible" (Jenkins, *Archaeologists and Aesthetes in the Sculpture Galleries of the British Museum, 1800–1939* [London: British Museum Press, 1992], 211; Graham, *Alfred Maudslay and the Maya: A Biography* [Norman: University of Oklahoma Press, 2002], 79).

2. Bruno Latour, "Drawing Things Together," in *Representation in Scientific Practice,* ed. Michael Lynch and Steve Woolgar (Cambridge: MIT Press, 1990), 54.

3. Palmerston to Chatfield, FO15/69, f. 53. As in the preceding example, material from the Foreign Office (FO) and Colonial Office (CO) archives, held at the Public Record Office at Kew, will be cited in the text as follows: (class, volume, piece, and, where available, folio). If no folio appears, the date will be given. Incoming and outgoing correspondence from the British Museum central archives in Bloomsbury will also be cited parenthetically, abbreviated CA and followed by the date.

4. The British Museum first acquired artifacts from Nineveh in 1847; over the next few years the collection grew steadily, culminating with the establishment in 1853 of a room specifically designed for its display. On these collections and the role of Austen Henry Layard, who served as Foreign Office under-secretary in 1852, see Shawn Malley, "Austen Henry Layard and the Periodical Press: Middle Eastern Archaeology and the Excavation of Cultural Identity in Mid-Nineteenth Century Britain," *Victorian Review* 22, no. 2 (1996): 152–70; and Frederick N. Boehrer, "The Times and Spaces of History: Representation, Assyria, and the British Museum," in *Museum Culture: Histories, Discourses, Spectacles,* ed. Daniel J. Sherman and Irit Rogoff (Minneapolis: University of Minnesota, 1994), 197–222.

5. Palmerston, however, in addition to taking an active interest in Central American mining, had already become acquainted with pre-Columbian ruins early in his

second stint as foreign secretary (1835–41), when he met several times with the Central American patriot and amateur antiquarian Juan Galindo, who, as I discuss later in this chapter, was then engaged in serious archaeological research. In 1838 he also exchanged letters with Jean-Frédéric Waldeck, who was doing archaeological research in Mexico. The Newberry Library in Chicago contains an 1838 letter from Palmerston's under-secretary, William Fox-Strangways, to Waldeck, informing him that "the Box of Drawings and Papers belonging to you have arrived from Mexico and are now safely deposited in this office" (W. Fox-Strangways to Jean-Frédéric Waldeck, 18 July 1838, Ayer Ms. 1238, Edward E. Ayer Collection, The Newberry Library, Chicago). As Robert Brunhouse explains, these were copies of original archaeological drawings later seized by Mexican officials, who feared that Waldeck was planning to contravene the law against the export of antiquities by shipping artifacts abroad (*In Search of the Maya: The First Archaeologists* [Albuquerque: University of New Mexico Press, 1973], 76). Waldeck sent the drawings to London with the help of Charles Ashburnham, a British consular official in Mexico who amassed a large collection of Mexican antiquities later donated to the British Museum in 1856. For more on Waldeck see Claude F. Baudez, *Jean-Frédéric Waldeck, Peintre: Le premier explorateur des ruines Mayas* (Paris: Hazan, 1993).

6. Edgar Allen Poe, "Review of New Books," *Graham's Magazine*, August 1841, 91; William Hickling Prescott, *The Correspondence of William Hickling Prescott*, ed. Roger Wolcott (Boston: Houghton Mifflin Company, 1925), 240. As for Dickens, Central America had been on his mind for some time. In 1851 Henry Morley, working from Stephens and Catherwood, described the ruins of Copán for Dickens's *Household Words*: "What Titanic wall is that whose image is reflected in the river? . . . the fixed stare of an enormous sculptured head encounters us . . . a statue twelve feet high, loaded with hieroglyphic and with grotesque ornament. . . . These are the ruins of Copan" ("Our Phantom Ship, Central America," *Household Words*, 22 February 1851, 518). For *The Woman in White*'s borrowings of Stephens, see Richard Collins, "The Ruins of Copán in *The Woman in White*: Wilkie Collins and John Stephens's *Incidents of Travel in Central America, Chiapas, and Yucatan*," *Wilkie Collins Society Journal* ns 2 (1999): 5–17.

7. John Lloyd Stephens, *Incidents of Travel in Central America, Chiapas, and Yucatan*, 2 vols. (New York, 1841), 2:115. Further citations to this work are given in the text.

8. [William Weir and W. H. Wills], "Short Cuts across the Globe," *Household Words* 1 (1850): 66; my emphasis.

9. Lincoln S. Bates, "Pioneering Adventures," *Americas* 38 (1986): 37; and Larzer Ziff, *Return Passages: Great American Travel Writing, 1780–1910* (New Haven: Yale University Press, 2000), 91.

10. Quoted in W. Baring Pemberton, *Lord Palmerston* (London: Batchworth Press, 1954), 141.

11. On the question of travel in relation to belatedness, see Ali Behdad, *Belated Travelers: Orientalism in the Age of Colonial Dissolution* (Durham: Duke University Press, 1994).

12. Elizabeth Williams, "Collecting and Exhibiting Pre-Columbiana in France and England, 1870–1930," in *Collecting the Pre-Columbian Past,* ed. Elizabeth Hill Boone (Washington: Dumbarton Oaks, 1993), 123–40.

13. Robert A. Stafford, *Scientist of Empire: Scientific Exploration and Victorian Imperialism* (Cambridge: Cambridge University Press, 1989), 85–87.

14. Charles Eliot Norton to Ephraim G. Squier, 2 November 1851, Ephraim George Squier Papers, Library of Congress.

15. Ralph Lee Woodward, Jr., *Rafael Carrera and the Emergence of the Republic of Guatemala* (Athens: University of Georgia Press, 1993), 231.

16. For the relevant diplomatic history, see Richard W. Van Alstyne, "British Diplomacy and the Clayton-Bulwer Treaty, 1850–60," *The Journal of Modern History* 11, no. 2 (1939): 149–83; idem, "The Central American Policy of Lord Palmerston, 1846–48," *Hispanic American Historical Review* 16, no. 3 (1936): 339–59; and Robert A. Naylor, "The British Role in Central America Prior to the Clayton-Bulwer Treaty of 1850," *Hispanic American Historical Review* 40, no. 3 (1960): 361–82.

17. The British Museum central archive is a case in point. During the period I used it (1997–2000) the archive was open just two days a week from 10 A.M. to 4 P.M., with seats for only two readers. The Public Record Office, by contrast, which holds other government records governed by the Public Records Act, is open for research six days a week. Although the museum could increase access to its files by transferring the archive to the PRO, where it properly belongs under British law, it has not done so.

18. Dominick LaCapra, *History and Criticism* (Ithaca: Cornell University Press, 1985), 11.

19. On the larger contest between the United States and Britain see J. Fred Rippy, *Rivalry of the United States and Great Britain over Latin America, 1808–1830* (London: Milford, 1929).

20. For a detailed bibliography of nineteenth-century works about Central America, see Ralph Lee Woodward, Jr., *Central America, a Nation Divided* (Oxford: Oxford University Press, 1998); for the maps, see Kit S. Kapp, *The Printed Maps of Central America up to 1860,* 2 vols. (London: Map Collector's Circle, 1974–75).

21. Juan Galindo, "On Central America," *Journal of the Royal Geographical Society* 6 (1836): 119.

22. On the history of Maya archaeology, see Robert L. Brunhouse, *Search;* idem, *Pursuit of the Ancient Maya: Some Archaeologists of Yesterday* (Albuquerque: University of New Mexico Press, 1975); Ignacio Bernal, "Maya Antiquaries," in *Social Process in Maya Prehistory: Studies in Honour of Sir Eric Thompson,* ed. Norman Hammond (London: Academic Press, 1977); idem, *A History of Mexican Archaeology: The Vanished Civilizations of Middle America,* trans. Ruth Malet (London: Thames and Hudson, 1980); Gordon R. Willey and Jeremy A. Sabloff, *A History of American Archaeology,* 3rd ed. (New York: Freeman, 1993); and Jorge Cañizares-Esguerra, *How to Write the History of the New World: Histories, Epistemologies, and Identities in the Eighteenth-Century Atlantic World* (Stanford: Stanford University Press, 2001).

23. Del Río's report was translated into English thanks to the combined efforts of

one Dr. McQuy, who took it to London, and the bookseller Henry Berthoud, who issued it with seventeen engravings made by Waldeck (Brunhouse, *Search,* 14).

24. Antonio del Río, *Description of the Ruins of an Ancient City, Discovered near Palenque . . .* (London, 1822), viii.

25. Ian Graham, "Juan Galindo, Enthusiast," *Estudios de cultura Maya* 3 (1963): 12. See also William Joyce Griffith, "Juan Galindo, Central American Chauvinist," *Hispanic American Historical Review* 40, no. 1 (1960): 25–52. Galindo also removed monuments from Maya sites and shipped them to Britain. An 1847 catalogue of antiquities in the Society of Antiquaries of London lists Galindo's gift of four ornamented tablets taken from Palenque, which he presented on 7 June 1832 (Albert Way, *Catalogue of Antiquities, Coins, Pictures, and Miscellaneous Curiosities in the Possession of the Society of Antiquaries of London, 1847* [London, 1847], 55). For a further description of these artifacts, see Juan Galindo, "A Short Account of Some Antiquities Discovered in the District of Petén, in Central America," *Archaeologia* 35 (1834): 570–71.

26. Galindo's status as a British citizen by birth eventually wrecked his attempt to aid the Central American Federation. At a crucial moment in his negotiations with Palmerston, he was turned away from the Foreign Office on the grounds that no British citizen could represent another country.

27. Juan Galindo, "Ruins of Palenque," *Literary Gazette,* 15 October 1831, 665–66.

28. Juan Galindo, "Description of the River Usumacinta, in Guatemala," *Journal of the Royal Geographical Society* 3 (1833): 62. Yet, as Ignacio Bernal states: "It was not necessary to vindicate the ancient culture [of the Mayas] because this culture had not been attacked [as had the Aztecs], but rather admired from the beginning, at least as far as its art was concerned" ("Maya," 26).

29. On the political rationale for such expeditions and a discussion of Miguel Rivera Maestre, a Guatemalan scientist, engineer, and geographer who played a key role in them, see Robert H. Claxton, "Miguel Rivera Maestre: Guatemalan Scientist-Engineer," *Technology and Culture* 14, no. 3 (1973): 384–403. For Gálvez's liberal policies, see Miriam Williford, "Las luces y la civilización: The Social Reforms of Mariano Gálvez," in *Applied Enlightenment: 19th-Century Liberalism,* ed. Margaret A. L. Harrison and Robert Wauchope, Middle American Research Institute Publications, no. 23 (New Orleans: Tulane University, 1972), 33–41.

30. Juan Galindo, "Central America," *Literary Gazette,* 18 July 1835, 456. In a version of this article published by the American Antiquarian Society, the author's patriotism was even clearer. He added that "the government of Central America intends publishing, in Castillian, a long report I have drawn up with relation to the ruins and history of this place, with various plans, views, and copies of figures and inscriptions" ("Letter from Colonel Galindo to the Hon. Thomas L. Winthrop, President of the American Antiquarian Society, Boston, Massachusetts," *Archaeologia Americana. Transactions and Collections* 2 [1836]: 545). Sylvanus G. Morley discusses the fate of that report and prints it, with explanatory notes, in *The Inscriptions at Copán* (Washington: Carnegie Institution, 1920), 593–604.

31. Galindo, "Description," 59. This article appears to provide the first published

description of the ruins of Yaxchilán, on the banks of the Usumacinta, just across the river from present-day Guatemala. Later in the century, as I discuss below, Alfred P. Maudslay removed carved stone lintels from Yaxchilán and shipped them to London, where they are now on display at the British Museum.

32. Juan Galindo to Thomas L. Winthrop, 25 April 1831, Galindo MSS, American Antiquarian Society.

33. Typical is the following: Stephens and Catherwood "gave birth to the science of American archaeology . . . rais[ing] the jungle curtain that had concealed for centuries the ancient civilizations of the Maya" (Richard O'Mara, "The American Traveller," *Virginia Quarterly Review* 74, no. 2 [1998]: 221).

34. Bruce A. Harvey, *American Geographics: U.S. National Narratives and the Representation of the Non-European World, 1830–1865* (Stanford: Stanford University Press, 2001); David E. Johnson, "'Writing in the Dark': The Political Fictions of American Travel Writing," *American Literary History* 7, no. 1 (1995): 1–27; Jennifer L. Roberts, "Landscapes of Indifference: Robert Smithson and John Lloyd Stephens in Yucatán," *Art Bulletin* 82, no. 3 (2000): 544–67.

35. Among the items Stephens and Catherwood shipped back were carved wooden lintels from the sites of Kabah and Uxmal; they were destroyed in the fire that consumed Catherwood's panorama in New York (Bernal, "Maya," 34; Carl C. Dauterman, "The Strange Story of the Stephens Stones," *Natural History,* December 1939, 288–96).

36. Quoted in David M. Pendergrast, *Palenque: The Walker-Caddy Expedition to the Ancient Maya City, 1839–1840* (Norman: University of Oklahoma Press, 1967), 31, 33.

37. J. Baily, "On the Isthmus between the Lake of Granada and the Pacific; Being an Extract from a 'Memoir on the Lake of Granada, the River San Juan, and the Isthmus between the Lake and the Pacific Ocean, in the State of Nicaragua, Central America'," *Journal of the Royal Geographical Society* 14 (1844): 127–29; idem, *Central America; Describing Each of the States . . . Their Natural Features, Products, Population, and Remarkable Capacity for Colonization . . .* (London, 1850); idem, *Map of Central America . . . Shewing the Routes between the Atlantic and Pacific Oceans . . . with Additions from the Latest Surveys of the Admiralty* (London, 1853); and Domingo Juarros, *A Statistical and Commercial History of the Kingdom of Guatemala,* trans. J. Baily (London, 1823).

38. Preserved in the Brinton Collection at the University of Pennsylvania is a manuscript copy, made by Karl Hermann Berendt, of Baily's "Sketches from Quiriguá," which includes some of Baily's drawings. See item 4042 in John M. Weeks et al., *The Library of Daniel Garrison Brinton* (Philadelphia: University of Pennsylvania Museum of Archaeology and Anthropology, 2002).

39. See Luigi Berliocchi, *The Orchid in Lore and Legend,* trans. Lenore Rosenberg and Anita Watson (Portland: Timber Press, 2000), and Merle A. Reinikka, *A History of the Orchid* (Coral Gables: University of Miami Press, 1972).

40. James Bateman, "Substance of an Address Delivered before the Royal Horticultural Society at South Kensington, on Tuesday, February 19th, 1867, by James Bateman,

Esq. F.R.S.," in *Orchid History Reference Papers,* no. 7, ed. R. M. Hamilton (Richmond, B.C.: R. M. Hamilton, 1992), 2; and Peter Hayden, *Biddulph Grange, Staffordshire: A Victorian Garden Rediscovered* (London: George Philip, 1989), 46. In August 2002 the *New York Times* reported that a new species of orchid was discovered in the highlands of Peru. Within three days of its discovery, "what had been a mossy slope of 500 of the new orchids had been stripped clean [by orchid hunters], even of inch-tall seedlings" (Carol Kaesuk Yoon, "New Orchid Species Leaves Admirers Amazed," *New York Times,* 13 August 2002, http://www.nytimes.com/2002/08/13/science/life/13ORCH.html [accessed 13 August 2002]).

41. Orchids and antiquities were found together in many British private collections. Bateman's Knypersely Hall contained a collection of Central American ruins, probably collected by Skinner (Hayden, *Biddulph Grange,* 123).

42. The noted American archaeologist Ephraim George Squier—who, like Stephens, enjoyed a diplomatic appointment in Central America—sought to capitalize on his knowledge of Nicaragua by forming a transit company centered on this region. Stephens devoted his energies and capital to the Panama route.

43. Through the labors of Canadian orchid historian R. M. Hamilton, a selection of Skinner's letters is now available in print. Especially interesting are Skinner's letters to William Hooker at Kew, which show the close interrelation between the cultures of natural history and the emerging interest in pre-Columbian archaeology. See George Ure Skinner, *Orchids and Ordeals in Guatemala and England, 1830–1867: 260 Letters by George Ure Skinner and Friends,* ed. R. M. Hamilton, Orchid History Reference Papers, no. 12 (Richmond, B.C.: R. M. Hamilton, 1993).

44. On the Ackermanns' adventures in Latin America, see John Ford, *Ackermann, 1783–1983: The Business of Art* (London: Ackermann, 1983), 84–89.

45. Byron's poems are cited from *The Poems and Plays of Lord Byron,* 3 vols. (London: J. M. Dent, 1910), 1:227 and 2:35, respectively.

46. Muriel E. Chamberlain, *Lord Aberdeen: A Political Biography* (London: Longman, 1983); and Lucille Iremonger, *Lord Aberdeen: A Biography of the Fourth Earl of Aberdeen, K.G., K.T., Prime Minister 1852–1855* (London: Collins, 1978).

47. George Ure Skinner to Lord Aberdeen: 23 July 1842; 25 September 1845; and 27 September 1845. Add. Mss. 43239 and 43244, British Library. In 1844, Captain Evan Nepean wrote Aberdeen describing a large collection of Mexican antiquities he had acquired from the Isla de Sacrificios, off the eastern coast of Mexico. The letter, along with an analysis of the collection by Samuel Birch, a keeper in the antiquities department at the British Museum, was published in the journal of the Society of Antiquaries. Comprising over 1,000 objects, Nepean's collection was acquired by the British Museum in 1844. See Evan Nepean and Samuel Birch, "Letter from Captain Nepean, to the Right Hon. The Earl of Aberdeen, K.T., President, Communicating an Account of Certain Antiquities Excavated, under His Direction, in the Island of Sacrificios: Followed by a Report Upon the Examination of Them, by Samuel Birch," *Archaeologia* 30 (1844): 138–43.

48. House of Commons, "Report from the Select Committee of the House of

Lords, Appointed to Inquire into the Operation of the Act 3 & 4 Will. 4, C. 85, for the Better Government of Her Majesty's Indian Territories," *Parliamentary Papers*, 1852–53, 21 June 1852, vol. 30, 301. The link between writing, influence from afar, and imperial administration is also evident in an extraordinary report by the Board of Trade on the subject of Latin America, issued in 1846, which was comprised almost entirely of verbatim excerpts from British travel accounts. The report did not confine itself to economic matters, but addressed the manners, customs, and racial character-istics of Latin American peoples, all filtered through the prejudices and exclusions of travel writing. See Board of Trade, *Commercial Tariffs and Regulations, Resources, and Trade, of the Several States of Europe and America, Together with the Commercial Treaties between England and Foreign Countries. Part the Sixteenth. States of Mexico* (London, 1846).

49. Quoted in D. M. Young, *The Colonial Office in the Early Nineteenth Century* (London: Longmans, 1961), 137.

50. Latour, "Drawing," 55.

51. See, among others: April Alliston, *Virtue's Faults: Correspondences in Eighteenth-Century British and French Women's Fiction* (Stanford: Stanford University Press, 1996); Elizabeth Heckendorn Cook, *Epistolary Bodies: Gender and Genre in the Eighteenth-Century Republic of Letters* (Stanford: Stanford University Press, 1996); and Robert Adams Day, *Told in Letters: Epistolary Fiction before Richardson* (Ann Arbor: University of Michigan Press, 1966).

52. Amanda Gilroy and W. M. Verhoeven, eds., *Epistolary Histories: Letters, Fiction, Culture* (Charlottesville: University Press of Virginia, 2000), 6, 13.

53. Harold Love, *Scribal Publication in Seventeenth-Century England* (Oxford: Clarendon, 1993), 177.

54. Thomas Richards, *The Imperial Archive: Knowledge and the Fantasy of Empire* (London: Verso, 1993).

55. See Young, *Colonial Office*, 137, 285–86; Ray Jones, *The Nineteenth-Century Foreign Office: An Administrative History* (London: Wiedenfeld and Nicolson, 1971), 23–39 and Appendix B; and Anne Thurston, *Records of the Colonial Office, Dominions Office, Commonwealth Relations Office, and Commonwealth Office* (London: HMSO, 1995), 30–40.

56. Kenneth Bourne, *Palmerston: The Early Years, 1784–1841* (New York: Macmillan, 1982), 430.

57. Quoted in Kenneth Bourne, "The Foreign Office under Palmerston," in *The Foreign Office, 1782–1982*, ed. Roger Bullen (Frederick, MD: University Publications of America, 1984), 21.

58. Ibid., 20.

59. Quoted in Bourne, *Palmerston*, 420.

60. Linda Colley, *Britons: Forging the Nation, 1707–1837* (New Haven: Yale University Press, 1992), 178. For more on this topic, see her chapter 4, esp. 177–82.

61. Edward Hertslet, *Recollections of the Old Foreign Office* (London: John Murray, 1901), 77. Further references to this work are cited in the text.

62. Quoted in Bourne, *Palmerston,* 477.

63. Latour, "Drawing," 56; emphasis in original.

64. Bourne, *Palmerston,* 446.

65. Ibid., 422.

66. The wily Chatfield arranged to have a British subject, who owned a mine near Copán, function as his front man. He was told to make an offer on the land, saying his interests were cattle grazing and tobacco cultivation.

67. Peter Brooks, *Reading for the Plot: Design and Intention in Narrative* (New York: Knopf, 1984).

68. Martin Green, *Dreams of Adventure, Deeds of Empire* (New York: Basic Books, 1979), 38; Joseph Bristow, *Empire Boys: Adventures in a Man's World* (New York: HarperCollins Academic, 1991).

69. René Girard, *Deceit, Desire, and the Novel: Self and Other in Literary Structure,* trans. Yvonne Freccero (Baltimore: The Johns Hopkins University Press, 1972); Eve Kosofsky Sedgwick, *Between Men: English Literature and Male Homosocial Desire* (New York: Columbia University Press, 1985), 23, 2.

70. Wodehouse's use of a private letter would not have seemed unusual to Palmerston, who was well known for encouraging ministers to write him unofficially, much to the consternation of Queen Victoria.

71. In the 1835 parliamentary report on the British Museum—one of several important nineteenth-century inquiries into the institution—the issue of foreign scientists arose during the question of J. G. Children, keeper of the zoological collections. Question: "Does it not sometimes occur that foreign naturalists of eminence would be very glad to come to some understanding with the British Museum to collect for them in their voyages or journeys of discovery? . . . I have no doubt that that would prove to be the fact, and that we should find plenty who would enter into that correspondence" (House of Commons, "Report from the Select Committee appointed to inquire into the Condition, Management and Affairs of the British Museum," *Parliamentary Papers,* 1836, vol. 10, 225).

72. Skinner, *Orchids,* 173.

73. Norman Hammond, following on Ian Graham's work, writes that the appearance of the report and drawings in London resulted from the publication in Berlin in 1853 of Méndez's account along with a related set of drawings. My research suggests, rather, that they emerged from the British Museum's inquiry to the Foreign Office about the status of its Mayan plot ("Nineteenth-Century Drawings of Maya Monuments in the Society's Library," *Antiquaries Journal* 64 [1984]: 86).

74. Ibid., 97–101. The report is reprinted in *Anales de la Sociedad de geografía e historia de Guatemala* 7, no. 1 (1930): 88–94.

75. Quoted in Jenkins, *Archaeologists,* 61.

76. Nancy Leys Stepan notes that among the photographic albums of racial types Louis Agassiz kept for his scientific studies were photographs of classical statues such as the *Venus de Milo* and *Apollo Belvedere,* interpolated with profile photographs of racial others to point up the contrastive logic of racial thinking (*Picturing Tropical Nature* [Ithaca: Cornell University Press, 2001], 94).

77. Ian Graham describes Maudslay's removal of one of the lintels from Yaxchilán thus: "as for the lintel, estimated by Maudslay still to weigh about a quarter of a ton even though reduced to half its original thickness, there was no other way to carry it than lashed to a pole borne on men's shoulders. Not surprisingly the men took several days to reach Sacluk. There Maudslay was able to reduce its thickness a little further with a saw he bought from a lumberman. . . . [Eventually it was] carried by sixteen Indians as far as El Cayo, British Honduras, whence it could be taken down-river to Belize for shipment" (*Maudslay*, 105).

78. "Dr. Karl Ritter Von Scherzer," *Geographical Journal* 21, no. 4 (1903): 463. Notable among Scherzer's contributions was the 1857 publication of a Spanish version of the *Popul Vuh*, which he had found in the library of the university in Guatemala. This was the text's first publication, though its existence had been known since the late eighteenth century (*Las historias del origen de los Indios de esta Provincia de Guatemala . . .* [London, 1857]). For Scherzer's role in bringing the text to light, see Sylvanus G. Morley, ed., *"Popul Vuh": The Sacred Book of the Ancient Quiché Maya* (Norman: University of Oklahoma Press, 1950).

79. Scherzer, *On Measurements as a Diagnostic Means for Distinguishing the Human Races* (n.p.: 1858), 2; emphasis in original. See also Joseph Barnard Davis, "On the Method of Measurements, as a Diagnostic Means of Distinguishing Human Races, Adopted by Drs. Scherzer and Schwarz, in the Austrian Circumnavigatory Expedition of the 'Novara,'" *The American Journal of Science and Arts* 2nd ser. 29, no. 87 (1860): 329–35. A summary of the *Novara's* accomplishments issued for the International Exhibition of 1862 observed that "it must create in the mind of a German an elevated feeling of pride and satisfaction, to witness, that it is the kindred Anglo-Saxon race, to which seems to have been reserved the diffusion of a new life over the earth" (International Exhibition of 1862, *Outline of the Principle Aims and General Scientific Results of the Novara Expedition, Undertaken During the Years 1857, 1858, and 1859* [n.p.: 1862]), 6.

80. In 1936, working from a garbled and incomplete manuscript in the library of Tulane University, the periodical *Maya Research* published a portion of the longest and most important of these reports, taken from Scherzer's diary (Carl Scherzer, "A Visit to Quiriguá," *Maya Research* 3, no. 1 [1936]: 92–101). To my knowledge, the report Scherzer actually submitted to the British Museum trustees (42 ms. pages, dated 18 November 1854) has never been published, though he excerpted freely from it in an 1855 pamphlet published in Vienna (*Ein Besuch bei den Ruinen von Quirigua im Staate Guatemala in Central-Amerika* (Vienna: 1855). For ease of reference, where there is agreement between the published version and the manuscript in the British Museum, I quote the former with page numbers. Otherwise, I provide folio numbers from the manuscript sent to the trustees and now in the British Museum central archives.

81. See Annie E. Coombes, *Reinventing Africa: Museums, Material Culture and Popular Imagination in Late Victorian and Edwardian England* (New Haven: Yale University Press, 1994), 43–62.

82. Scherzer, "A Visit," 98.

83. Coombes, *Africa*, 44.

84. Scherzer, "A Visit," 98.

85. For Stevenson's donation, see the registers in the British Museum, Department of Ethnography (1857.4–14). Over the next few decades, the museum's ethnographic collections boomed, rising from about 3,500 to more than 38,000 by the end of the century. Among the most important Mexican collections to enter the museum was that bequeathed by Henry Christy on his death in 1865. Christy had met Edward B. Tylor in Havana and the two traveled together across Mexico in the mid-1850s, toward the end of the plot examined here; Tylor's account appears in *Anahuac: Or, Mexico and the Mexicans, Ancient and Modern* (London, 1861). Christy's collection was global in reach, but the ancient Mexican antiquities, several of which are featured in the Mexican Gallery, are particularly renowned.

86. On these objects, see John W. Boddam-Whetham, *Across Central America* (London, 1877), 301; Valerie Meyer-Holdampf, *Tikal-Abenteuer und Entdeckung: Auf den Spuren der Alten Mayavölker* (Frankfurt: Fouqué Literaturverlag, 2000), 138–71; and Sylvanus Griswold Morley, *The Inscriptions of Peten* (Washington: Carnegie Institution, 1938), 77–83.

87. A set of the Guatemalan stereographs and the accompanying booklet (*Description of a Series of Photographic Views of the Ruins of Copan* [London, 1863]) are contained in the Princeton University Library. The Guatemalan diary of Caroline Salvin, his wife, has now been published in a splendid bilingual edition (Caroline Salvin, *A Pocket Eden: Guatemalan Journals 1873–1874* [South Woodstock, VT: Plumsock Mesoamerican Studies, 2000]).

88. Roger Fry, *Last Lectures* (Cambridge: Cambridge University Press, 1939), 87.

89. Anne Cary Maudslay and Alfred Percival Maudslay, *A Glimpse of Guatemala, and Some Notes on the Ancient Monuments of Central America* (London, 1899), 86. Of the Indians themselves, Alfred Maudslay had this to say: "Ignorant, lazy, dirty, and drunken as these peoples undoubtedly are, I found them to be cheerful, kindly, and honest" (139).

90. Alfred Maudslay's magisterial disdain for the Central American officials who came around to observe his work (129–31) is echoed by his contemporary Zelia Nuttal, who complained at length about the conditions under which the Mexican government "accepts volunteer scientific work," which included the requirement that her excavations be overseen by the inspector of archaeological monuments, as required by Mexican law ("The Island of Sacrifices," *American Anthropologist* 12, no. 2 [1910]: 257–95; see esp. 277–79).

91. Quoted in Williford, "Las luces," 38. For the expeditions, see Claxton, "Miguel Rivera Maestre," 393–94; and J. Antonio Villacorta C., *Historia de la República de Guatemala (1821–1921)* (Guatemala City: n.p., 1960), 354.

92. "Disposiciones oficiales que se han venido dictando desde el año de 1845 para la conservación de los monumentos y vestigios arqueológicos existentes en Honduras," *Revista del archivo y biblioteca nacional de Honduras* 18, no. 4 (1939): 180; for the history of these laws, see Daniel F. de la Borbolla Rubin and Pedro Rivas, *Honduras:*

Monumentos históricos y arqueológicos (Mexico City: Consejo Internacional de la Filosofía y de las Ciencas Humanas, 1953), 16, 27.

93. "Disposiciones," 180. For a particularly strong reading of these laws and the "depredation" they were intended to stanch, see Ricardo Agurcia Fasquelle, "La depredación del patrimonio cultural en Honduras: El caso de la arqueología," *Yaxkin* 8, no. 2 (1984): 83–91.

94. Sara Suleri, *The Rhetoric of English India* (Chicago: University of Chicago Press, 1992), 12.

95. William Bullock, *Six Months' Residence and Travels in Mexico* (London, 1824), 341–42.

96. Ibid., 342.

97. Boddam-Whetham, *Central America,* 179. Cf. Maudslay and Maudslay, *Glimpse,* 131.

4. FREAK SHOW

1. Royal Archives, Windsor Castle (ref: RA PP/VIC/2/5/4198), courtesy of the gracious permission of Her Majesty Queen Elizabeth II.

2. In the United States, Matthew Brady and Charles Eisenmann made a specialty of photographing human freaks; Brady's studio was located across the street from Barnum's American Museum. For a discussion of human monstrosity in the U.S. context, see Bill Brown, *The Material Unconscious: American Amusement, Stephen Crane, and the Economies of Play* (Cambridge: Harvard University Press, 1996), 199–245.

3. "The Aztecs! A Newly-Discovered Tribe of Human Beings," Handbill, Human Freaks Box 4, John Johnson Collection, Bodleian Library; Richard D. Altick, *The Shows of London* (Cambridge: Belknap Press, 1978), 341–42.

4. Robert Bogdan, *Freak Show: Presenting Human Oddities for Amusement and Profit* (Chicago: University of Chicago Press, 1988), 132.

5. "The Aztec Lilliputians," *London Times,* 8 July 1853, 8c; "Lilliput in London," *Household Words* 7 (1853), 573. The bright light of publicity shone on the Aztec Children from July to December 1853. See articles in the *Illustrated London News* (30 Jul. 1853; 9 Jul. 1853; 23 Jul. 1853); *Household Words* (3 [1851] and 7 [1853]); the *Athenaeum* (9 Jul. 1853; 16 Jul. 1853; 1 Oct. 1853); *Illustrated Magazine of Art* (1 [1853]); *Liverpool Mercury* (21 Jun. 1853); *Notes and Queries* (121 [1858]; 123 [1858]; 132 [1858]); and the *Times* (7 Jul. 1853; 11 Jul. 1853; 14 Jul. 1853; 19 Jul. 1853; 25 Jul. 1853).

6. For Altick, whose prolific labors in the archive of Victorian popular culture have enabled much recent work on freakery, the exhibition illustrates "how unequal a combatant scientific opinion is when matched against the determination and sheer noise of showmen" (*Shows of London,* 284). See also Erin O'Connor's discussion of monstrosity, broadly speaking, in *Raw Material: Producing Pathology in Victorian Culture* (Durham: Duke University Press, 2000), 148–208. The basic theatrical history for the Aztec Children is given in Bogdan (*Freak Show,* 127–34) and Ricky Jay, *Jay's*

Journal of Anomalies (New York: Farrar, Strauss, and Giroux, 2001), 83–94. Juan Comas reproduces contemporary documents with commentary, Nigel Rothfels discusses the children's sojourn in Germany, and Evelleen Richards discusses their relationship to evolutionary theory (Comas, *Dos microcéfalos "Aztecas": Leyenda, historia, y antropologia* [Mexico City: UNAM Instituto de Investigaciones Históricas, 1968]; Rothfels, "Aztecs, Aborigines, and Ape-People: Science and Freaks in Germany, 1850–1900," in *Freakery: Cultural Spectacles of the Extraordinary Body*, ed. Rosemarie Garland Thomson [New York: New York University Press, 1996], 158–72; and Richards, "A Political Anatomy of Monsters, Hopeful and Otherwise: Teratogeny, Transcendentalism, and Evolutionary Theorizing," *Isis* 85, no. 3 [1994]: 377–411).

7. William Bullock, *Six Months' Residence and Travels in Mexico* (London, 1824), 443.

8. In mid-Victorian Britain, medical and ethnological curiosities frequently shared the same exhibitionary space: in 1853, the year Máximo and Bartola were first exhibited in London, visitors could attend Reimers' Anatomical and Ethnological Museum in Savile House, which consisted of "upwards of 300 superb and nature-like Anatomical Figures, in Wax, &C." along with a waxwork "Gallery of All Nations" (quoted in Altick, *Shows of London*, 341).

9. B. C. Brodie, "Address to the Ethnological Society of London, Delivered at the Anniversary Meeting on the 27th May 1853," *Journal of the Ethnological Society of London* 4 (1856): 102–3; James Hunt, "Anniversary Address to the Anthropological Society of London," *Journal of the Anthropological Society of London* 2 (1864): xciii. The Ethnological Society of London's prospectus made explicit the link between ethnology and colonialism, suggesting that "to complete the circle of Scientific Institutions" in the metropolis, there was need of one "whose sole object should be the promotion and diffusion of the most important and interesting branch of knowledge, that of man,— ETHNOLOGY," a science Britain was well suited to prosecute given its "numerous and extensive Colonies and Foreign Possessions" (Richard King, "Address to the Ethnological Society of London, Delivered at the Anniversary Meeting on the 25th May, 1844," *Journal of the Ethnological Society of London* 2 [1850]: 15–16).

10. Rosemarie Garland Thomson, "Introduction: From Wonder to Error—a Genealogy of Freak Discourse in Modernity," in *Freakery*, 3.

11. O'Connor finds the freak ultimately a "twisted allegory" reflective of the "imaginative needs of a culture in a violent, chronic state of flux," but also asserts that freaks "own[ed] themselves by selling themselves" (*Raw Material*, 150–52). Many however, such as the Aztec Children and Julia Pastrana, were owned, bought, and sold by others, and thus could not be said to have any such agency.

12. Exemplifying the desire to separate archaeology from spectacle, Robert Brunhouse claims that the exhibit and Stephens's book "appealed to different audiences." While the public expected to be fooled, "Serious readers . . . knew that they could rely on the veracity of Stephens and the accuracy of Catherwood" (*In Search of the Maya: The First Archaeologists* [Albuquerque: University of New Mexico Press, 1973], 112).

13. While the 1813 edition of James C. Prichard's *Researches into the Physical History of Mankind* contained only a few pages on American races, the third edition (5 vols. [London, 1847]) devoted one of its five books to the subject.

14. See Felix Driver, *Geography Militant: Cultures of Exploration and Empire* (Oxford: Blackwell Publishers, 2001), 49–67.

15. Thomas S. Kuhn, "The Function of Measurement in Modern Physical Science," *Isis* 52, no. 2 (1961): 161.

16. George W. Stocking, "What's in a Name? The Origins of the Royal Anthropological Institute (1837–71)," *Man* 6 (1971): 372.

17. In 1848 *Punch* ran a cartoon entitled "Deformito-Mania," in which an unruly mob presses around the Egyptian Hall; its walls, notes *Punch,* "are placarded from top to bottom with bills announcing the exhibition of some frightful object within, and the building itself will soon be known as the Hall of Ugliness" (quoted in Altick, *Shows of London,* 254).

18. Thomas Carlyle, "Occasional Discourse on the Nigger Question," *Fraser's Magazine for Town and Country* 40 (1849): 670–79; Charles Dickens, "The Noble Savage," in *Reprinted Pieces,* vol. 34 of *The Works of Charles Dickens* (New York: Charles Scribner's Sons, 1911), 120–27.

19. Nancy Leys Stepan, *Picturing Tropical Nature* (Ithaca: Cornell University Press, 2001), 94.

20. Robert Burford and Henry Courtney Selous, *Description of a View of the City of Mexico; and the Surrounding Country, Now Exhibiting at the Panorama, Leicester Square* (London, 1853).

21. George W. Stocking, *Victorian Anthropology* (New York: Free Press, 1987), 3. Sounding very much like Palmerston (see chapter 3), Thomas H. Huxley argued in 1865 that with white Europeans "has originated everything that is highest in science, in art, in law, in politics, and in mechanical inventions. In their hands, at the present moment, lies the order of the social world, and to them its progress is committed" ("On the Methods and Results of Ethnology," in *Man's Place in Nature and Other Anthropological Essays,* vol. 7 of *Collected Essays* [London, 1895], 232). For the ethnological exhibits at the Crystal Palace, see R. G. Latham, *The Natural History Department of the Crystal Palace Described: Ethnology* (London, 1854).

22. John Conolly, *The Ethnological Exhibitions of London* (London, 1855), 5. Conolly, who taught practical medicine and psychiatry at the University of London, wrote widely on insanity and was instrumental in opposing the use of restraints in clinics. He also authored the first psychiatric study of Shakespeare: *A Study of Hamlet* (London, 1863).

23. Antoinette Burton, "Rules of Thumb: British History and 'Imperial Culture' in Nineteenth- and Twentieth-Century Britain," *Women's History Review* 3, no. 4 (1994): 486.

24. Edward Said, *Orientalism* (New York: Vintage Books, 1979), 177.

25. John Lloyd Stephens, *Incidents of Travel in Central America, Chiapas, and Yucatan,* 2 vols. (New York, 1841), 2:195–96.

26. Pedro Velásquez, *Memoir of an Eventful Expedition into Central America* (London, n.d.). There are several extant versions of the pamphlet. Further references to this edition will be given in the text.

27. Victor W. Von Hagen, *Frederick Catherwood, Archt.* (New York: Oxford University Press, 1950), 3–34.

28. "A Mysterious City," *Household Words,* 19 April 1851, 96; Richard Cull, "A Brief Notice of the Aztec Race," *Journal of the Ethnological Society of London* 4 (1856): 125.

29. R. G. Latham, "Ethnological Remarks Upon Some of the More Remarkable Varieties of the Human Species, Represented by Individuals Now in London," *Journal of the Ethnological Society of London* 4 (1856): 149.

30. Jacques Derrida, *Of Grammatology,* trans. Gayatri Chakravorty Spivak (Baltimore: The Johns Hopkins University Press, 1976), 145.

31. George W. Stocking, "Reading the Palimpsest of Inquiry: *Notes and Queries* and the History of British Social Anthropology," in *Delimiting Anthropology: Occasional Essays and Reflections* (Madison: University of Wisconsin Press, 2001), 169–70.

32. Dr. [Thomas] Hodgkin, "On Inquiries into the Races of Man," British Association for the Advancement of Science [hereafter BAAS], *Report,* 11th Meeting (1841), 52, 53–54.

33. Prichard's paper was subsequently published with the title "On the Extinction of Human Races," *Edinburgh New Philosophical Journal* 28 (1839): 166–70. For the humanitarian context here, see Patrick Brantlinger, *Dark Vanishings: Discourse on the Extinction of Primitive Races, 1800–1930* (Ithaca: Cornell University Press, 2003), 68–73.

34. Quoted in BAAS, "Queries Respecting the Human Race, to Be Addressed to Travellers and Others. Drawn up by a Committee of the British Association for the Advancement of Science, Appointed in 1839," in BAAS, 1841 *Report,* 332.

35. "Foundation Meeting of the Ethnological Society, 1843," *Man* 44 (1944): 25.

36. BAAS, 1841 *Report,* 333; see also James C. Prichard, "On the Various Methods of Research Which Contribute to the Advancement of Ethnology, and of the Relations of That Science to Other Branches of Knowledge," BAAS, *Report,* 17th Meeting (1848), 232–33.

37. Hodgkin, "Inquiries," 54.

38. BAAS, "Queries," 332. Prichard's questionnaire, through various permutations, had a long shelf life. It was reprinted in the first edition (1849) of the Admiralty's *Manual of Scientific Inquiry;* E. B. Tylor enlarged it for the fourth edition of 1871. By 1889, when the Royal Geographical Society issued the sixth edition of its own *Hints to Travellers,* Tylor's piece, now called "Anthropology," ran to twenty-two pages, with an additional thirteen pages of questions by A. W. Franks (the British Museum's Keeper of Ethnography), Francis Galton, and J. G. Frazier (John F. W. Herschel, ed., *A Manual of Scientific Enquiry: Prepared for the Use of Her Majesty's Navy and Adapted for Travellers in General* [London, 1849]; E. B. Tylor, "Anthropology," in Royal Geographical Society, *Hints to Travellers, Scientific and General* [London, 1889], 371–92).

39. Dickens, "Noble Savage," 127, 120. For a reading of this essay in relation to

figurations of the Orient, see Jeff Nunokawa, "For Your Eyes Only: Private Property and the Oriental Body in *Dombey and Son*," in *Macropolitics of Nineteenth-Century Literature: Nationalism, Exoticism, Imperialism,* ed. Jonathan Arac and Harriet Ritvo (Philadelphia: University of Pennsylvania Press, 1991), 139–58.

40. See May Castleberry, ed., *The New World's Old World: Photographic Views of Ancient America* (Albuquerque: University of New Mexico Press, 2003).

41. Anne McClintock, *Imperial Leather: Race, Gender, and Sexuality in the Colonial Conquest* (New York: Routledge, 1995), 30.

42. "Aztec Lilliputians," 8c.

43. Cull, "Brief Notice," 123. Jonathan Mason Warren observed that "the peculiar form of their heads" is "exactly represented in the Travels of Mr. Stevens [sic], as carved on some of the monuments in that region" (*An Account of Two Remarkable Indian Dwarfs Exhibited in Boston under the Name of Aztec Children* [Boston, 1851], 17).

44. BAAS, "Queries," 333.

45. Photographic profile shots were in use in criminology by the 1840s (Nancy Armstrong, *Fiction in the Age of Photography: The Legacy of British Realism* [Cambridge: Harvard University Press, 1999], 26, 213–17; Simon A. Cole, *Suspect Identities: A History of Fingerprinting and Criminal Identification* [Cambridge: Harvard University Press, 2001], 20 ff.; and Alan Sekula, "The Body and the Archive," *October* 39 [1986]: 3–64).

46. J. Barnard Davis, "On Some of the Bearings of Ethnology Upon Archaeological Science," *Archaeological Journal* 13 (1856): 317–18.

47. The catalogue to the 2002 Royal Academy Aztec show incorrectly identifies this as the exhibit of Henry Christy (Adrian Locke, "Exhibitions and Collectors of Pre-Hispanic Mexican Artefacts in Britain," in *Aztecs,* ed. Eduardo Matos Moctezuma and Felipe Solis Olguin [London: Royal Academy of Arts, 2002], 83). See British Museum, *Synopsis of the Contents of the British Museum,* 63rd ed. (London, 1856); and Charles Bedford Young, *A Descriptive Catalogue of the Collection of Mexican Antiquities Now Exhibiting at No. 57, Pall Mall* (n.p., 1855). Young's exhibit was reviewed in the *Athenaeum* (10 Mar. 1855), the *Times* (23 Feb. 1855), and the *Illustrated London News* (27 Jan. and 10 Feb. 1855).

48. Conolly, *Ethnological,* 41.

49. Davis, "Bearings," 318 and idem, "Anthropology and Ethnology," *Anthropological Review* 23 (1868): 395–96.

50. Anthony Pagden, *European Encounters with the New World from Renaissance to Romanticism* (New Haven: Yale University Press, 1993), 31; Hugh Honour, *The European Vision of America* (Cleveland: Cleveland Museum of Art, 1975), 21.

51. Thomson, "Introduction," in Thompson, ed., *Freakery,* 2.

52. Bodgan, *Freak Show,* xi.

53. "The Aztec People," *Athenaeum,* 9 July 1853, 825; my emphasis.

54. Lori Merish, "Cuteness and Commodity Aesthetics: Tom Thumb and Shirley Temple," in Thomson, ed., *Freakery,* 186–87. For attention to how "the expansion of

ethnology and ethnography implicated the child and childhood" in mid-Victorian Britain, with special reference to *Jane Eyre* and the culture of spectacle, see Cora Kaplan, "'A Heterogeneous Thing': Female Childhood and the Rise of Racial Thinking in Victorian Britain," in *Human, All Too Human,* ed. Diana Fuss (London: Routledge, 1996), 169–202, esp. 193–94.

55. "Lilliput in London," 576.

56. "Aztec People," 824–25.

57. Warren issued his findings in the *American Journal of Medical Science* and the *Proceedings of the Boston Society of Natural History* [BSNH]. This and further references are to a separately published pamphlet (*An Account of Two Remarkable Indian Dwarfs Exhibited in Boston under the Name of Aztec Children* [Boston, 1851]). There are also important connections here back to John Lloyd Stephens and W. H. Prescott. Samuel Cabot, the young physician who had accompanied Stephens and Catherwood on their second trip to Central America, chaired the BSNH meeting at which the Aztec Children were discussed, and John Collins Warren (1778–1856), father of Jonathon Mason Warren and also on the faculty of the Harvard Medical School, had requested Prescott in 1840 to fill in a missing link in his "craniological chain" by procuring a pre-Columbian skull from Mexico for his Anatomical Museum. According to a subsequent letter, the request for the skulls was successful (William Hickling Prescott, *The Correspondence of William Hickling Prescott,* ed. Roger Wolcott [Boston: Houghton Mifflin Company, 1925], 137, 237).

58. Another anatomist, James Redfield, in his *Comparative Physiognomy; or, Resemblances between Men and Animals* (New York, 1852), compared the children to mice (65–69).

59. Richard Owen, "Description of the So-Called Aztec Children," *Journal of the Ethnological Society of London* 4 (1856): 128–37. Further references to this work are given in the text.

60. Stephen Jay Gould, "Human Equality as a Contingent Fact of History," in *The Flamingo's Smile: Reflections in Natural History* (New York: W. W. Norton, 1985), 189. Cf. Huxley's criticism of Owen for using misleading craniological images (Huxley, "Man and the Apes," *Athenaeum,* 30 Mar. 1861, 433).

61. Samuel George Morton, *Crania Americana, or, a Comparative View of the Skulls of Various Aboriginal Nations of North and South America* (Philadelphia, 1839), 81.

62. Stepan, *Tropical Nature,* 95.

63. M. de Quatrefages, "The Formation of the Mixed Human Races," *Anthropological Review* 2 (1864): 22.

64. Dalton later discussed Máximo and Bartola in the chapter on the brain in his standard and frequently re-issued medical textbook, *Treatise on Human Physiology* (Philadelphia, 1861), 409–10.

65. Charlotte Brontë, *Jane Eyre,* ed. Michael Mason (London: Penguin, 1996), 345; ch. 27. The joining of race with sexuality was further strengthened in a show that debuted in 1857, the exhibition of Julia Pastrana, the Bear Woman, or Nondescript, a hirsute native of Mexico. See Rosemarie Garland Thomson, "Narratives of Deviance

and Delight: Staring at Julia Pastrana, the 'Extraordinary Lady,'" in *Beyond the Binary: Reconstructing Cultural Identity in a Multicultural Context*, ed. Timothy B. Powell (New Brunswick: Rutgers University Press, 1999), 81–104; and Jan Bondeson, *A Cabinet of Medical Curiosities* (New York: W. W. Norton, 1997), 216–44.

66. Philip D. Curtin, *The Image of Africa: British Ideas and Action, 1780–1850* (London: Macmillan, 1965), 377.

67. Robert Knox, *The Races of Men: A Fragment* (London, 1850), v.

68. Robert Knox, "Some Remarks on the Aztecque and Bosjieman Children Now Being Exhibited in London, and on the Races to Which They Are Presumed to Belong," *The Lancet*, Jan.–Jun. (1855): 357–60; this passage, 358. Further references to this work are given in the text.

69. See Charles Darwin, *Journal of Researches into the Natural History and Geology of the Countries Visited During the Voyage Round the World of H.M.S. Beagle*, 11th ed. (London: John Murray, 1913), 390.

70. Dr. Carl Scherzer, *Travels in the Free States of Central America: Nicaragua, Honduras, and San Salvador*, 2 vols. (London, 1857), 2: 234.

71. Ibid.

72. A Traveller in the New World, "The Aztecs," *Anthropological Review* 5 (1867): 253.

73. Robert J. C. Young, *Colonial Desire: Hybridity in Theory, Culture, and Race* (New York: Routledge, 1995), 2.

74. Ephraim G. Squier, *Notes on Central America; Particularly the States of Honduras and San Salvador* (New York, 1855), 55.

75. Herbert Spencer, *Herbert Spencer on Social Evolution*, ed. J. D. Y. Peel (Chicago: University of Chicago Press, 1972), 163.

76. Davis, "Bearings," 323.

77. Robert Knox, *The Races of Men: A Philosophical Enquiry into the Influence of Race over the Destinies of Nations*, 2nd ed. (London, 1862), 487.

78. William Bollaert, "Observations on the Past and Present Populations of the New World," *Memoirs Read before the Anthropological Society of London* 1 (1863–64): 85; 77–79. Bollaert was also one of the many ethnologists with a serious interest in museums. In 1860 he wrote Roderick Murchison offering to compile a descriptive catalogue of the British Museum's American antiquities (William Bollaert to Roderick Murchison, 3 October 1860, Ayer Ms. 3022, Edward E. Ayer Collection, The Newberry Library, Chicago). For a list of Bollaert's contributions to ethnology, see "Biographical Sketch of Mr. W. Bollaert," *Journal of the Anthropological Institute of Great Britain and Ireland* 6 (1877): 510–13.

79. W[illiam] Bollaert, "The Llama, Alpaco, Huanacu, and Vicuña," *The Sporting Review*, Feb. 1863, 123–32. Also apposite here is a parallel concern with hybridity that flourished at the same time in zoos and private collections of animals. See Harriet Ritvo, *The Animal Estate: The English and Other Creatures in the Victorian Age* (Cambridge: Harvard University Press, 1987), 235.

80. James Hunt, "Memoirs of the Anthropological Society of London," *Anthropological Review* 5 (1867): 93–94.

81. Scherzer, *Travels,* 96.

82. Ibid., vi–vii.

83. Quoted in Bogdan, *Freak Show,* 131.

84. Ibid., 132–33.

85. Marianna Torgovnick, *Gone Primitive: Savage Intellects, Modern Lives* (Chicago: University of Chicago Press, 1990), 9.

86. "Can the Aztecs Speak?" *Illustrated London News,* 30 July 1853, 66.

87. Coco Fusco, *English Is Broken Here: Notes on Cultural Fusion in the Americas* (New York: New Press, 1995), 37, 56. Further references to this work are given in the text.

88. Guillermo Gómez-Peña, Roberto Sifuentes, and Matthew Finch, "Aztechnology," *Art Journal* 60, no. 1 (2001): 37; Guillermo Gómez-Peña, *The New World Border: Prophecies, Poems, and Loqueras for the End of the Century* (San Francisco: City Lights, 1996), 97.

89. Gómez-Peña, *New World Border,* 97.

90. Fusco, *English,* 44.

91. Gómez-Peña, "Aztechnology," 37.

92. Michel Foucault, *The Order of Things: An Archaeology of the Human Sciences* (New York: Vintage, 1970), 312.

CODA

1. Lilias Rider Haggard, *Norfolk Life* (London: Faber and Faber, 1943), 65.

2. Morton Cohen, *Rider Haggard: His Life and Work,* 2nd ed. (London: Macmillan, 1968), 146.

3. Lilias Rider Haggard, *The Cloak That I Left* (London: Hodder and Stoughton, 1951), 152.

4. Cohen, *Haggard,* 139–41.

5. Throughout his career Haggard concerned himself with museums, writing letters to the *Times* about them, figuring them in his novels, and donating collections to the British Museum and the Liverpool Museums.

6. John Forrester, "'Mille e tre': Freud and Collecting," in *The Cultures of Collecting,* ed. John Elsner and Roger Cardinal (Cambridge: Harvard University Press, 1994), 227.

7. Martin Green, *Dreams of Adventure, Deeds of Empire* (New York: Basic Books, 1979), 228.

8. H. Rider Haggard, *The Days of My Life,* ed. C. J. Longman, 2 vols. (London: Longmans, Green, and Co., 1926), 1:78. Further references to this work are given in the text.

9. Cohen, *Haggard,* 95.

10. Quoted in Brian V. Street, *The Savage in Literature: Representations of 'Primitive' Society in English Fiction 1858–1920* (London: Routledge and Kegan Paul, 1975), 11.

11. For the modernist fascination with Mexico, see Helen Delpar, *The Enormous*

Vogue of Things Mexican: Cultural Relations between the United States and Mexico, 1920–1935 (Tuscaloosa: University of Alabama Press, 1992).

12. Drewey Wayne Gunn, *American and British Writers in Mexico, 1556–1973* (Austin: University of Texas Press, 1974), 43.

13. Although critics have largely ignored these novels, they have had a powerful effect on other readers. Graham Greene credited *Montezuma's Daughter* with luring him to Mexico, and the historian of Mesoamerica Michael Coe notes that the eminent archaeologist Sylvanus Morley claimed to have been set on the path of his life work by *Heart of the World* (Graham Greene, *A Sort of Life* [London: Bodley Head, 1971], 53; Michael Coe, *Breaking the Maya Code* [New York: Thames and Hudson, 1992], 98). Alfred Maudslay, perhaps with Haggard in mind, acknowledged the competition posed by novelists to the work of archaeology: "The novelist has already tried his hand both on Ancient Mexico and Yucatan. . . . Surely here there is scope for the more chastened scientific imagination" (Anne Cary Maudslay and Alfred Percival Maudslay, *A Glimpse at Guatemala, and Some Notes on the Ancient Monuments of Central America* [London: 1899], 126).

14. Anne McClintock, *Imperial Leather: Race, Gender, and Sexuality in the Colonial Conquest* (New York: Routledge, 1995), 257.

15. Henry Adams, *Henry Adams and His Friends: A Collection of His Unpublished Letters,* ed. Harold Dean Cater (Boston: Houghton Mifflin, 1947), 332; Gunn, *American and British Writers,* 40.

16. Quoted in Alfred Tischendorf, *Great Britain and Mexico in the Era of Porfirio Díaz* (Durham: Duke University Press, 1961), 19.

17. Ibid., 76.

18. Desmond Young, *Member for Mexico: A Biography of Weetman Pearson, First Viscount Cowdray* (London: Cassell, 1966). Pearson, who arrived in Mexico just prior to Haggard, was also a major collector of Mexican antiquities.

19. Tischendorf, *Great Britain,* 128–30.

20. H. Rider Haggard, "Introduction" to Mrs. John Beveridge Gladwyn Jebb, ed., *A Strange Career: Life and Adventures of John Gladwyn Jebb by His Widow,* 4th ed. (Edinburgh, 1895), xv–xvi.

21. Cohen, *Haggard,* 131.

22. Haggard, "Introduction," xvi.

23. Although we will never know how much of the story is true (Haggard was fond of tall tales), both Haggard and Jebb present it as a crucial narrative in their accounts of Mexico. Jebb's *Strange Career* gives greater detail, along with other stories of buried treasure and lost antiquities (268–82). The best assessment of Haggard's veracity may be Oscar Wilde's: "As for Mr. Rider Haggard, who really has, or had once, the makings of a perfectly magnificent liar, he is now so afraid of being suspected of genius that when he does tell us anything marvellous, he feels bound to invent a personal reminiscence, and to put it into a footnote as a kind of cowardly corroboration" (Oscar Wilde, "The Decay of Lying," in *Oscar Wilde,* ed. Isobel Murray [Oxford: Oxford University Press, 1989], 218–19).

24. Haggard, "Introduction," xvii.

25. H. Rider Haggard, *Montezuma's Daughter* (New York, 1984), 11, 16. Further references to this work appear in the text.

26. For influential assessments of the primitivist project see Elazar Barkan and Ronald Bush, eds., *Prehistories of the Future: The Primivitist Project and the Culture of Modernism* (Stanford: Stanford University Press, 1995); and Marianna Torgovnick, *Gone Primitive: Savage Intellects, Modern Lives* (Chicago: University of Chicago Press, 1990).

27. D. S. Higgins, *Rider Haggard: A Biography* (New York: Stein and Day, 1983), 148.

28. Charles Darwin, *Journal of Researches into the Natural History and Geology of the Countries Visited During the Voyage Round the World of H.M.S. Beagle,* 11th ed. (London: John Murray, 1913), 147.

29. See also W. H. Kingsley's *Westward Ho!; or The Voyages and Adventures of Sir Amyas Leigh of Burrough, in the County of Devon, in the Reign of Her Most Glorious Majesty Queen Elizabeth* (London, 1855).

30. L. R. Haggard, *Cloak,* 159.

31. Ibid.

INDEX

Aberdeen, Lord (George Hamilton Gordon), 79, 84, 85, 176n47
Academy of San Carlos, 57
Ackermann, George, 78, 166n38
Ackermann, Rudolph, xxi, 85, 152n25
Agassiz, Louis, 178n76
Aglio, Agostino. *See* Bullock, William
Alamán, Lucas, 28–29, 30, 57–58
Altick, Richard, 36–37
Anthropological Society of London. *See* Hunt, James
anthropology: and museum exhibitions, 9; and polygenesis, 116, 126, 128–29; and profile illustration, 116, 185n45. *See also* Aztec Children; Davis, Joseph Barnard; ethnological questionnaires; Ethnological Society of London; ethnology; Fabian, Johannes; race; Scherzer, Karl Ritter von
Antiquaries of London, Society of, 62, 79, 90, 174n25
antiquities: Central American attitudes toward, 67–68, 73, 97–101; international competition for, 69, 74–76, 77, 90; laws protecting, 30–33, 98, 161n76, 161n80, 172n5, 180n92, 181n93; Mexican attitudes toward, 24,

28, 29–33; traffic in, xiv, 28, 53. *See also* British Museum; Bullock, William; Copán; Maudslay, Alfred P.; Quiriguá; Tikal
Appadurai, Arjun, xxii–xxiii, 19, 28
archaeology, xv; ascendancy of, in United States, 141; relation to ethnology, 116, 126
archives: constructedness of, xix; and empire, 79, 80, 83; organization of, 61. *See also* Colonial Office; Foreign Office; imperial administration; Latour, Bruno; Palmerston, Lord
Armstrong, Nancy, 37
Atlantic world: circulation of objects in, xv, xxii, xxix, 6, 28. *See also* antiquities; British Museum; collecting; networks
Austen, Jane, 16
Aztec Children, xxviii, 103–31; examined by Robert Knox, 126–27; examined by Richard Owen, 121–22, 124–25; examined by Jonathan Mason Warren, 120–21; racial descriptions of, 123–30; at Reimer's Anatomical and Ethnological Museum, 103, 182n8; and Scherzer, Karl Ritter von, 127

Aztecs, xiii, 6, 154n6. *See also* British Museum; Bullock, William; Haggard, H. Rider; Humboldt, Alexander von; Mexico

Baartman, Saartjie (Hottentot Venus), 17–18
Baily, John, 76, 85, 175n38
Bal, Meike, xxiii, 49. *See also* focalization
Barker, Henry Aston, 41, 59. *See also* panorama
Barker, Robert, 36. *See also* panorama
Barthes, Roland, 6
Bateman, James, 77, 85, 176n41
Beaufoy, Mark, 3
Beddoe, John, 116
Belzoni, Giovanni Battista, 18, 20–21
Benedict, Barbara, 14
Benjamin, Walter, 36, 37, 38
Bentham, Jeremy, 37–39
Bhabha, Homi, xvii
Black Legend, 22, 24, 72
Blom, Frans, 113
Boddham-Whetham, John, 96, 101
Bogdan, Robert, 119
Bollaert, William, 128–29, 187n78
Boruwlaski, Joseph (Polish Dwarf), 17
Bristow, Joseph, 86
British Association for the Advancement of Science, 107, 111
British Empire. *See* imperialism
British Honduras (Belize), 76, 78; strategic importance of, xviii, 62, 86, 151n10. *See also* Central America
British Museum: acquisition of Bullock's collection, xxvi, 6, 27; artificial curiosities, gallery of, 27; catalogues, 26–27; Elgin Marbles in, 15, 27, 79, 158n41; employment of foreign scientists, 178n71; ethnographical room, 27, 107; ethnography department, 27, 28, 95, 150n7, 151n13; founding, 14; gifts from Mexican

national museum, 162n88; and Mayan ruins, 62, 71, 78, 86–97; and Mexican collection of Charles Bedford Young, 118; Mexican Gallery, xiii–xiv, 9, 97, 149n4; and postmodern freak shows, 133; and pre-Columbian collections, 6, 9, 150n7, 157n28, 172n5, 176n47, 180n85, 187n78; Rosetta Stone in, 15; *Synopsis of the Contents of the British Museum,* xxiv, 27; troubles during 2002–04, 149n6; use of Karl Ritter von Scherzer and Moritz Wagner, 88, 90, 94–96. *See also* collecting; museums
Broca, Paul, 116
Brontë, Charlotte, 124–25
Brooks, Peter, 85
Bry, Theodore de, 24
Buckland, William, 27
Buffon, Comte de, 128
Bullock, William, xxv, xxvi, 72; and antiquities law, 30–31; anti-Spanish rhetoric, 24–26, 47–48; and British Museum, xxvi, 30–31; catalogues, 27; comments on *Coatlicue,* 100; compared to Humboldt, 155n8; coverage in press, 2; display of Mexican native, 5, 9, 105; dissemination of British goods in Mexico, xxi; early museum career, 13–15; exhibition of Egyptian artefacts, 18, 21; exhibition of Laplanders, 18–19; exhibition of Mexican artefacts, 2, 4–11, 19–33; exhibition of Napoleon's carriage, 17; influence on W. H. Prescott, 49; and informal imperialism, 2–3, 22; journey to Mexico, 1–2; and G. F. Lyon, 156n20; move to London, 15–16; and plaster casting, 158n39; and possessive individualism, 16; return of Mexican codices, 162n85; rhetoric of progress, 25–26; role in Burford's panorama, 2; *Six Months' Residence*

Robert D. Aguirre is associate professor of English at Wayne State University. His articles on British and American literature have been published in *Genre, Biography,* and *Victorian Studies.*